Black Writers, White Audience

BLACK WRITERS: WHITE AUDIENCE

A Critical Approach to African Literature

Phanuel Akubueze Egejuru

An Exposition-University Book

Exposition Press
Hicksville, New York

PR
9344
E35

FIRST EDITION

© 1978 by Phanuel Akubueze Egejuru

Library of Congress Catalog Card Number: 77-94306

ISBN 0-682-48977-8

Printed in the United States of America

To my mother

CONTENTS

PREFACE

This is a critical study which attempts to analyze the influence of readership on African novels. The areas examined are: audience composition, publication, language, subject matter and its handling, and genre.

The study concentrates on pertinent works from the Anglophone and Francophone countries in Africa south of the Sahara. Representative novels by seven authors from the English sector are studied in some detail, namely: Chinua Achebe, Ayi Kwei Armah, Cyprian Ekwensi, Onuora Nzekwu, Gabriel Okara, Wole Soyinka, and Amos Tutuola. From the French sector, novels by the following authors are discussed: Laye Camara, Cheik Hamidou Kane, Mongo Beti, Ferdinand Oyono, Ousmane Sembène, Abdoulaye Sadji, Ahmadu Kourouma, Nazi Boni, and Yambo Ouologuem. L. S. Senghor's *Poèmes* and *Negritude et Humanisme* are discussed in connection with the influence of audience on language.

Interviews with President Senghor, Sembène, Kane, Camara, Pathé Giagne, Achebe, Ngugi Wa Thiong'O, and Ezekiel Mphahlele are incorporated into the study whenever they help to illuminate a point.

The study shows that the modern African novelist is a committed artist who is under constant pressure to meet the demands of a dual audience made up of Europeans and the Western-educated African elite. The two audiences exert different influences on the writer. In the overall evaluation of the influence of readership on the writing, it is found that the European audience exerts more influence on the writer from the fact that the writer uses the European language, publishing houses, and literary genre.

However, the trend of later novels set in Independent Africa shows less European influence in subject matter and its presentation. And as the writer's local audience expands along with his regional publication resources, he would be less preoccupied with the desire to satisfy the literary taste of the European audience even though he may still have to contend with the European language and genre.

FOREWORD

In *Black Writers: White Audience—A Critical Approach to African Literature*, Dr. Phanuel Egejuru critically examines the effect on the African novelist of the fact that the language in which he writes, his publishers, the art form in which he expresses himself, and a significant proportion of his readership are non-African.

One important influence which is implied in the book but which probably qualifies for a chapter of its own is that of the literary critic. He was at least in the early years, also non-African, and had scanty (if any) knowledge of the culture of the African creative writer. Nevertheless he unabashedly pontificated on what constituted authentic African writing. By helping to build up and project the public image of the writers he admired and deliberately disregarding or even denigrating those he did not; by attempting to prescribe guidelines for African writing, these critics wielded excessive influence especially on inexperienced African writers naturally seeking recognition. The African writer was thus in the unhappy position in which his success as a writer was determined not by his fellow Africans but by a handful of European and American literary critics with preconceived ideas about what African writing should be.

This book is a welcome addition to the growing body of literary criticism by Africans on African writers. Having, as it were, sucked the same breast as the African novelist she is reviewing, the author approaches her study with a store of inside knowledge which many foreign critics lack woefully. This fact comes out very clearly in her observations on the works of Chinua Achebe and other Igbo writers. Her knowledge of French (as well as English) is an additional feather to her cap.

11

One feature of the study which makes it particularly commendable is the additional trouble taken by the author to interview eight of the novelists whose works she studied. It is one thing for a critic to speculate about an author's intentions (as many critics do, and often with little success); it is something else to give the author the opportunity to speak for himself. The reports of the interviews make interesting reading; they also bring the novelists reviewed much closer to the reader.

I commend the book to students and critics of African literature as well as to the African writers themselves. It has compelled me to take another look at the mirror, so to say, in an attempt to see how I would have come off if any of my four published novels had come under Dr. Egejuru's searchlight.

Not all will agree with the author's conclusions, but I believe most readers will agree that it is a painstakingly researched, provocative, and interesting book.

Chukwuemeka Ike,
Registrar (& Chief Executive),
West African Examinations Council,
Accra, Ghana.

INTRODUCTION

Since the second half of the twentieth century, Africa has been a subject of interest in the academic world. Among the various fields of study such as history, anthropology, sociology, and so on, African literature has been the most controversial subject of debate. This controversy is partly due to the particular nature of literature as a subject and partly due to the peculiar situation of the African writer as compared to writers in other parts of the world.

Unlike history, anthropology, sociology, and many other fields of study, literature has linguistic and national implications. A historian or a sociologist can write about any people in any language. But more important than that is the fact that his audience is universal. On the other hand, *The American College Dictionary* defines literature as "The entire body of writings of a specific language, period, people, subject . . . e.g., the literature of England." Thus a literary writer must write in a specific language, in most cases his native language. He also has a select audience, usually the people who share the same language and culture with him.

One could cite a few examples of writers who wrote in foreign languages. We find as far back as the second century, Apuleius,* a Numid from North Africa, who wrote his *Golden Ass* in Latin. We also find Erasmus (1466?-1536), the Dutch humanist and satirist, who wrote in Latin. Saint Augustine of Hippo wrote his *Confessions* in Latin. Several African scholars of the Middle Ages in Timbuktu wrote in Arabic. In contemporary literature

---

*Information by Hassan el Nouty, Professor of French and Specialist in French African Literature.

we find authors like the Irish Samuel Beckett writing in French while the Polish Joseph Conrad wrote in English. In each case the language choice was significantly dictated by an assumed audience.

These examples show that modern African writers are not the first people to write in foreign languages. However, the situation of the African writers is still unique. Because for the first time in literary history, we have a whole body of literature identified with an entire continent—Africa, and yet this literature is written in foreign languages. None of the other writers, cited as examples of writers in foreign languages, ever constituted a body of literature accredited to their own countries. Their works are listed with the rest of the literature of the people whose language they used.

We therefore find the peculiar situation of the modern African writer who, in order to express his African experience and vision of life, is compelled by historical circumstances to use the language and imitate the literary tradition of an external audience.

The language factor is very important because the choice of language invariably qualifies the choice of audience. In this case the African writer who writes in English or French automatically has as his audience all the people that speak that language. Incidentally his audience comprises Africans and Europeans who are affiliated by language but disaffiliated by culture.

By writing in European languages, African writers cannot escape being read by Europeans even if the work is intended solely for the local audience. But the issue is not the fact of "other readers" but the pre-awareness that they must be catered to. Most of the writers find it hard or humiliating to admit this fact, but a close study of several African novels shows that there is often a deliberate effort on the writers' part to present their works in a way to please either an external audience or their local audience.

Among the most patent things that show the tendency to cater to the European audience are: (a) Insertion and explanation of anthropological materials which should be taken for granted by a local audience; (b) the use of a glossary to explain African terms; (c) the use of the pronouns "our" or "us" to mean Africans; and (d) such phrases as "In Africa, girls and women do. . . ."

We find thus that the presentation of subject matter and sometimes the choice of it are very much influenced by the particular audience which the writer has in mind; that is, he takes into consideration the literary taste and sensitivity of the audience that he wants to address.

The popular genre in modern African literature is the novel. European critics like George Lukacs associate the beginning and development of the novel with the bourgeois class, which is more interested in the novel than any other class of the society. By choosing the novel rather than the theater, for instance, the African writer announces his preferred audience—the bourgeoisie, composed of European bourgeoisie and the Western-educated African elite. This choice eliminates the African masses, most of whom do not understand the foreign languages and are not familiar with the novel genre.

With this Afro-European audience, the writer is faced with the problem of pleasing his two audiences. For although the two share the same literary tradition and sometimes the same literary tastes, they often react differently to the same work. This is partly due to the kind of relationship that grew up between Europeans and Africans as a result of colonialism.

For the European bourgeois at home, Africa is an unknown land with different people and strange customs. They tend therefore to appreciate those works which "teach" them about African people and their customs. For the African elite who have constantly watched the colonial rulers look down on everything African, they tend to appreciate the works that show off all that is good about Africa, works which show that Africa has dignity. In short, works that contradict the poor and distorted image that Europeans have about Africa. This demand of the African elite audience is very important in that it makes of the writer a committed artist with the obligation to present, as much as he can, a balanced view of Africa to the outside world.

Since the writers' audience—African and European, likes to

read about Africa, though for different reasons, the result is that the topic of African literature is always Africa. But while drawing upon Africa, the writer is under pressure from his audience to choose particular areas of Africa—customs and experiences —and handle them in a way that appeals to the particular audience that he wants to please.

With his borrowed literary tradition and his borrowed language to express his African experience, the African writer finds himself in the difficult situation in which his audience exerts a great deal of influence on his writing.

From the preceding remarks, the aim of this study could be thus stated: To examine the relationship between the African writer and his audience; to find out the extent to which he is influenced in his writing by the literary tradition, tastes, language, and sensitivity of his audience.

Black Writers: White Audience

1

AUDIENCE

"Certainly most African writers up to now have in practice written to a Western rather than an African audience."[1] A brief survey I made among the African elite also shows that the African writer today is largely addressing a non-African audience. Most of the African writings that I have studied show by their subject matter and the manner of their presentation that the African writer is very much aware of his external, European bourgeois audience as well as his African elite audience. But what is most surprising is that most of the authors whom I interviewed claimed to be writing exclusively for an African audience. It was only with much reluctance that some of them admitted the existence of a double audience made up mostly of the European bourgeois and the Western educated African elite.

It will be helpful for the purpose of comparison with their works to write out the answers of some of these writers to my questions on audience. President L. S. Senghor was the first writer I questioned.

QUESTION: Who is your audience?

PRESIDENT SENGHOR: First of all, when I write, I address an African audience and I believe that for someone to really "feel" my poems he has to be an African, or rather, I would say that he has to be Senegalese. You see, I write in a certain geographic, historic, physical, moral, and aesthetic environment, but beyond one's ethnic group and country, one has to reach all men. And that is why the first exigency is that of sincerity. But I would say that sincerity alone is not sufficient.

What distinguishes prose from poetry is not sincerity, it is a certain "manner of saying," and if we meet the exigencies of Negro-African aesthetics, and since I am a Negro-African writer, I will reach Negro-Africans, but I will at the same time reach other men. The Africans would be touched because they will recognize themselves in what I write. But other men will also be touched because they have the impression that it is a new way of saying things human.

QUESTION: Would that mean that when you write, you think of an African audience as well as an audience that is outside Africa?

PRESIDENT SENGHOR: Exactly.

QUESTION: Does this create any problem for you?

PRESIDENT SENGHOR: No, no. That has never posed a problem.

QUESTION: Would this mean that you expect nothing from them by way of reaction?

PRESIDENT SENGHOR: I do, because I have the impression that I am delivering a message; therefore, I expect my audience to understand my message. But I don't think there is an opposition between my African and non-African audiences. And the best proof is that I am read as much by Africans as by non-Africans. And the majority of students who write theses on me are Europeans in general and women in particular. I have to say though, that the most comprehensive audience is the African one. The best writings on my poems come from Africans: the best thesis is that of an American Black woman; the best article is that of a Nigerian professor, and in fact the Africans are the ones that understand me better.[2]

At the beginning of the interview, President Senghor preferred to imply rather than mention his "other" audience. It required a reiteration of his answer before he started to refer to it as non-African, and later he specified it as European. This reluctance to recognize the existence of an external audience is a general attitude of African writers. Perhaps this is a normal reaction on their part since the writer is looked upon as the spokesman of his people. If they should admit of having a European audience it would simply mean a betrayal of their people and a shirking of their responsibility toward Africa.

President Senghor states that he is read as much by Africans as by Europeans. He says that at least half of his poetry books are sold in Africa, and he quoted 50,000 copies at least.[3] From his answer, it is clear that he is mostly read by European and African academicians. His books are set in the French lycées and universities, they are also set in Senegal and in some universities in the United States of America. Now, if we should compare the ratio of Senghor's readers in Africa to the ratio of readers in Europe and America together, it would most likely run in the thousands for the Western world, to one or less for Africa since the number of academicians in Europe and America together is by far greater than that in Africa.

In a brief survey I conducted among some university students in Dakar to find out who was the most popular author in Senegal, all the students said that Senghor's books are imposed on the university. They said that many students prefer to read Sèmbene and some other French-African writers like Oyono and Mongo Beti. When I later asked Mr. Sèmbene the same question, he said that in a recent survey on the popular Senegalese writers, President Senghor came third while Mr. Sèmbene came first. He added that Senghor is taught in the university, but that people do not just go out to buy his books of poetry.

In actual fact, Senghor is not the only African author whose works are confined to the academic sector of the society. It is true of all African writers because the Western-educated African elite is the only foreign language reading public in Africa at the moment. Like Senghor, Achebe claims that he sells more books in Africa than overseas. This is because his books are now set in school syllabuses in West Africa. In 1964, his *Things Fall Apart* became the first novel by an African writer to be included in the required syllabus for the West African School Certificate Examination. He is also widely studied in several universities in Africa. When the book appeared first in hardcover, it was sold at fifteen shillings a copy, and for the average African it was too expensive to buy. Perhaps, it is because of this high price that

Larson contends that the novel was "written for readers outside Africa";[4] these outsiders are mainly Europeans and Americans, for they alone can afford to buy the book. By 1964, the novel has appeared in paperback and has sold at five shillings a copy. Achebe claims that he sold 20,000 copies in Nigeria alone.[5] By the time his fourth book (*A Man of the People*) appeared, Achebe has become so popular in Africa that it would be hard for any critic to say that he is writing for an external audience. Furthermore, his subject matter in that novel and how he handled it show that he is addressing his local Nigerian audience.

The fact that Achebe is very popular in Africa and overseas makes it hard for one to say offhand that he has a larger audience in Africa or outside Africa, and it would require tedious research before one could come out with definite figures on Achebe's audience in and outside Africa. At the moment he is the only authority on the issue of his audience, and as the editorial advisor of African Writers Series he is in a better position to know how many of his books are sold in different parts of the world.

On the question of audience Achebe's answer is rather vague for he chose not to pinpoint any particular group of readers as his audience. In his reply to the question of who his audience is, he said:

ACHEBE: My audience is anybody who wants to read. I no longer think of any particular group of people although I do think that I have more readers in particular places, e.g., Nigeria; but my audience is not limited to Nigeria anyway. Anybody who is interested in the ideas I am expounding is my audience.

QUESTION: Did you arrive at this conclusion after you wrote more novels, other than the first one?

ACHEBE: Yes, I suppose so. One thing about this kind of problem. . . . I didn't have any particular idea in mind to expound to start with. But I knew vaguely that I wanted to talk to people who live in different places, they will be English-speaking to begin with because I was writing in English. But English-speaking with a difference. After the first book came out, this kind of question is asked more and more and one begins to think more clearly of who constitutes one's audience. And I think it is at that point that I finally came to the conclusion that you really shouldn't worry; anybody who wants to read you is your audience.

QUESTION: That is, in the beginning, you had no preconceived audience in mind?

ACHEBE: Not consciously, maybe subconsciously. I mean anybody who opens his mouth to talk has to know that there is an audience; it doesn't have to be in terms of clearly seeing the faces. It is in a way unclear in the sense of faces but it is clear in the sense that you are talking and anybody who is talking is talking to someone, even to himself.

QUESTION: You said your readers are English-speaking with a difference, that is, the literate group in case of Nigerians where you have more readers. Don't you think this is a very small fraction of the entire people?

ACHEBE: As far as I am concerned that is neither here nor there. I mean you get up and talk and you can pick your audience . . . and if you are writing you are thinking of people who can read; there's nobody who can get up and talk to every single person in the world, not even in his own country. So the size of audience may be important but it is not the main thing.

QUESTION: In other words, you have written for this audience because it reads English?

ACHEBE: Yes.

QUESTION: I would imagine that you have a certain message which you intend to communicate to this audience. Would you say that you do satisfy their expectations of you?

ACHEBE: Well, that's not the understanding that I should be expected to make a statement on. It's really for you. But I do have an idea of the kind of feedback which one gets from all kinds of people who stop you on the street to say they have read such and such from you and people who write to you and say: "this is what I think of your books."

QUESTION: I would like to know if you share the same feeling as many writers who say that they have an obligation toward their audience?

ACHEBE: Oh, yes, definitely, I think I have a responsibility to my audience, but it's not very easy to define; in other words, what I mean is: I want to do what I think is right, to hold up values that I think are important and wholesome, to stand for things that are meaningful. If I am telling a story I want to tell a story that is valuable in terms of ideas it conveys; this is what I think is my responsibility to myself and to my audience—to do the best.

QUESTION: To do the best you said. Would you then say that your audience somehow influences you in your creative work?

ACHEBE: I suppose in an indirect way; this does not entail monitoring your audience to give them what they want; in other words I have to satisfy myself that what I am saying is true and important and if those who read me agree that what I am saying is true and important and well said, then I am obviously very happy. If they don't, I would still say it. First of all, because the conviction is mine, the vision is mine. I put this vision to you. You don't have to agree. So I don't know if this means that I am open to influence by my audience; in an indirect way, yes, but not in the sense of taking dictation.

QUESTION: I really mean in your choice of topic, its handling, the expressions you use, etc., thinking of some audience which might not understand you?

ACHEBE: No. I don't bother about that at all. The subject matter is immaterial. The way I handle it, all this is dictated to me by the story, by what I am saying not by the level of understanding of some audience that I might have in mind, because this is speculative to begin with. I simply do the thing the best way I know, and that's the only condition.

QUESTION: What do you say to the fact that the author explains "kola nut" to a Nigerian audience? And the use of a glossary. Don't you think that that presupposes a foreign audience?

ACHEBE: Well, that is slightly different from what I was answering. The question of glossary is something for the publisher; in my own case, he says: "We want the people to understand it." There was none in the first novel and when a glossary was done, it was done by someone else. It is a different kind of thing. Once a novel is seen in terms of its educational value that's a different explanation for the whole thing.

QUESTION: The formula which you use to introduce a proverb, e.g., "among the Ibo we say this . . ." Would this imply that you are talking to an external audience?

ACHEBE: No! That's not true, as you must know, because the formula of introducing a proverb in Ibo is precisely that: "ka ndi be anyi si ekwu" (As our people normally say). It is a matter of form of expression which varies from place to place. If you find me explaining something for the benefit of foreigners, that's a sign of underdevelopment as a writer, but I don't think you find too many examples.

As can be seen from Achebe's well-thought-out answers, his audience is somehow universal. However, there is some element of selection in that this audience is English-speaking, with or without a difference, because the writer is writing in English. And here at once one sees the powerful grip of a language that makes a writer think of a particular audience, at a subconscious level at least. Even though this audience is not all that defined, since you can always talk to anybody who wants to listen to you, Achebe still feels a sense of responsibility toward it—to do what is right and to uphold wholesome values. Here, this faceless audience exerts some degree of influence, even if indirectly, on the writer, who suffers some uneasiness as to whether this audience would agree or disagree with what he has to say.

Achebe does not deny that one may or does find some turns of phrases in his first novel, which indicate the writer's awareness of a foreign audience that might require further help from the writer in order to understand what he was saying. But this is what he attributes to artistic immaturity or underdevelopment. Yet it is clear that if he were writing in Ibo for an Ibo audience in particular, this problem of authorian intervention to explain would never have arisen. Thus showing the indirect influence of his readers whose language he is compelled to use.[6]

As it has already been shown in figures, it is important to note that the number of books sold by Senghor and Achebe is relative to their school audience. If one should exclude the school and university audiences, it is most unlikely that both writers would sell more books in Africa than would other writers. As has already been mentioned, Senghor is not the most popular writer in Senegal and people prefer to buy novels by other writers than his books of poems. It is equally unlikely that the average Nigerian reader would prefer Achebe's *Things Fall Apart* to Ekwensi's *Jagua Nana*. In fact, *Jagua Nana* has been the only novel printed in series in a national paper, the Nigerian *Sunday Times*. Ekwensi's first attempt at a novel, *When Love Whispers*, reached a best-seller standard when it appeared in 1947. It aroused people's interest in Onitsha Market literature, which comprises pamphlets ranging from twenty to fifty pages. They are noted for their bombastic English and catchy titles such as: *The Broken Heart*, *When Love Whispers*, *Veronica*, *My Daughter*, *Okeke, the Magician*, *Money Hard to Get*, etc. Their subjects vary from adolescent love and romance, courtship and marriage, to money-making and how to write business letters.

A number of critics of African literature regard the Onitsha Market pamphlets as the beginning of novels in Nigeria. Some like Charles Larson consider them "among the best depictions of realism that African novel has seen to date".[7]

In terms of African audience, more credit should be given to these pamphleteers because they are the only writers who could claim an exclusively local audience. They are published by local publishers and sold mostly by the traders in Onitsha Market and by some local bookstores. They are very popular among secondary-school children, literate traders, and civil servants whose level of education (standard six) is not high enough to handle the more sophisticated novels such as Soyinka's *The Interpreters* or Okara's *The Voice*.

Statistics are not available for the sale of Onitsha Market novels, but from what I know about them, it is not unlikely that they would outsell the more sophisticated novels whose readership is confined to the very academic sector of the society, as opposed to the less academic audience that constitute a majority of the literate public.

Mr. Ousmane Sembène reacted vehemently to the suggestion that he is writing for two audiences.

QUESTION: Who is your audience?

SEMBENE: For me, first of all, there is one audience; it is my country. It is not the consideration of others, and it is often false problems that are created for those artists who, from the onset, want to be universal. Yet there is no work created in this perspective of universality. First, the artist can only express his people and his time. Now that I am writing in Wolof, I can only write for a Wolof audience. When unfortunately I write in French, I write first of all for my people and by correlation for all those who speak the French language.

QUESTION: Now that you are writing for a Wolof audience, does that make it easier for you in terms of what you present to your readers, of language and of manner of presenting your subject matter?

SEMBENE: The audience has never posed any problems for me. I am free to choose my subjects and to treat them as I like, because it is not fair to blame the audience for anything. The audience has never asked the artist for this or that kind of work. They only ask for bread, cinema, hospitals, etc. It is left to the artist to show them the inside of things.[8]

If Mr. Sembène had written all his books in Wolof, and if other African writers were writing in African languages, there would be no question of an external audience influencing, let alone, controlling, African writing. However, Sembène's Wolof writing is a two-monthly magazine (*Kaddu*) in its sixth issue. The works for which he is known, *Les Bouts de Bois de Dieu, Le Mandat, Le Docker Noir,* are all written in French. He said that his Wolof audience is larger than his French audience in Senegal and this was confirmed by the co-editor of the *Kaddu,*

Mr. Pathé Giagne, another radical Senegalese writer whom I interviewed. This is quite understandable since Wolof is the most widely spoken language in Senegal. Mr. Sembène considers it unfortunate that he writes in French, for he realizes the implications of using a foreign language to write a literature which you intend solely for your own ethnic group. It may be true that his audience does not dictate his subjects, but he cannot escape exigencies of the French language, which is inevitably that of the French reading public.

Mr. Laye Camara was more direct in his answer to the question on audience. He said:

> It is evident that there are two sets of audiences at the moment: the foreign, or European, and the African audiences. But what is most important to me is what Africa herself thinks of what I say. I would say that art is a kind of suffering through which the individual liberates himself in view of another suffering. A person has something to say, he is seized by the urge to express it in order to liberate himself; at that very moment he does not think of an audience, he thinks of himself. Finally, the audience intervenes.[9]

Mr. Camara was obviously thinking of his book *L'Enfant Noir* when he talked of the artist being seized by a certain desire to liberate himself of his "suffering," because at various conferences he has insisted that it was homesickness that inspired him to write his first novel. He repeated his experience to me:

> I was in Paris. I was feeling homesick and *L'Enfant Noir* was the result. The only way to overcome the difficulty was to go into my room in the evening and recall the sweetness of Africa, my parents, and my friends. By thinking of them I forgot my unhappiness.[10]

This proves that Camara was only preoccupied with himself when he wrote his first novel. In short, he had no audience in mind. But as will be shown later under subject matter and its treatment, certain passages in *L'Enfant Noir* tend to show that the author was mostly addressing a non-African audience. He says that he cares very much about what Africa thinks of what he says. He probably started to think this way when he realized that "Africa" was going to read his book. Since "Africa" is not a person, one would assume that Camara means Africans. He shows his concern over the opinion of his fellow Africans by his desperate effort to defend himself against those African intellectuals who accused him of evading the issue that occupied all the other African writers—colonialism. His reply to these accusations and the work he produced in *Le Regard du Roi* will be treated in a later chapter on the influence of audience on choice of subject.

Cheik Hamidou Kane also told me that he was not thinking of any audience when he wrote his *L'Aventure Ambigue*, because he had no intention of publishing the book. He only did so at the instigation of friends. He insisted very strongly that the book that he is now writing is strictly intended for the African elite audience, which he maintains is the only audience available in Africa at the moment.

When asked if he knew any African novelists writing exclusively for the African audience, Kane replied:

> The African novelist has no audience in Africa because the Africans are not familiar with the tradition of the novel. The writer is therefore obliged, if he wants to be read, to write for the audience whose literary tradition he has borrowed. In this case he has to use the technique and the recipe which allow this audience to understand him. He must also pay attention to their sensitivity.[11]

It is true that Mr. Kane did not mention subject matter, but it is implied in the author's concern for the sensitivity of his audience because he has to write what appeals to them.

Like many other writers, Ezekiel Mphahlele was very direct in his answer on the question of audience.

QUESTION: Who is your audience?
MPHAHLELE: My audience is an African audience first and fore-

most. When I write and because I am writing about things that concern Africans, I have them in mind all the time and nobody else.

QUESTION: In this case you do not mean the local audience in South Africa?

MPHAHLELE: No. I am talking about the African audience at large. There is a sense in which when you write about your local setting; of course, you are thinking that there is a potential local audience and even though my books are banned in South Africa, I do have them in mind but there is a point at which they fused with the general African audience.

QUESTION: In other words you do have a specific audience in mind?

MPHAHLELE: Yes.

QUESTION: Does this audience in any way influence you in your choice of topic and presentation of it?

MPHAHLELE: No. Not in any direct sense at all; that means, I don't say, when I have found something that I want to write about, I ask myself whether my African audience will like this or not. The ruling passion in me when I write is my faithfulness to reality. I base my writing on things that either have happened in my presence or that I heard about from my contemporaries or people I live with or read about, which means it will be about people or happenings of today. These are things that suggest themes to my mind.

QUESTION: Do you feel you have a certain obligation to your readers?

MPHAHLELE: No. Here again it is always difficult to say at which time you have a sense of commitment that gets hold of you. I would say that the first commitment I find . . . , first of all, is that I take my African audience for granted; that is, I am writing out of an African experience and it is something that they tune into naturally, say more naturally than they would tune into Shakespeare, that is to the extent that I feel my audience in those terms. Secondly my commitment at the next level is my commitment to my subject, that is, to be faithful to it and not to falsify it; and I think in my effort not to falsify it comes an element here of how I think it will come across to my audience. . . .

QUESTION: There is here a direct influence, wouldn't you say?

MPHAHLELE: Yes. The audience comes in but it is always difficult to put your finger on that kind of commitment because if you are more committed to your subject than to your African reality, you are therefore in a sense committed to your African audience. They don't say to you silently, "You've got to be writing for us," even though you know that finally that is where it is going to end up. It is more of a commitment to your African reality I would say than to an audience as a group of readers that you can enumerate.

QUESTION: I am sure you expect a certain reaction from your audience. From the books you have published, do you think they react the way you had expected?

MPHAHLELE: That's always a difficult thing to really determine. I think I don't know; I suspect that a number of African writers have the same difficulty, that we seldom know what the enlightened man thinks about our work in any intelligent way. We hear rumors, we hear scattered voices of people we meet, at your back, "That's a good book," that kind of thing. But they don't constitute a feasible, tangible African audience to that extent, but I don't really know what people think in Africa about my works. All I can say is that they are reading some of these things at school; the school market is still the most viable market; outside of school one doesn't know. And then there aren't any enlightened book reviews in African papers, so one doesn't get them and if one doesn't, what does one go by?

QUESTION: So you don't really know whether more Africans read your books or more non-Africans?

MPHAHLELE: I wouldn't know at all unless one is published on both sides of the Atlantic, then one knows one is getting across to a large number on both sides, but there is no way of knowing, not any way of knowing what Africans think. I don't know whether the writer who lives in his own country

all the time and writes there is any more fortunate than we
who are outside; whether he actually comes in close grips
with the comments about his works or not, I would suspect
none.

QUESTION: I don't think writers have enough readers among
Africans outside of school. If one is not fortunate enough to
have his book set in schools, do you think he has any chance
of being read at all in Africa?

MPHAHLELE: You don't get read at all!

QUESTION: From the contents of *Down Second Avenue*, would
you consider yourself in that book as the voice of the suffering
people of South Africa?

MPHAHLELE: Yes I could. I certainly could. I really could, yes.
That is one book I happen to know did strike the chord
among my own readers in South Africa. Then I did hear
echoes, a lot more echoes about their reaction to the book
and they were more fascinated by it than about anything
else I have written outside.[12]

QUESTION: In most African novels one finds certain turns of
phrases which presuppose some external audience which is
not African. Do you think they are not really thinking of
Africans?

MPHAHLELE: No, I think it is more of a recognition that you
have other African readers who don't speak your language,
and will not know what you mean when you use your local
terms. The other thing is that you don't want to bamboozle
your editor. This is one thing that comes together with publishing abroad.

QUESTION: Would you say, then, that the audience exercises a
certain amount of influence on the way a writer presents
his topic?

MPHAHLELE: That's right.

For Mphahlele there is no doubt in his mind as to who
his audience is—it is an African audience, but it is a very minute
one made up of students. And even getting this audience depends
on whether one is lucky enough to be assigned in the schools.

Therefore, if one doesn't get read in school, one isn't read at all!

Mphahlele's answer is the same as that or almost the same as Senghor's and Achebe's who claim more readers in Africa because their works are studied in schools. From this statement, one could conclude that if the school audience is eliminated, the few African writers whose works are studied in schools would not have any readers at all in Africa.

Besides, as Mphahlele points out clearly, the fact of being published on the other side of the Atlantic makes it difficult for the African writer to know if he is getting across to his supposed African audience! One wonders then if this does not mean a total absence of readers in Africa, that is, if one takes the "people" into consideration.

Ngugi Wa Thiong'O is even more specific in his answer to the question on audience:

QUESTION: Who is your audience?

THIONG'O: It is very difficult for any one writer to know who his audience is. But I take it that mine is the East African audience. I have in fact an African audience in mind. At least those who can read, but they are primarily a Kenyan East African audience. Or rather people who are in some ways affected by the kind of conditions and issues that I write about.

QUESTION: In other words you do have some message which you wish to communicate to a particular audience?

THIONG'O: Not so much a direct, didactic message but a message in a more general sense that you are making people aware of the issues around them, aware of those things that are shaping their own lives.

QUESTION: Since you are inspired by the situation and issues that affect an entire region of Africa or precisely a cross section of East Africa . . . Kenya, could you in that case consider yourself as the voice of the people of East Africa?

THIONG'O: I don't consider myself as the voice of the people. What I do like to think is that I can raise issues that are meaningful to the people. When I write, I like to think that I

am touching the heart of the matter, then I should be able
to discuss the moving issues of Kenya and East Africa.

QUESTION: In that sense I will assume you are committed to
this audience somehow?

THIONG'O: In a sense, yes. In so far as one is making this
audience look fundamentally at the tensions and conflicts
underlying their daily, social, political, economic actions. You
are in fact committed to that audience; otherwise, there is
no sense addressing yourself to the issues affecting them.

QUESTION: Since you are really committed to this audience, would
you say that it influences your choice of subject and the way
you handle it?

THIONG'O: Yes. I suppose in two ways: (1) The choice of
subject matter is likely to be that which is again a pressing
problem in the community about which I am writing. I
can't find myself setting my novel in the moon or in America
or Britain although in the future I might feel like doing it.
Britain for instance is too far removed from the pressing
problems around me today so the audience can influence the
choice of subject in that I want to discuss that which has
been affecting my community or rather those issues that
shaped the development of the community. (2) In terms
of technique of presentation, an audience does not affect me
in this way, but on the whole I do try to get that narrative
technique structure which is part of the people's narrative
inheritance.

QUESTION: In other words you are influenced by the African
traditional narrative form?

THIONG'O: Yes. Insofar as oral tradition is part and parcel of
one's cultural upbringing it is bound to affect one's narrative
technique. But there is another immediate way the audience
can affect one's narrative technique; I have in mind, in the
village when people tell stories and you are around to listen,
you will somehow be impressed or affected to the extent that
you may find yourself telling stories in the same way.

QUESTION: This oral tradition you said you are now trying in your works. I don't find it in *Weep Not Child*. Where have you really tried it?

THIONG'O: I didn't use the technique in *Weep Not Child* and *River Between*. There I was using the traditional novelistic third person biographical kind of structure. It is only in *A Grain of Wheat* that I tried the technique of narratives within narrative as a conscious narrative structure.

QUESTION: I would imagine you expect some kind of reaction from your audience with respect to what you have written. Do you think they are responding in the way you had expected?

THIONG'O: With the novel this is difficult to say because the novel is a very individual art form. It is not public reading. But occasionally we get letters from people who make comments on what you have written, taking one aspect of the novel that affected them. The other form is the review and articles on the novel.

QUESTION: You said you are writing exclusively for East Africa, or rather for those who are affected by the situation you describe. Would this mean that you have more readers in East Africa than from some other external audience?

THIONG'O: I think the word "mainly" will be more appropriate than "exclusively." In terms of readership I think I am read more in East Africa or in Africa generally than outside. This may well be because the book is set in the school syllabus and it is difficult to find readers who are not part of the school system.

QUESTION: Judging from the ways the writers put in certain phrases, it does appear that they are not trying to reach a local audience. For instance explaining the significance of "Bride Price." What would you say to this? Don't you think the writer has some non-African audience in mind?

THIONG'O: Not necessarily. Of course there are writers who do that because their readers are outside Africa. There is also the popular belief that African writers are writing for a non-African audience. There are writers who want to reach that mythic, non-African audience. Another thing that conditions them is not so much this non-African readership but other national commitments, because we cannot assume that the cultural symbols of one community apply to the rest.[13]

Of the writers so far interviewed on the question of audience Ngugi Wa Thiong'O seems to be the only one who is seriously "involved" with his local East African audience. All the same, his claim to more readers from East Africa has the same explanation as the other writers whose books are set in the school syllabus. Again we find the same limited school audience without which perhaps Ngugi wouldn't get read at all by the East African people whose life experiences he is exploring in his novels. It is rather ironic that his local audience, which he says influences his choice of subject matter, does not get to read him because he writes in English. This leaves him, with the rest of his brother writers, only an external English-reading audience, who probably find the subject matter quite alien to their own situation and will only read his novel for the purpose of "learning" about current issues in East Africa.

We see then that the African writer is very much controlled by an external audience whose existence he consciously tries to erase. Yet, with this strong hold on him, he still insists that he is mainly interested in writing for his fellow Africans. Perhaps for the African writer there is a great deal more to writing than publication, genre, language, technique, and subject matter. One has to go into the works to find out what is left and perhaps that is where the influence of the African audience would be found!

So far, the survey shows how defensive most African writers are on the question of a double audience. It has been suggested that this may be due to the writers' loyalty to their people and continent. But more important than that is their desire to show that they are now independent of the colonial masters, politically and otherwise. It is only when one reminds these writers that they are still using the language of the colonialists that they admit, *à la regueur*, that they have a double audience.

It was President Senghor himself who raised the problem of opposition between two audiences: "Je ne pense pas qu' il y ait une opposition entre mon public africain et mon public non-africain."[14] He made this statement because he knows that there is bound to be an opposition where there are two sets of people with different cultural backgrounds. It is this very opposition that constitutes the biggest problem for the African writers, though they will not admit it. Their personal artistry suffers while they exert themselves trying to reconcile or satisfy their two audiences. Senghor who is much aware of this opposition says he does not encounter it. He may be right, for with his theory of *metissage culturel*, he knows how best to reoncile opposing forces. From the outset he knew what the problem was and he set out to deal with it. When I told him that I did not know the difference between French thinking and African thinking, he said:

> In reality, we are achieving a symbiosis between French thought and sentiment and African thought and sentiment. We are coming out with a cross-breed culture and that is not bad.[15]

Senghor's position is thus different from that of other writers because they consciously try to suppress the fact that they are working toward a symbiosis, if not of culture in general at least of literature in particular. Evidence of this literary symbiosis is found in the works, and a careful study shows that these works are *entre deux mondes*, neither African nor European, but having elements of both. The work for the critic is to find out the degree of influence which each audience exercises over the African writer.

NOTES

1. Edgar Wright, "African Literature I: Problem of Criticism," *Journal of Commonwealth Literature*, No. 2, (December, 1966), p. 108.
2. Interview with Senghor by author, Dakar, December, 1972.
3. *Ibid.*

4. Charles Larson, *The Emergence of African Fiction* (Bloomington: Indiana University Press, 1971), p. 27.
5. Chinua Achebe, "The Novelist as a Teacher," *New Statesman*, (January 29, 1956), p. 162.
6. Interview with Achebe by author, Amherst, Massachusetts, September, 1974.
7. Larson, p. 92.
8. Interview with Ousmane Sembène by author, December, 1972.
9. Interview with Laye Camara by author, December, 1972.
10. *Ibid.*
11. Interview with Cheik Hamidou Kane by author, Abidjan, December, 1972.
12. Interview with Ezekiel Mphahlele, Philadelphia, September, 1974.
13. Interview with Ngugi Wa Thiong'O. Nairobi, December, 1974.
14. Interview with President Senghor.
15. *Ibid.*

2

PUBLICATION

One could say that publication is among the most decisive factors in the production of literary material. The extent to which publication controls the writer is best demonstrated by Diderot and his *Encyclopédie*. Diderot's audacity as a writer had already earned him some months in the prison of Vincennes after the publication of his *Lettre sur les Aveuges*. To make sure that the *Encyclopédie* was finished and to avoid too much censorship from the editor, Diderot resorted to all kinds of ruses, using the method of *renvoi* or treating serious subjects under trivial headings. It is quite evident that the *Encyclopédie*, as revolutionary as it was, would have been much more so if the editors had not intervened to modify its contents.

Some other bold writers like Voltaire had to be locked up twice in the Bastille after being banished to the provinces for daring to write so boldly about the Regent. This power of the press did not end with the eighteenth century because it is still in full force in the twentieth century, irrespective of its "free press." Today the writer can still go on and put down whatever his imagination presents to him, but it is up to the editor to accept and print the matter as given to him or to modify it to meet the demands of the press.

Like other writers, the African writer has to consider the requirements of his editor when he is writing. But it appears that for every problem a European writer encounters, the African doubles or triples it. For instance, in Europe there are many publishing houses, and the author can always take his work to another publisher if he is rejected by some other. The African writer does not have this opportunity in his country. At the moment there are few publishing houses in Africa.

In East Africa we have the East African publishing house which publishes in English and Kiswahili. In Nigeria we have Oxford University Press, Ibadan branch; Ibadan University Press; University of Ife Press, the government publishing house at Lagos and in some other state capitals in Nigeria. There are also privately owned ones like Mbari Publications, Abiodun Works, the Caxton Press of West Africa Ltd.—all of Ibadan. There is also the most recent one at Enugu, Nwamife publishing house run by Nwankwo and Ifejika.

In Ghana we find the Ghana Publishing Corporation and the privately owned Anowuo Educational Publications, which puts out ten to twenty books a year, all written by Ghanaians about Ghanaian life and society.[1] The proprietor of Anowuo, Asare Konadu, is one of the few Africans who is aware of the influence of the foreign press on African literature. Konadu's objective is to "help Ghanaian authors reach their countrymen without having to sell to a London publisher and please a partly foreign readership."[2]

None of the above local publishers has published any major works in African literature. Most of the publications in African literature of English expression are done by Heinemann, Longmans, Macmillan, and various companies in the U.S.A.

In French West African countries, the story is much the same if not worse. With the possible exception of Cameroon, which has small publishing houses like Librairie au Messager, Abbia, and the Clé publishing house, there are no publishing facilities in French West Africa. At the moment, Senegal is only trying to set up a publishing house which would publish in French and in some six other languages of Senegal. All major literary works by Francophone writers of Africa are published in France or Canada. Among their popular editors are Le Seuil, Juillard, Plon, and Presence Africaine.

Until African countries establish publishing houses to handle materials in African and international languages, African writers will continue to sell to foreign publishers and please a foreign readership. This simply means that both the African writer and African literature will remain enslaved to foreign presses. The writer's artistic potentiality is very much undermined by the exigences of the foreign editor who determines the language and the format, and to a great extent the theme. African literature will be static because the writers are constrained to produce works which would sell in the country where the book is produced. For instance, most major works in African literature are first published in hard cover because Europeans and Americans "try them first"! If they are found interesting enough, then they are published in paperback and shipped to Africa, and any book that does not "make it" in hardcover is doomed. The distribution of these works is also carried out by foreign agents.

None of the writers whose works are examined in this book has published anything at home. Nonetheless, those who were interviewed had varied opinions on the influences of publication on their work. In answer to the question on the influence of place of publication, C. H. Kane gave the following answer:

I very much believe that it does influence the content and the structure of the work. Take the case of Mr. Kourouma from the Ivory Coast; Kourouma had not the opportunity of publishing his book *Les Soleils des Independances* in Africa because there are no publishing houses there. And even if there had been, they would not have accepted his book considering its political overtones. Mr. Kourouma could not get his book accepted in France either, because the French editors found that the book was written in a French whose structure has been affected by the author's mother tongue—the Joula. Kourouma wrote in French but the grammatical structure, the proverbs, the images, all had been carried over from his mother tongue. The result is that when a Joula who speaks French reads the book he understands it very well and much better than any other Ivorien who speaks Baoule or Peul. For this reason the author had difficulties getting his book accepted in France because the French editors said that they did not understand the book; that their audience could not understand all those proverbs and nuances. Kourouma finally had his book published in Canada where people speak a kind of French which is different from that spoken in France.[3]

Mr. Kourouma's experience shows what the French-African writers are bound to encounter if they tried to create some form of "Africanized" French. They could not hope to capture the rhythm of African speech in French as Achebe does in English; strew their narrative with proverbs and idioms and still get published by French publishers. Books like Tutola's *The Palm Wine Drinkard* or Okara's *The Voice* could never hope to be published in France if they had been written in French, yet they were published in the U.S.A. and even considered among books of "new experiment with the English language."

The reason why the French publishers refuse books whose language structure deviates very much from classical French is because the French language itself is not as permissive or accommodating as the English language. Whereas the French regard any local adaptions as a violation of the pure French, the English regard such adaptations as contributing to the enrichment of the language.

Apart from violating the foreign language, the African writer is also limited in his subject matter. It is the publisher who often decides what books would be interesting to his European readers. An example of this is Ouologuem's *Le Devoir de Violence*. Most often such books deal with the exotic aspect of Africa. At first they are published in hardcover and sold to Europeans because they are very expensive for the Africans. If they are found interesting enough to the Africans they are then published in paperback and sold at cheaper rates.

The writer is also limited by the politics of his country and that of the continent as a whole. As Mr. Kane pointed out, if there had been publishing houses in Africa, Kourouma would still not have got his book published there because of its political contents. Thus, in the event that a writer criticized his government he could not hope to get such a book published in his own country or anywhere else in Africa. But he could easily go to foreign publishers because his government cannot prevent publication and distribution of books abroad.

If on the other hand an African writer appeared very anti-

British, anti-American, or anti-French, if he dared take his book to the publishers of any of the countries he had antagonized, it is understandable that those publishers would either refuse the book or censor it. In such a case the writer would either give up the publication or accept a lot of modifications to have his book published.

Mr. Pathé Giagne, a politically inclined Senegalese author, publishes at Presence Africaine because of his friendship and affinities with Alioun Diop, the editor. Giagne maintains that the "place of publication is already the choice of audience but often one does not choose in Africa. Since there are very few publishing houses in Africa, one is obliged to published in Europe. The place of publication is also important because one could know how to address such and such a public and evidently this will affect his work."

QUESTION: If you were to publish in Africa would that make you modify your writing?

GIAGNE: I do not think so and that is why most of us prefer to publish outside because we are not censored.

QUESTION: Are you saying that there is censorship in Africa?

GIAGNE: I do not know. In Africa the press is often state controlled and once the state controls the press you can be sure there will be no compromise.

QUESTION: Does it mean that publication outside gives more freedom to the writer?

GIAGNE: Not necessarily. It depends on the content. In Senegal, theoretically there is no censorship, . . . but one thing is sure: the African writer at the moment has no choice but to publish in foreign countries.[4]

There is a note of finality and pessimism in these writers' acceptance of the fact that they are condemned to publish their works in foreign countries. None of them seemed eager to have publishing houses in Africa because the conditions they envision would be worse than what they now find outside. In this case it is very likely that African literature will have to remain static after the writers have exhausted those topics and writing techniques which appeal to the foreign publishers and audience.

Ousmane Sembène publishes in France, but has no preference for any particular editor. He says that the place of publication does not influence a work. Yet he makes statements which indicate that his publishers do suggest some modifications which he refuses: "Je n'ai jamais accepté de modifications. Tous les éditeurs sont des écrivains ratés." He expresses the same fears as the other writers on the would-be condition of the press in Africa in general and in Senegal in particular. "With the present government, since it is a one-party government it goes without saying that everything which has to be published will follow the same line. One could only write what pleases the publishing house. That is normal; it is a political problem because each time a writer writes, he is circulating an ideology."[5] At this point one sees that Ousmane Sèmbene has already contradicted himself, because all he is now saying is that the place of publication influences a work. He admitted that publishing in Europe gives more freedom to the writer.

President Senghor states categorically that the place of publication does not influence a work in any way. Asked the kind of press he would like to have in Africa, he said: "We are obliged at the first instance to create these publishing houses with the help of European publishers. It is little by little that we shall learn to manage a publishing house ourselves but it requires a long apprenticeship."

QUESTION: Do you think this house would be controlled by the government?

SENGHOR: Yes, but only partly.

QUESTION: Do you imply that the government will constitute a censor?

SENGHOR: No. It will not be geared toward politics, all the same one couldn't just publish anything.[6]

Again Senghor contradicts himself as Sèmbene did. For, if the government would not allow the writers to publish "just anything" that would force all those who intend to publish there to modify their work or seek publication abroad. The president maintains however, that his government has not yet censored any works. Moreover he has himself passed films that criticized the government and even presided over soirées where there had been movies criticizing the government indirectly. He concludes that they are not concerned with politics but with the moral and aesthetics of the public and, as such, the government will censor all writings that encourage violence, drug abuse, prostitution, and things of that nature.

The pessimism of the Franco-African writers is tempered by the optimism of the Anglo-African writers. Unlike their Francophone brothers, the Anglophones would definitely prefer to publish with a local publisher where they exist. And, in fact, some of them who were interviewed have taken positive steps either to establish a publishing house or to encourage the few that have already started production, like the East African publishing house, by giving their manuscript to them. But it is sad to note that the confidence which the African writer had sought to place in his local publisher has ended in a failure at the first attempt. Nevertheless, Achebe insists that the local publisher must be given a chance to develop. The apparent inefficiency of the local publisher, so far tried, leaves the Anglophone writer in the same position as the Francophone writer—publishing abroad and having to put up with the demands of foreign publishers.

For purpose of comparison between the views of Francophone and Anglophone writers on publication, it will be helpful to set down the answers given by the Anglophone writers as well.

Chinua Achebe is one writer who, in conjunction with another writer, Okigbo, had taken the initiative to establish a publishing house in their country but their effort was halted as a result of the Nigerian civil war. Like other Anglophone African writers I interviewed, Achebe feels very strongly that local publishing houses should be encouraged. He had published his works up to date abroad because he had no alternative. His answers on question of publication are of interest:

QUESTION: Where do you normally publish your works?

ACHEBE: When I began to write there was only one place to publish—Britain. The first draft of *Things Fall Apart* was ready in 1957 and I happened to be going to B.B.C. for a course, so I took it with me and showed it to a B.B.C. staff member who was a novelist and that helped to get it published. So first it was Britain; later they found American publishers for me. Today the situation is different. At a conference at Ife University I read a paper suggesting that time has come to change from foreign to local publishers.

QUESTION: Why do you think it is necessary to publish with local publishers?

ACHEBE: I think in terms of total development of literature; this is one way of getting the story from the writer to his audience. The most important element in this dialogue is the writer and his reader, all the others—publishers, book sellers, etc., are there to encourage this contact to take place between writer and reader.

And if the writer is abroad and most of his readers are at home, then it stands to reason that the man to do the best job in terms of getting him in touch with his people will also share the same kind of experience as the writer and his readers. In other words, I don't see how this process of communication, which is intimate and delicate, can be helped by somebody coming from a different culture and situation. But in the absence of anybody else, yes. But ultimately I think the ideal situation is that they should all be operating from the same cultural complex. This is a very pretentious way of saying that there are certain facets in this business of getting the words from the writer to his reader which might be interfered with really if somebody who is not really in tune with what is being said could get involved in it. . . . An editor or publisher does exercise editorial corrections. If his ideas and notions are foreign to the writer and reader, then he is liable to impose certain factors that are really not necessary in this process of communication between writer and reader.

QUESTION: Therefore you do think that the publisher has a certain amount of influence on what the writer puts down?

ACHEBE: Yes. What they (the French writers) are saying is like what the Nigerian managing director of Longmans said to the effect that anything the Nigerian publisher can do, the British publisher can do better. That's so much nonsense; in a way it's true but only in a very limited sense that, as of now, because of the situation we have inherited, if you want exposure as a writer you are more likely to get it from a British publisher than from a Nigerian publisher. Even if you want efficient servicing of your book you'll get it better from a British publisher. But that does not alter the basic fact I mentioned before. Ultimately you have to begin to deal with a local publisher and you have to help him by entrusting him with things even if he is not in a position to do it as well as a foreign publisher. To begin with, your ultimate interest lies in his having a go at it. This does not of course mean that the publisher himself doesn't have the responsibility. The indigenous publisher must understand that this is a big responsibility and therefore must do everything he can to justify the confidence which the writer expresses in him by giving him the manuscripts. He must do a good and honest job. But given that, there is no other way but helping him develop.

QUESTION: The fear is not that he will not do a good job but that he will interfere with the content by withholding facts.

ACHEBE: That's assuming you will have a government publishing house, but that's not the only way. You can have a private publisher; in theory, the whole thing is to be independent, but if that is the main concern, that one is likely to be limited in one's ability to speak one's mind, then that's a very real problem but I don't think one can rule out the necessity for trying by simply putting up that argument. Because I don't think the indigenous publisher has actually been tried in any

effective way outside of Egypt, and there they were more
concerned with government control which was not very satis-
factory; e.g., the minister in Cairo boasting that they were
publishing a new book every six hours! I hope every country
will find a solution.

If the French-African writers think there's no way in which
they can have independent publishing, that's something I
cannot argue about. In Nigeria there's no reason why we
shouldn't have a go at it anyway. As things are today we could
possibly have independent publishers and this is one thing I
tried to do at the beginning of the Nigerian crisis with
Okigbo. . . .

QUESTION: You wouldn't say that the desire for international
recognition motivates some writers to publish abroad, apart
from the fact that they don't have the facilities at home?

ACHEBE: It is really difficult to say which is responsible for what.
At the time I began writing, there was no publisher, so you
really didn't have a choice. Now it is possible to change the
situation—to print a good book in Nigeria. The first two
issues of *Okike* magazine were all done at Ibadan Nigeria.[7]

Ezekiel Mphahlele has actually tried to get one of his books
published by an African publishing house as a way of encouraging
the development of local publishers, but his experience with them
is not very encouraging and rather goes to reinforce what the
Nigerian managing director of Longmans said—that foreign publishers do a better job. Below is what Mphahlele has to say on
publication:

QUESTION: Where do you normally publish your works, and do
you have any preference as to where you publish?

MPHAHLELE: I began with Faber with two books then came to the
U.S.A. and I published with Macmillan. Finally I tried the
East African publishing house but they are utterly unreliable.
It came to a point that I became very sad that I gave my
stuff to them. I went to them thinking I was supporting an
African publishing house and hoped I would use them to

publish my works subsequently. . . . mine was not the only complaint. I wish I could publish in an African publishing house, I really wish I could but this East African one has not been a helpful one.

QUESTION: If you had the opportunity to use an African press, would you prefer that to a non-African publishing house?

MPHAHLELE: Yes. I would; e.g., I've sent my new novel to Okpaku in New York. I hope it will be all right. Publishing in South Africa is out of the question.

QUESTION: Since most of these writers are publishing abroad, don't you think that these foreign publishers influence the writer in the way he handles his material?

MPHAHLELE: To some extent they do. Until one matures, you may give it to the publisher without thinking and he will ask you to change certain things. But if you've faithfully stuck to your subject and to your reality and you are confident in yourself, once you reach that stage, you would really not have much to worry about interference from publishers. But the younger ones would certainly be influenced.

QUESTION: Did you ever have any difficulty having any of your works accepted for publication?

MPHAHLELE: Oh, yes. I must say, though, that I have been lucky so far because I really have not had a rough time. Once I was rejected by one publisher, but was accepted by Macmillan.

QUESTION: Apart from the fact that we do not have facilities to publish at home, don't you think that the desire for international recognition motivates some writers to publish abroad?

MPHAHLELE: Oh, yes, it does. I could appreciate that until we have developed a certain consciousness, that is, an African audience exists, until one can say that, the international reputation is important.[8]

Like his fellow Anglophone writers Ngugi Wa Thiong'O has published his works, to date, overseas, but he obviously would prefer to publish at home if the facility is there. Below are his answers to the question on publication:

QUESTION: Where do you normally publish your works?

THIONG'O: Heinemann.

QUESTION: Would you say that the publisher influences the writer in the way he presents his subject, the language he uses?

THIONG'O: I suppose indirectly, when the publisher also determines the market area. But I think at present we have a lot of British firms such as Heinemann who have made it clear that they are publishing for African markets.

QUESTION: Suppose you had the choice to publish at home and abroad, which would you rather choose?

THIONG'O: Home obviously. But there are some problems, mechanical errors. . . .

QUESTION: What kind of press would you like to see in East Africa? Free enterprisers or government-controlled?

THIONG'O: Fortunately we do not yet have the problem of government restrictions. I have not seen any book refused publication in Kenya or any book the Kenyan government has banned or prevented from circulation because of its political sentiments so far. I am not saying that it is not a real problem, I am just saying that so far it has not happened. I am not saying that a publishing house is the real answer to this because, who knows, if you write a book which may be excessively critical of certain aspects of the government . . . the book might be suppressed. I don't have that unlimited faith in our democracy.[9]

None of the writers interviewed have had their works censored. In other words, they have not written anything that fell outside the literary norms established by their publishers. One would imagine that they had to do a lot of compromising in the composition of their works so as to meet the demands of the publishers. As in many other aspects of writing yet to be considered, it is seen that the place of publication greatly limits the liberty and the artistic scope of the writer. But unlike writers in Europe or America, the African writer has little or no opportunity to publish in his home country. Being published by foreign publishers again leaves him at the mercy of a foreign audience, for as Giagne puts it, "The choice of place of publication is already the choice of audience."

NOTES

1. Stephen H. Grant, "Publisher for Many," *Africa Report*, vol. 17, no. 1, (January 1972), p. 27.
2. *Ibid.*, p. 26.
3. Interview with Cheik Hamidou Kane by author, Abidjan, December, 1972.
4. Interview with Pathé Giagne by author, Dakar, December, 1972.
5. Interview with Ousmane Sembène by author, Dakar, December, 1972.
6. Interview with President L. S. Senghor by author, Dakar, December, 1972.
7. Interview with Chinua Achebe by author, Amherst, September, 1974.
8. Interview with Ezekiel Mphahlele by author, Philadelphia, September, 1974.
9. Interview with Ngugi wa Thiong'O by author, Nairobi, December 1974.

3

LANGUAGE

Language is the most controversial issue in African literature today. This is because the majority of African writing is done in European languages—English, French, and Portuguese. Since the literature of a people must be written in the language of that people, the use of foreign languages in African Literature poses the problem of identifying with the African continent literary works produced in foreign languages. But more important than the problem of identification is the fact that the African writer is virtually controlled in his expression by a non-African audience whose language he uses.

In this chapter, the following topics will be discussed:

I. The need for European languages.
II. Some advantages of European languages.
III. French-African writers: The rigors of French and its demands on the African writer.
IV. English-African writers: The flexibility of English and its advantages to the African writer.
V. The control of African writing by European languages.

THE NEED FOR EUROPEAN LANGUAGES

There are many people, including African writers and critics, who feel that African literature should not be written in foreign languages. Among the most outspoken critics against foreign languages are Miss Christina Ama Ata Aido of Ghana and Obi Wali of Nigeria. In her introduction to Armah's *The Beautiful Ones Are Not Yet Born*, Miss Aido says:

> Naturally, one would wonder where the African writer who is writing in English, French, or Portuguese really stands, since however positively he may be using any of these languages his position is essentially negative.[1]

Miss Aido implies that it would be better for the African writer to write in an African language. Like her, Obi Wali maintains that

> until these writers and their Western midwives accept the fact that any true African literature must be written in African languages, they would be merely pursuing a deadend which can only lead to frustration.[2]

Critics who condemn the African writers for using the languages of the ex-colonial masters tend to overlook the historical circumstances that forced the writers into their present position.

That African writing is carried on today in European languages and tradition is one of the various facets of the *fait colonial*. The writer has no choice but to use the language of the ex-colonial masters, because for most of them and in particular those from the French sector, this is the only language they have learned to read and write. In the French colonies, for instance, the use of the vernacular in the schools was forbidden. Instruction was therefore carried on in French right from the first year in school. This practice was part of their assimilation policy which theoretically aimed at building a greater France whose citizens are united by language and culture if not by race. With this kind of policy, literacy in French African colonies became synonymous with proficiency in the French language. The result of this was that the teaching of African languages in schools, not to talk of their development as written languages, was entirely neglected.

In the English sector, the situation was slightly different. Unlike the French, the British did not totally neglect the African languages. During the first three or four years of school, instruction is given in the vernacular while English is taught like any other subject in the curriculum. It is only during the last three years of school that English becomes the medium of instruction while the vernacular is then taught as one of the other subjects. The teaching of the vernacular is continued in the secondary school and could be taken as an optional paper in the West African School Certificate or in the General Certificate of Education. However, the limitation of this policy is that most of the African languages, with the possible exception of Hausa, have no standardized grammatical and phonological structures. This means that instruction at a higher level in these languages is at present impossible.

Except for a few isolated cases in the French territories (Ousmane Sembène now has a journal in his native Wolof), one could say that the Anglophone is in a better position than his Francophone counterpart. For he could by choice, and with a great deal of effort, express his ideas in writing fairly well in his mother tongue; that is, if he is only interested in writing for his own language group. In spite of this possibility for the Anglophone, publications in African writings today show that the writers from the ex-British and French colonies are in the same position, because they are both writing in the language of their ex-colonial rulers.

Apart from the high proficiency of the writers in the use of these European languages, there are some other very important reasons why they have no choice but to use them. One of these is the long-standing linguistic problems of Africa. It would take many years of research for anyone to come up with an accurate number of indigenous languages spoken in West Africa alone. And each of these languages has many dialects. The situation is such that the new nations find it more convenient and economical to retain the European language as their official language. Apart from the political and social implications of choosing one language against several others, the leaders see the foreign language as one of the strongest bonds of their national unity. Robert G. Armstrong in his article "Language Policies and Lan-

guage Practice in West Africa" comments: "It has been the
official, explicit policy of the governments of the Francophone
countries that literacy means literacy in French. Most of these
countries regard this policy as the foundation of their national
unity as it undoubtedly is."[3] Mr. Armstrong's statement is confirmed and reinforced by that of President Senghor, who, in reply
to those who reprimanded him for using French to express his
Negro-Africanness, said: "Je répondrai que nous n'avons pas
choisi. Et s'il avait fallu choisir, nous aurions choisi le français."[4]

With the exception of Tanzania which chose Swahili as its
national language, on equal footing with English, the other
African nations are still using the language of the colonizers as
their official language. But the leaders of these nations, unlike
Senghor, would not come out and say that they have no choice
or that if everything is considered they would choose the foreign
language.

The other very important reason, which African writers feel
humiliated to accept, is that many of them cannot express their
ideas adequately in their mother tongue. They fail, however, to
realize that this is not their fault if we consider the kind of
education they received. It may be true that the Anglophone
learns to read and write the vernacular during the first three or
four years of school, but one could hardly say that a child at
that period of formation is capable of the sustained reasoned
argument of the writer. By the time he reaches what one may
call the age of logical reasoning, his line of thinking is gradually
being shaped by the foreign language. At the time he graduates
from the university, all his "academic" thinking is done in the
foreign language.

In one of his articles, Senghor claims that one of the short-
comings of the British educational policy in Africa is that "l'élève
qui entre au lycée ou à la grammar school, ne pense pas encore
en anglais."[5] Senghor may be right, but the fact is that most of
the present African writers did not stop their education with
the elementary school. One may cite Amos Tutuola as one African
writer with only an elementary school education, but any student

of African literature knows that Tutuola stands apart from the rest with his "special" English which defies classification. Several, if not all African writers, went to the university.

That the average Western-educated African cannot express his ideas well enough in his mother tongue is again confirmed by Senghor when he said that "beaucoup, parmi les élites, pensent en français, parlent mieux le français que leur langue maternelle."[6] Senghor himself belongs to this group and unlike other writers he is not ashamed to confess that he thinks in French and expresses himself better in French than in his mother tongue. This inability of a number of the elite to express themselves well in their native language is again explained by the colonial factor. But apart from this predicament, the Western-educated African has acquired new ideologies, such as marxism, socialism, negritude, etc., and these cannot be readily and adequately translated into the vernacular. This means that he must limit the expression of his modern thoughts to the use of the foreign language from where most of the new ideologies are borrowed.

In his article "The Dead End of African Literature," Mr. Obiajunwa Wali recalls the decision reached at the conference of African Writers of English Expression held in Makerere College, Kampala, in June, 1962: "It was generally agreed that it is better for an African writer to think and feel in his own language and then look for an English transliteration approximating the original." After quoting the above statement whose purpose was to support his subsequent argument, Mr. Obiajunwa dismissed it in the next line as "naïve and misguided."[7] The statement is not only naïve and misguided, it assumes too much of the writer's ability to think, feel, and write in his mother tongue given the kind of education he has received. It also reduces the entire African writing to mere translation of "Africanity" into foreign languages.

It is unwise to hold it against the African writer who writes a novel or a play in the language and literary tradition of the ex-colonial rulers. Because his British or French education places him in an impasse as far as the use of that language and its literary forms are concerned. Since they are now part of his acquired culture, they come to him automatically regardless of his audience. However this does not mean that the writers are content to write forever in the foreign languages. Comments by most of them, especially those I interviewed, show that they are very eager to use the African languages as soon as they have been grammatically and phonologically codified.

SOME ADVANTAGES OF EUROPEAN LANGUAGES

In spite of the controversy over the use of European languages by the African elite, it must be remembered that there are certain advantages that the African gets by using them. Before the educated Africans started to feel the humiliation of expressing their "Africanity" in the languages of the ex-colonial masters, it did mean a great deal to them at the beginning to be able to use those languages. Being able to use the language of the colonizer was one of the ways of proving to him that the colonized people were educable. In this way, knowledge of the foreign language became a powerful means of contradicting the colonizer's idea of the mental inferiority of the colonized. Having thus established their ability to learn, they also undertook to contradict the Western idea of cultural inferiority of the Negro. This they did by pointing out in their writings those aspects of their culture that the colonial teachers tried to make them despise because they were "barbaric" and "primitive"! This desire to show that African culture is also good was, in fact, the origin of modern African literature. In using the foreign languages which are international, the African culture gains a wider publicity, while the writer has a wider audience.

As the spokesman for the French-African writers, President Senghor has outlined in detail, both in conferences and in his writings, the reasons and the advantages of writing in French. In his postface to *Ethiopiques*, he asks and answers the question why Africans write in French:

> Pourquoi, dès lors, écrivez-vous en français? Parce que nous sommes des métis culturels, parce que, si nous sentons en nègres,

nous nous exprimons en français, parce que le français est une
langue à vocation universelle, que notre message s'adresse aussi
aux français de France et aux autres hommes, parce que le français est une langue de gentillesse et d'honnêteté. Qui a dit que
c'était une langue grise et atone d'ingénieurs et de diplomates?
. . .

Le français, ce sont les grandes orgues qui se prête à tous les
timbres, à tous les effets, des douceurs les plus sauves aux fulgul-
rances de l'orgue. Il est tout à tour ou en même temps, flûte,
hautbois, trompette, tam-tam et même canon. Et puis le français nous a fait don de ses mots abstriats—si rares dans nos lan-
gues maternelles, ou les larmes se font pierres précieuses. Chez
nous les mots sont naturellement nimbés d'un halo de sève et de
sang; les mots de français rayonnent de mille feux, comme des
diamants. Des frises qui éclairent notre nuit.[8]

One may not agree with all that Senghor says about French but
he does point out most of the obvious advantages that the African
writer derives by writing in French. One of the outstanding
advantages is that French, or English for that matter, furnishes
the writer with a number of abstract and rare words that are
lacking in his vernacular language. In his process of acculturation
the African comes across certain words and expressions that do
not appear in his native language. For example, words like: radio,
television, cinema, bomb, etc., have no equivalents in the African
languages, because they strictly reflect the level of Western tech-
nological development.

In his modern politics, the African is also confronted with
foreign words like: democracy, republic, socialism, etc. In philosophy and science he still has the same problem and even his
own coined word *Négritude* is of Latin etymology. Thus, the
African, in his process of modernization, has to rely very heavily
on foreign vocabulary because "the content of modernity comes
to them in some foreign language, usually a European one."[9]

Senghor had earlier said that even though he had no choice
but to use French, that if he had been given that choice, he still
would have chosen French. He gives his reasons for this: French
is rich in its resources, especially the vocabulary which abounds
in synonyms. He declares, however, that the African language

is very rich indeed; but in a most paradoxical statement, he says that the very force of this language is also its weakness:

> Ce sont des langues poétiques. Les mots, presque toujours con-crets, sont enceints d'images. L'ordonnance des nits dans la proposition, des propositions dans la phrase y obéit à la sensibilité plus qu à l'intelligibilite aux raisons du coeur plus qu'aux raisons de la raison.[10]

His other reason is that the French syntax is precise and because of this,

> les intellectuels noirs ont du emprunter ces outils français pour vertébrer les langues vernaculaires. A la syntaxe de juxtaposition des langues négro-Africaines s'oppose la syntaxe de subordination du français, à la syntaxe du concret vécu celle de l'abstraite pen-sée: la syntaxe de la raison à celle de l'emotion.[11]

According to Senghor, the Negro-African words are all flesh without bones, therefore the writers had to borrow the bony French words to give support to their fleshy ones.

Finally he argues that French is a language of humanism and that it always expresses a moral. In this case, the African will find it very useful to express his African thoughts which often tend to be moralistic.

By outlining the advantages of French, Senghor was only trying to prove that the African writer, since he cannot at the moment write and publish in his mother tongue, has nothing to lose by expressing his "Africaness" in French, because it is a language with rich resources and can furnish the writer with fairly enough vocabulary to express his native experience. He further pointed out that, contrary to current opinion, language is not necessarily linked with race. He cites the Gaulois who abandoned their Celtic language for Latin; and the French, which is born of this Latin, has through her masterpieces in literature, produced one of the most beautiful monuments of humanity. There were also the Berbers of North Africa who abandoned the language of Hannibal for Arabic.*[12] It is interesting to note that Africanists like Jaheinz Jahn are of the same opinion that it does not matter what language a writer uses: "What is important is that we find in his work those aspects of culture which we set out to look for in his work."[13]

One very important advantage of the foreign language is that it not only creates an international audience for the African writer, but it also creates his African audience. If, for example, every Nigerian writer writes in his native language, we could not speak of Nigerian literature the way we are doing now. We would actually have Yoruba, Ibo, Hausa, Ijaw, and Efik literatures. A Yoruba could only read Ibo literature in translation and vice versa.

An interesting example of this lack of communication is found in an article in *Nigeria* magazine, no. 91, December, 1966, by E. C. Okwu. Mr. Okwu narrated his experience when he went to watch a Yoruba play with some friends from other parts of West Africa. The Yorubas were enjoying themselves and laughing their heads off, while Mr. Okwu found it "quite mortifying to sit and watch others apparently and thoroughly enjoying themselves at what did not make any meaning to me." Mr. Okwu said that his friends were even more bewildered than he was." It is therefore significant to note," he continues, "that even in our comparatively small geographical unit we cannot share artistic experience in its original form owing to our language barriers."[14]

Thus, English has cut down the linguistic barriers and made it possible for Nigerians and people from the ex-British colonies to read what their writers are writing. If they had to wait till their countries created national languages from the African languages, these writers would not have written by now. And even if the countries succeeded in creating the *lingua franca* overnight, it will still take years of learning before a man like Achebe, who has thought and expressed himself in Ibo all his life, begins to

---

*Contrary to Senghor's assertion, the Berbers did not speak the language of Hannibal, which was Semetic. They spoke Berber, a Hamitic language. I am grateful to Professor El Nouty for this information.

produce the same quality of work he is now producing in English, in Hausa, or Yoruba, should any of these languages be chosen as the Nigerian national language instead of Ibo. Thus while these writers would be learning and reorientating themselves in the new language, the artistic potentiality of the nation would be wasting away. But by writing in these foreign languages, these writers are storing their genius and therefore preserving it for later generations who will translate them into the vernacular languages that will be transcribed.

FRENCH-AFRICAN WRITERS: THE RIGORS OF FRENCH AND ITS DEMANDS ON THE AFRICAN WRITER

L. S. Senghor

From Senghor's writings one can easily see that he has actually "tasted" and "chewed" as well as absorbed the French language into his system. As such, one would assume that he could express any complex Negro-African thought in French. Renato Berger says that Senghor "uses French with a godlike easiness,"[15] and mentions in parenthesis that Senghor was asked by the French government for the stylistic revision of the French constitution. However, in spite of his facility with French, Senghor made me understand when I interviewed him, that he still has to work very hard in order to adequately transpose his African poetic experience into French. He has a lot of modifications to make, and when I asked him whether French had ever posed any problems for him in his literary creativity, he said:

> I am obliged to modify the French language in such a way that it meets the demands of Negro-African aesthetics. I am led to make African music with French language which is musical but not very expressive. There is in this case a very difficult problem. For instance the French language is not tone marked, it is an abstract language, and from this abstract language one has to construct a concrete and vivid language. From this monotonous language one has to make a melodious language. We have here all the problems of language, that is why it is very difficult to be a great writer in French.[16]

The problem which Senghor claims to have with the French language is not unique to him because it has been the problem of French writers since the symbolists. It was in their attempt to escape the rigors of French and versified poetry that the symbolists turned to *vers libre*. Nevertheless, if French puts Senghor to task, one can imagine the magnitude of difficulty it will create for others who have not mastered French as much as he has. If they have to make many modifications to find adequate expressions, it means that they lose a great deal in transliteration. Senghor confirmed this when he said, "Very often when I write a poem, there is a difference between the poem as I conceived it in my imagination and the poem that is written down. It appears in such a way that I am disappointed and satisfied at the same time."[17]

This is of course true of many African Francophone writers, because they were discouraged from thinking in their mother tongue. Therefore, like Senghor, they only feel *en Négro-Africain*. This perhaps accounts for their having to work so hard, since feelings are more difficult to express than thought.

One would assume that Senghor's Negro-African feelings would be present in all his poems. Yet, apart from the subject matter, it has always been difficult if not impossible to distinguish a poem by Senghor from those written by French poets. Take for instance a portion of his poem which treats the theme of separated lovers:

Epitre À La Princesse

Je me rappelle rue Gît-le-Coeur, lorsque tu levais ton visage, ce front de pierre et de patine sous l'hiver blond. Et cette voix grave de toutes les angoisses, mais comme le grondement des cascades généreuses à l'aube du monde. Et tes yeux comme la lumière sur les collines bleues d'Assise. Ta voix, tes yeux qui chaque jour me faisait naître. J'ai grand besoin des murmures de Mai à Montsouris, de la splendeur des Tuileries à la fin d'été ou simplement sous broussailles et lianes pour retrouver mon obélisque, de l'angle pur du front de la Concorde.
(*Poèmes*, p. 143)

These lines could well have been written by a French symbolist poet like Verlaine or Rimbaud. If we compare this piece with a poem like Verlaine's "Nevermore," we find a great deal of similarity in tone and cadence. But the fact that Senghor's poem reminds one of some nineteenth-century French symbolist poet does not necessarily mean that he imitated them. Besides, from the age of seven, Senghor lived under the influence and guidance of French teachers. And having lived in the same environment and having received the same kind of education, there is no doubt that he should produce the same quality of work that French poets did produce. The point here is that Senghor's writing is mostly controlled by his French language and culture and by extension his French audience. Judging from his language, he could not have had an African audience in mind when he wrote such poems as the one already cited, not to mention others like "Rêve de Jeune Fille," "Neige sur Paris," "La Mort," etc. Let us take "Rêve de Jeune Fille" as an example:

> Je m'imagine que tu es là. Il y a le soleil
> Et cet oiseau perdu au chant si etrange. On dirait une
> après-midi d'été, Claire. Je me sens devenir sotte, très
> sotte. J'ai grand désir d'être coucher dans les foins,
> Avec des taches de soleil sur ma peau nue, Des ailes de
> papillons en larges pétales Et toute sortes de petites bêtes
> de la terre Autour de moi.
> (Poèmes, p. 222)

Why couldn't this poem be attributed to any French poet? Nothing shows that the poet comes from a different cultural background. In "Priere aux Masques," the declamatory tone and the sonority of the verses override rhythm, which is often associated with the Negro and on which Senghor himself has written so much. I would disagree with Frederick Ivor Case who said that his (Senghor) "love poems are rich in rhythm and penetrating imagery that are essentially Negro-African."[18] Because, as an African, I did not find much African rhythm and imagery in his love poems. Unless of course Mr. Frederick considers

"Femme Noire" a love poem, while I consider it a romanticized portrait of a Black woman. Commenting on "Femme Noire," a Senegalese said that Senghor was not looking at a Black woman when he wrote that poem. If he were looking at an African Black woman, he could not have missed that part of her—the posterior, which attracts the African male. Besides, an African does not refer to his woman as "Black woman" just as the white man does not refer to his as "White woman." The poem therefore is merely an abstract portrait of the Black woman.[19] There is not a single African image in "Rêve de Jeune Fille," one of Senghor's love poems said to be laden with African imageries!

It is significant to note that Senghor denies the influence of French poets. He very firmly denied the intimations of those who said that he imitated Saint-John Perse. But he later admitted that when he finally discovered Saint-John Perse, he was swept off his feet by the man's work: "Je confesserai aussi qu' à la découverte de Saint-John Perse, après la libération je fus ébloui comme Paul sur le chemin de Damas."[20]

There is no reason to doubt Senghor if he says that he never knew Saint-John Perse before he wrote some of his important poems. It is quite understandable that his poems resemble those of other French poets because they all drank from the same source—French language and literature. He admitted during our interview that Paul Claudel was among the poets he admired very much but that he was not the poet he liked most. He firmly said:

> I have not been, so to say, influenced by European poets. I liked European poets inasmuch as they resembled Negro poets. I have chosen, by preference, Irish poets because they are much closer to the "soul" of the Negro-African.[21]

He finally said that he received his inspiration exclusively from Negro-African poets:

> Those who influenced me the most are the poetesses of Serere, my native soil. And in particular I remember the gymnique poets —Maron N'Diaye, Siga Diouf, Koumba N'Diaye—who composed

poems during the wrestling matches. They are my three great
inspirators. You see that it is African poetry that inspired me.[22]

Perhaps it is this claim to African inspiration that explains
why Senghor indicates on top of several of his poems, the kind
of African musical instruments to accompany the piece in order
to add an African flavor to what might otherwise be a European
piece. Thus we find on top of the poems: *pour un toma, pour
flutes et balafong, pour kora, pour tam-tam*, etc.

Senghor may feel *en Négro-Africain* but his classical and
impeccable French hide his Negro-Africanness. The feeling which
one gets from reading most of his poems is summed up by
Frederick Ivor Case who said that "Senghor has allowed the
voice of the European to dominate his expression and the African
is revealed with some difficulty."[23] His claim that he is obliged
to bend the French language to meet the Negro-African aesthetics
is not reflected in his works because his French obscures rather
than illuminates his Negro-African aesthetics. The impression
that many Africans get from his poems also contradicts his claim
that he is writing first for Africans and believes that "for one
to really feel my poems, one has to be an African if not
Senegalese."[24]

Nevertheless, in spite of the "European" which overshadows
the "African" in Senghor's works, it must be pointed out that
there are a number of his poems which show that he had Africa
or Africans in mind when he wrote them. Among these are:
"Prière aux Masques," "Femme Noire," "Totem," "Joal," "Chaka,"
"Elégie des circoncis," and "Nuit de Sine." Judging from Senghor's declared intention to express his Africanness, one can say
that his very mastery of French has helped to hide rather than
expose his Negro-African feeling.

Cheik Hamidou Kane

Except for a few writers like Nazi Boni and Ahmadou Kourouma, who have dared to experiment with the French language,
the rest of French-African writers are in the same position as

Senghor. They could not or have not yet said like Ezekiel Mphahlele, "If we've got our focus on our social milieu this will have an effect on our style, we shan't be writing Oxford English. We should be able to change, to experiment with style, to give English a new ring and to hell with being published abroad or not."[25] The French-African writer unlike his Anglophone counterpart, is more constrained in his literary creation by the rigors of the French language. When I interviewed Cheik Hamidou Kane, he explained his problems with the language:

QUESTION: Do you think that the exigencies of the French lanugage force the African writer to modify his work?
KANE: It is not only the exigencies of language, let us say that of French culture as a whole and the French audience.

(Mr. Kane argues that since the African is writing a "novel," which is strange to his culture, logically he has no African audience in that respect. He is therefore obliged to write for a non-African audience, and he must utilize the writing technique of his audience if he wants to be understood. He also has to pay attention to their sensitivity. The writer is thus controlled by an external audience whose language he uses.)

QUESTION: Does it then not constitute a problem that he should be writing for an audience with whom he has no cultural ties?
KANE: That is a problem. For instance I did not follow any European model when I wrote my book. But when I read it over, I realized that there was perhaps an influence of my mother tongue on my French language. And I believe that it happened unconsciously.
QUESTION: That means that your French was modified?
KANE: That is to say that it is my use of French which was modified.
QUESTION: Does that not modify your thinking?
KANE: Perhaps my thinking is also modified to some extent by my use of French. But I have to say that the way in which I write and speak French is modified by my mother tongue, even if it is not the language in which I write.

QUESTION: Would you say that this modification of French to suit your sensitivity comes easily?

KANE: I believe that it is even done quite unconsciously. I do not have any difficulties thinking in French but I believe that when I think in French and transcribe it into writing, I find that my thought is influenced by my mother tongue.

QUESTION: If you had to translate or transpose an African image into French, do you succeed in finding the *mot juste*?

KANE: I could try to describe something when I am writing and to do that I use an image which is neither African nor French. It is an image which has been presented to me by my inspiration and this inspiration is the fruit of my sensitivity, my culture, the language which I use, and the fruit of my mother tongue which I do not use. The image a person uses has to symbolize what he feels and wants to communicate to his reader. This image is offered to him by his traditional culture and also by the culture which he has acquired from the Western culture.

QUESTION: Do you think the Africans would create some form of Africanized French in order to be able to express more adequately their African sensitivity?

KANE: No, I do not think so. What we have to do and have started to do is to transcribe our languages. But that is not all. These languages have to be taught in the schools and it is necessary that people use them. But while we are waiting, there is going to be more African literature in French or English or Portuguese and these in some ways would be influenced by the African sensitivity of the writer, who in turn would be influenced by the taste of his African audience, which in its own turn would be influenced by the aesthetics that one finds in the African public.

QUESTION: What do you consider to be the link between you and traditional African literature?

KANE: In the only book I have published, *L'Aventure Ambiguë*, there is perhaps a certain form of narration, a certain rhythm in the phrase itself which are reflections of my mother tongue; there is for instance this kind of recourse to repetition all of

which I believe are the marks of traditional African literature.
As a writer I did not set out to look for them but I found
that when I wrote, they just came out.[26]

Perhaps there is a certain rhythm of verset, and a certain
rhythm in the phrase that are carried over from the author's
mother tongue, and probably a Peul French speaker could discern
them, but I could not find these rhythms and repetitions. However there are very obvious passages which are verbatim translations from the author's mother tongue. For example in the
manner of greeting:

> "La paix règne-t-elle dans votre demeure maître des Dial-
> lobé?"
> "Je rends gâce à Dieu, Grande Royale. La paix règne-t-elle
> chex vous de même?"
> "Grâces soient rendues au Seigneur."
> (*L'Aventure Ambiguë*, p. 34)

When the disciples go out in the mornings to beg for their
food, they carry it on in the Islamic tradition, they repeat certain
litanies used specifically for begging. Thus Samba Diallo recites
some of the lines and his comrades respond:

> *Samba Diallo:* La paix de Dieu soit sur cette maison. Le pauvre
> disciple est en quête de sa pitance journalière. Gens de Dieu,
> songez à votre mort prochaine. Eveillez-vous, oh éveillez-vous.
> Azrael l'Ange de la mort, déjà fend la terre vers vous, il va
> surgir à vos pieds . . .
> *Chorus:* Qui nourrira aujourd'hui les pauvres disciples? Nos
> pères sont vivants et nous mendions comme des orphelins.
> Au nom de Dieu, donnez à ceux qui mendient pour Sa
> Gloire. Hommes qui dormez, songez aux disciples qui passent
> . . . (p. 23).

One can also imagine the fury of the Islamic teacher when Samba
Diallo has mispronounced some of the words he was reciting:

> Ah!—Ainsi, tu peux éviter les fautes? Pourquoi donc en fais-
> tu?—Hein—Pourquoi? Répète avec moi: "Dieu, donnez-moi"

"Dieu, donnez-moi l'attention . . ."
"Encore . . ."
"Dieu donnez-moi l'attention . . ." (p. 16)

Much as these lines reflect the author's traditional Islamic culture, it is not impossible for a French writer to reproduce them in the same way just for local color. Therefore it is not necessarily the influence of the author's mother tongue.

In chapter four he paints a picture of a village meeting of elders, but he omits many important aspects of a traditional village meeting. The meeting is announced by the village crier who beats his tam-tam round the village. We are only told that Samba Diallo heard the tam-tam which shook the ground. A writer like Achebe would have spelt out the sound of the ogene and the delivery of the message. Nazi Boni would have done the same as it appears in his *Crépuscule des Temps Anciens*:

Konkon! konkon! konkon! konkonkonkon!
Hééhééeé!
boééééé! . . . Waloho! . . .
(p. 41)

Mr. Kane omits this aspect of the crier's job probably due to inhibitions of language. At the time he wrote *L'Aventure Ambiguë*, he never thought that anyone could take liberties with the French language as Nazi Boni did. He realizes this big omission in his first book and he kept repeating during our interview that the book he is now writing would be a "traditional griot in writing"; in other words, the texture would be richly African.

The village meeting is summoned by the heroine, la Grande Royale, who has invited the women to attend. To begin with, she apologizes for breaking the tradition because a woman is not supposed to attend the men's meetings, let alone summon a village meeting herself! Before she starts with the main topic, she dismisses the traditional opening of a village meeting with: "Gens du Diallobé, je vous salue" (p. 55). If it were Achebe or Nazi Boni, they would have reproduced the actual greeting.

This omission again on the part of the author shows how much a slave the author is to the demands of his borrowed language. It also contradicts the author's claim that his mother tongue affected his writing. For, if one does not find this influence in such common things as greetings and formal address, it will be more difficult to identify it within the body of the narrative.

Kane does use dialogue extensively. But the line of these dialogues does not throw much light on the typical African manner of expression as they do in Achebe's works. The Africans in Kane's novel sound very much like French people. A good example of this is when Samba Diallo and the Chevalier engage in a philosophical discussion on Pascal, Nietzsche, and on industry. The reader is surprised to hear the Chevalier, who never went to the French school, pass judgment on the West in these words:

> L'Occident est en train de bouleverser ces idées simples dont nous sommes partis. Il a commencé timidement par reléguer Dieu "entre guillements" puis, deux siècles après, ayant acquis plus d'assurance, il décréta "Dieu est mort." De ce jour date l'ère du travail frénétique. Nietzsche est contemporain de la revolution industrielle. Dieu n'était plus là pour mesurer et justifier. N'est-ce pas cela, l'industrie? . . . Après la mort de Dieu voici que s'announce la mort de l'homme. (*L'Aventure Ambiguë*, p. 113)

Here the Muslim-educated Chevalier speaks like a French existentialist philosopher! It shows the influence of the author's French literary heritage which unconsciously or consciously directs his line of thought. Kane could not possibly have an African audience in mind while writing this French philosophic debate.

Mr. Kane said that he had no audience in mind when he wrote *L'Aventure Ambiguë* but a greater portion of his book tends to prove that he was partially addressing a European audience. The story is situated in the Islamic society of the Diallobé which resembles in certain aspects, at least in social classification, the European societies of the Middle Ages. It is in the description of these Muslim characters that the influence of the French language and tradition is clearly demonstrated. These descriptions are very impressive and perfect because there are no restrictions in language. The vocabulary he uses has its parallel in French culture.

For example, the noble origin of Samba Diallo is spelt out in so many words. It is surprising how the little boy's nobility is felt by everyone around him, even his playmates and also little Jean Lacroix, a French boy. All are overwhelmed by his personality. In the French classroom Jean Lacroix has been wondering who the strange boy might be, so when Samba slowly turned to look at him for the first time:

> Ce fut comme une révélation! Le trou de silence, la brèche de paix, c'était lui! Lui qui, en ce moment même attirait tous les regards par une espèce de rayonnement contenu, lui que Jean n'avait pas remarqué mais dont la présence dans cette classe l'avait troublé dès les premiers jours. (p. 64)

Samba's rival and would-be successor, Demba, makes fun of his noble gesture and manner of speech when they quarrel; Demba says of him: "Quelle magnaimité! même quand il congédie, il congédie noblement . . ." (p. 26). Finally the author elaborates on the hero's aristocratic origin thus:

> Tous les disciples savaient combien il lui déplaisait que soit fait cas de son origine patricienne. Assurément, il était le mieux né de tout le foyer du Maître des Diallobés. Nul dans ce pays, ne le lui laissait ignorer. . . . La noblesse de son origine lui pesait, non point comme un fardeau dont il eut peur, mais à la manière d'un diadème trop encombrant et trop visible. . . . Il désirait la noblesse, certes, mais une noblesse plus authentique, non point acquise mais conquise durement et qui fut plus spirituelle que temporelle. . . . Il ne se passait pas de jour que quelqu'un ne fît de remarque sur la noblesse de son port ou sur l'élégance racée de son maintien, en dépit des haillons dont il se couvrait. . . . Il savait que Demba l'enviait. Ce fils de paysan. . . . (p. 27)

In this description of Samba Diallo, the image of nobility is concretized by a piling up of adjectives and nouns denoting of noble rank—patricienne, noblesse, diadème, élégance racée, etc., and finally the distinction between him and Demba is sharply drawn by calling the latter, "Ce fils de paysan." It is quite unlikely that non-Islamic African readers could identify with Samba Diallo's social position because the animist societies are not divided between aristocracy and peasantry. But a European reader is on familiar grounds when he reads this passage because the institution represented by the hero has a parallel in his own society, and the language used in drawing the parallels is very appropriate, thus making the similarity more striking.

There is also the impressive portrait of La Grande Royale whose very name speaks of her social status:

> On la nommait La Grande Royale. Elle avait soixante ans et on lui en eût donné quarante à peine. On ne voyait d'elle que le visage. . . . La Grande Royale qui pouvait bien avoir un mètre quatre vingts, n'avait rien perdu de sa prestance malgré son âge. . . . La violette de gaze blanche épousait l'ovale d'un visage aux contours pleins. . . . Les traits étaient tout en longeur dans l'axe d'un nez légèrement busqué. . . . Un regard extraordinairement lumineux répandait sur cette figure un éclat imperieux. . . . Elle avait pacifié le Nord par sa fermeté. Son prestige avait maintenu dans l'obéissance les tribus subjugées par sa personalité extraordinaire. C'est le Nord qui l'avait surnommée La Grand Royale. (pp. 30-32)

La Grande Royale is taken out of the stereotyped position of the subjugated Muslim woman and made the virtual ruler of the Diallobe society. Here the author's intention is to prove to his French readers that the African woman is not a mere chattel attached to the man, that she could be actively involved in politics, and unlike the French women of the salon who ruled France indirectly through the king and his courtiers, La Grande Royale ruled her people directly.

The portraits of Samba Diallo, La Grande Royal, and that of the Chevalier are perfect and the reason why the author succeeds in painting them so perfectly is that he has the appropriate vocabulary. Moreover it will impress a French audience which can easily find parallels to these personalities in the French society. It is especially in the portrayal of the Chef that the author takes his French audience to the knights of the Middle

Ages with whom he actually compares the Chef. It is little Jean
Lacroix who notices the semblance of the Chef to the engravings
of knights in history manuals. Jean looked at him steadily and
noticed he was tall even though he was sitting:

> On sentait sous ses-vêtements une, stature puissante mais sans
> empatement. Les mains étaient grandes et fines tout à la fois. La
> tête qu'on eût dit découpée dans du grès noir et brillant, achevait,
> par son port, de lui donner une stature hiératique. Pourquoi, en le
> regardant, Jean songea-t-il à certaine gravure de ses manuels
> d'histoire représentant un chevalier du Moyen Age revêtu de sa
> dalmatique? (p. 66)

From this point on, the Chef is qualified with "le chevalier
a la dalmatique," later "Chef" was called Chevalier throughout
the book. As beautiful as the portrait of the Chevalier is, it is
completely removed from anything an African reader could
imagine. The African sees him through the eyes of a little French
boy who compares him to what is familiar to himself. If the
author had wanted to present the Chef through the eyes of one
of the African characters, one wonders if he could have found
appropriate images in the foreign language to transpose those
images he could have used in his mother tongue. This image of
chevalier à la dalmatique totally contradicts Kane's assertion
that the images he uses are neither French nor African, that they
are the fruits of his inspiration and of his mother tongue.

One the whole, *L'Aventure Ambiguë* is indeed one of the
most penetrating novels in African literature. As far as the language of the book is concerned, the book is certainly a *chef-
d'oeuvre* of French classicism in African literature. But it is dis-
appointing that even though the author has a good mastery of
the French language, he has not been very successful in finding
the conceptual tools in the very interior of that language to
convey his message to the average African reader whom he
claims as his audience. On the other hand he is understood by
the French audience because he uses the vocabulary that describes their own institution.

Laye Camara

"Nul moyen de s'y tromper, un Européen n'écrit pas comme cela."[27] This statement was made by President Senghor in regard to Laye Camara's style. It echoes but in reverse form, what Martin Banttam says of Nigerian playwrights:

> One really has to state the obvious and say that it is only logical that Nigerian playwrights should write as Nigerians and one must not be confused by the fact that they write, sometimes in English; this is not to say that they write like the English.[28]

These two statements are among many which point to the fact that African writing has its own peculiar characteristics, therefore the African writer should definitely not be confused in language and style with his European counterpart with whom he shares the same language.

Laye Camara is perhaps the foremost French-African author who has achieved this particular distinction of the African writer. His first autobiographical novel, *L'Enfant Noir*, has been praised by many critics in different words. Robert Pageard speaks of the effect it produced on the French audience: "*L'Enfant Noir* a surtout été apprecié en France pour sa fraicheur, et l'on s'est étonné de voir capté avec une telle perfection le génie discursif du français classique . . ."[29] And Lilyan Kesteloot says of it: "C'est une réussite de style tant pour la composition générale . . . que pour l'écriture dont les qualités les plus frappantes sont l'aisance, la simplicité et le naturel." And to describe his childhood, his parents, and a culture laden with mysteries, Camara "n'a pas besoin de grands mots ni de savantes figures de style, mais son langage direct nous touche au coeur."[30]

Mr. Pageard is astonished to see Camara capture with such perfection "le génie discursif du français classique." If he had known anything about the art of storytelling in Negro-Africa, he would have added that Camara has attained it with greater perfection even in a foreign language. When one compares the

language of *L'Enfant Noir* and that of *L'Aventure Ambiguë*,
one is struck by the sharp contrast between the simplicity of
the former and the erudition of the latter. But just as the simplicity of language matches the idyllic innocence of Laye, so
does erudition match the aristocratic bearing of Samba Diallo.
Both writers do not distort the French language in any form
and both are trying to express their African sensitivity in a foreign
language. But it is in Camara's novel that every African reader
recognizes those qualities and traditions that belong in common
to Negro-Africa—uncomplicated lifestyle of village folks, communal labor, respect and concern for one another. One of the
most pathetic scenes is where the author shows the young boys'
concern for their sick playmate. It is described in a simple and
touching language of *L'Enfant Noir*:

> Nous nous relayions au chevet de Check et nous regardions notre
> malhereux ami se tordre sur le lit, son ventre ballonné dur, était
> glacé comme une chose déjà morte. Quand les crises augumen-
> taient, nous courions, affolés chez le médecin: venez, docteur!
> . . . Venez Vite! . . . Mais aucun médication n'opérait, et nous
> pouvions tout juste prendre les mains de Check et les serrer, les
> serrer fortment pour qu'il se sentit moins seul en face de son mal,
> et dire: Allons! Check. . . . Allons! Prends courage! Cela va
> passer. . . . (p. 167)

Camara is at his best when he paints different kinds of
scenes or when he describes incidents. Among the most moving
scenes is the one in which Laye's father and Laye go to tell the
mother that Laye would finally go to France to finish his studies.
There are many powerful descriptive passages but the ones that
stick to the mind are the ones at the very beginning where Laye
is playing with the family sacred snake and that of the initiation
ceremony when the boys are terrified by the "roaring lions."

The significant point about Camara's style is that he achieves
his effect without recourse to the artificial verbatim translations
of vernacular expressions into the foreign language, as it is now
widely practiced by several African writers, especially Nigerians.

Though Camara's French remains classical, like Kane's, his simple
style permits the average reader to understand and share the
author's experience.

In his criticism of *Le Regard du Roi*, Senghor comments on
the same simplicity of Camara's style. However he notices certain imperfections in the book. He says that at the very beginning of the book he did not "feel Africa," for Camara has borrowed many European images and metaphors which do not fit
into an African context. For, Africans do not say "ne me quittez
pas d'une semelle, sentir l'escroquerie à plein nez, ne rougis
pas."[31] In spite of these pitfalls, Senghor concludes that what
saves the book is the Negro rhythm that animates the narration
and gives it its authenticity. Senghor agreed that Camara has
not only mastered the French language but has been able to
make it respond to his Negro aesthetics.

After reading Camara's works one may agree with Senghor
that Camara is one of the most successful French-African writers
who have been able to express their African sensitivity without
distorting the foreign language. One has to admit that it takes a
tremendous amount of work to attain such perfection as Camara
has. And in my interview with him he made a most honest
avowal of the difficulties he encounters with the French language.

QUESTION: Does your use of French create any problem for you
   as an African writer?

CAMARA: Evidently it does. Personally I think I am quite inte-
   grated into the culture of my people and I can easily talk
   about it in Malinke. But it is the French language that creates
   problems for me. When I give a conference in French, I first
   of all have to write it out. If I were giving it in Malinke I
   would not do that. I have to work very hard in order to
   write good French because one loses a lot in transposition.

QUESTION: Why do other writers say that they do not lose anything in transposition?

CAMARA: They do not understand your question. They are only
   thinking of the structure of the language. It may be true that
   you could express yourself in French or English but when you

want to translate your own African culture into French or English there is a problem because what you want to express has no equivalent in the foreign culture. You are obliged to leave certain things unexpressed. For instance it is hard to find images that could truly translate the image you have in mind. For example, "Her blouse is as white as snow." This is a foreign image for the African who has never seen snow. On the other hand the African says, "Her blouse is as white as the moon in its full phase." This image does not signify much for a European because the moon is not clear in Europe as it is in Africa. Besides the moon is overshadowed by artificial lights in Europe.

QUESTION: What could the writer do in a situation like that?

CAMARA: The writer is obliged to do some acrobatics, i.e., jump from one image to another. If he uses a French image he has to repeat it or find its closest equivalent in the African language. He has to do this to satisfy his two audiences.

QUESTION: You then agree that the demands of the audience force a writer to modify his language or the structure of his work?

CAMARA: It certainly does.

QUESTION: Do you think that the African writer would one day find a solution to this language problem?

CAMARA: That is the question. We are still culturally alienated. We have not yet decided on a cultural politics which is basically African. We need a language of communication born on African soil but since there is none at the moment, we have to speak French, English, Portuguese, etc. Besides, we live in a planetary civilization in which case the international languages have to be retained.

QUESTION: You don't then think that there would be an African literature in African language?

CAMARA: Yes I do. I wrote my thesis in Malinke then translated it into French.[32]

It is remarkable that with the level of perfection which Camara has reached in his use of French, he still feels that he

loses something in transposition. It is therefore hard to imagine
what *L'Enfant Noir* would have been if it had been written in
Malinke. Camara's preference to write in Malinke, as he did in
his thesis, shows that the foreign language has not given him
enough scope to exercise to the fullest, his artistic potentiality.

Ousmane Sèmbene

Ousmane Sembène is one of the French-African writers who
feels very strongly against using a foreign language in his writing.
He has taken the initiative to start a magazine in Wolof—the
KADDU. He boasts of a larger audience in Wolof than in
French. His attitude toward the use of French is clearly shown
in the way he answered my questions on language.

QUESTION: Does it bother you to use the French language in
   your writings instead of Wolof?
SEMBENE: Unfortunately, in order to get acquainted with world
   literature, I am obliged to do so through the French language
   which is my exile because I exile myself internally when I use
   French.
QUESTION: Does that mean that the manipulation of French
   creates problems for you?
SEMBENE: "Not at all! However that is their own problem. If it
   becomes necessary to violate the French language it has to
   be violated but that would only be temporary. I am sure
   that African literature will not remain forever in French and
   English. In the future, I am sure that these two languages
   will lose their influence.

Mr. Sembène is in fact one of the few French-African writers
who defied the rigors of French. In his works he violates the
French language whenever he feels it is necessary to do so. It
is in his work that one often comes across *le petit nègre*, the
equivalent of pidgin English. In addition to the *petit nègre* many
local expressions are carried into the body of the narrative with
explanations in parentheses or footnoted at the bottom of the
page. There is quite a bit of vulgarism among the characters in

Les Bouts de Bois de Dieu. An example is the scene where the women strikers are marching to Dakar. The first group arrived at the resting place and are waiting for the rest to arrive. The latecomers wanted to squeeze in under the shed and in so doing they roused those who had already dozed off. Then there is an exchange of angry words in which vulgar expressions are freely used:

> "He! vous êtes les dernières et vous voulez toute La place!"
> "On vient de traverser l'enfer, on veut se coucher!"
> "Et nous? Nous l'avons pas traversé, l'enfer?"
> "Poussez-vous un peu!"
> "Ah!, regardez celle-là, elle me met son derrière au nez! Si elle lache un peu, elle me dessèche d'un coup."
> "Awa, ce n'est pas parce qu'on est grosse que tout est permis! Poussez tes fesses! Une aiguille n'y entrerait pas!"
> "Mesure tes paroles, Yacine."
> "Mesure ton derrière, Awa! . . ." (p. 302)

It is true that the language of these women is vulgar or dirty, but it is very common among women of their background, semi-urbanized, women whose husbands belong to the lowest income group. These women often do some retail trading in the markets and there they use the kind of foul language which Sembène captures in various scenes. Now, if the author had tried to translate the women's words into "pure" and "decent" French, the entire scene would have been lost to the reader.

A similar picture is painted of two men whose conversation about the courtesans is overheard by Bakayoko. The courtesans are now turning away their customers because they have no money:

> "Tu te rends compte, cette salope? Elle me dit de venir, je fais le mur, elle avait filé avec son civil. Je lui casserais la gueule à celui-là."
> "Bah! il n'y a que les sous qui comptent! Moi je m'en fous, ce soir, j'ai mon coup à credit. Avec cette greve elles vont toutes y passer . . ."
> "Parle pas de ces garces! Et demain, de bonne heure, de garde a la gare."

"Ils nous les cassent tous tant qu'ils sont avec leur greve."
"Pourquoi ne me parles—tu pas de Penda?"
"Tu la connaissais bien?"
"Je la connaissais. Pourquoi me la demandes—tu?"
"C'etait une putain."
"Qui te l'a dit?"
"Toutes le femmes de la concession le savent Elles disent
gu'il n'y avait que le chemin de fer qui ne lui etait passe dessus,
je me demande comment?" (p. 342)

The last comment on the dead girl contains a figure of speech
widely used in Africa to describe the state of girls found to be
sexually promiscuous. Here Sèmbene says—it is only the railway
track that has not passed through Penda, the dead girl. We find
exactly the same image in Achebe's *Arrow of God*. Obika's wife
is happy and proud because her husband found her "at home"
(virgin), if not she would have suffered the fate of "Ogbanje
Omenyi whose husband was said to have sent to her parents
for a matchet to cut the bush on either side of the highway
which she carried between her thighs" (*Arrow of God*, p. 151).

Here again it is by resorting to popular expressions that
Sèmbene is able to paint a vivid picture of some aspects of
African social life.

In a humorous scene between the precocious Ad' jibidi'ji and
her grandmother, Sèmbene lets the reader know how some older
people feel about the use of French by the Africans. In this
scene, the little girl is protesting to her grandmother that she
has not been as lazy as the grandmother thought. After enu-
merating all she had been doing, she ends with, "Alors?" The
word stung the old woman and she speaks as if to tear the word
out of the girl's lips:

Aloss, aloss! . . . Tu me parles à moi, la mère de ton père, et
tu me dis "aloss . . . voulo"? Les toubabous quand ils s'adressent
à leur chien disent "aloss . . . voulo," et toi, ma petite fille, tu
me traites comme un chien! Aloss, aloss. . . . Je te parle en
Bambara et tu me réponds dans ce language de sauvages, de
voulos!" (p. 20)

The old woman is one of the older Africans who detest the sound of European languages. She calls French the "language of savages," an interesting reversal, because the white man is the one who regards the African languages as those of savages. Niakoro mispronounces the word, as is always with the illiterate people. In the book, the villagers call N'Deye Touti "Mad'mizelle" (mademoiselle). This is a sign of respect because she has been to school. The same practice is found in Nigeria where the working girl is called "Miss" as a sign of respect for her new social position. We find it in Achebe's No Longer at Ease when Obi's sister becomes a teacher and "everyone said that she should no longer be called Esther because it was disrespectful, but "Miss." So she was called Miss. Sometimes Obi forgot and called her Esther whereupon Charity told him how rude he was" (No Longer at Ease, p. 62).

Thus, in the single word "Mad'mizelle" or "Miss," with its special connotation, the author creates a social distinction with its special connotation. The author creates a social distinction between the educated and the noneducated women. Such a distinctive word would not be found in the vernacular, since everybody received the same education before the Europeans came.

One finds a number of petit nègre expressions in Sembène's works—toubab (white man), toubabesse (white woman), les rapides (autocar); there are also a lot of mispronunciations like "sef" for chef, "sustement" for justment, "dimasse" for dimanche, "les risses" for les riches, "M'sieu" for monsieur, etc. One of the commonest practices of the semiliterate French speaker is to drop the ne in a negative sentence. This is found very often in the speech of semiliterate Africans in Sembène's novels. We find many of these in Le Mandat; e.g., c'est pas moi, fais pas cela, j'ai pas, faut pas faire ça and so on. In Véhi-Ciosane, the ex-serviceman sings a song in petit nègre:

Li plus b'o de touss lis tangos
que z'ai dansé, c'ce ci lui
que z'ai danzé dans ton bras.
(p. 60)

By making his characters speak different versions of French, Sembène creates a class distinction as it exists in the French society where the language of the upper class differs from that of the lower class and that of the *Parisien* from that of the peasant in the countryside. The use of language in this way by the African writers is very significant, because language is never used that way in the African societies where everybody speaks the same language. At best, one could distinguish the speech of an older person from that of a younger one because the former adorns his speech with proverbs and other figures of speech while the latter does not. But the way an older person uses the language is only a sign of maturity and orderly thinking, it does not denote social class.

In Western novels, we know the kind of person a character is by his language. Sembène uses language in this way to portray a character. Thus, the Frenchmen who worked with the African show by their language that they are as vulgar as the African laborers. For instance, the prison guard is angry with Konate, the secretary of the Workers' Union, for addressing him in the familiar *tu* so the guard shouts:

> Quoi! tu tutoies un Blanc! Sale bougnoul! le droit ici, je le prends, et toi, tu obéis, macaque!
> (*Les Bouts de Bois*, p. 360)

When the guard catches Fa Keita praying instead of marching, he forces him to bend and pray so that he could kick him in the pants; the old man hesitates and the guard says to him: "Alors, tu la fais cette priere ou merde?" And as the old man obeys he gives him a kick that sends him head first across the wire fence. (*Les Bouts de Bois*, p. 361).

At the end of the strike, the Africans demand the dismissal of some French officers. Mr. Isnard who has been dismissed curses in anger:

"Les salauds, les salauds . . . après tout ce que j'ai fait pour eux?! Mais bon Dieu! Qu'est-ce qui se passe, qu'on laisse ces sauvages decider? Ils ne savent même pas ce qui est bon pour eux" (*Les Boutide Bois*, p. 377).

Sembène makes excessive use of vernacular words in the body of the narrative and he explains them in parentheses. This process interrupts the reader because the local word which is explained in French serves only as a local color. For example in a short conversation as the one below, one finds many authorian interventions:

> "Il était malade?"
> "Deded (non, non) mère. Il va venir. Nous l'avons trouvé chez Voulimata (la quatrième épouse). Il a demandé de tes nouvelles."
> "C'est tout ce qu'il vous a dit?"
> "Vav (oui)!"
> (*Le Voltaique*, p. 62)

This kind of intervention is time consuming, both for the writer and the reader. But it shows that kind of acrobatics which Camara suggests that the writer should do in order to satisfy his two audiences. The writer would not have this double work if he were writing in his mother tongue. I specifically asked Sembène why he resorts to this technique very frequently, and he said:

> It is a violation which the author commits, in that he is addressing his people in a foreign language. In as much as he is not expressing himself in his mother tongue he is obliged to explain. Because there are always words that escape translation, the writer is obliged to explain unfortunately. And this is not peculiar to the African writer.[34]

Of course this may not be peculiar to the African writer, but the extent to which it is used in what is supposed to be an original African writing is quite superfluous. However, Sembène touched the main issue—that it is the imposition of the foreign language, and by extension the foreign audience, which creates the extra work of authorial intervention. The time the writer spends in jumping from one language to another could be used in improving his literary talent. One could thus say that many African writers are not actually producing their best because their artistry is very much constrained by the rigors of a foreign language.

Nazi Boni

Nazi Boni is one of the few African writers who have experimented with the French language in a way that makes the influence of the mother tongue appear to dominate that of the foreign language. The style of his *Crépuscule des Temps Anciens* places him on the same level as Achebe. Both writers have succeeded better than others in their language to capture the authentic traditional African village life. The language structure in the work of both authors is so similar that if Nazi Boni's book were translated into English or Ibo, one would find passages that read word for word in Achebe's *Things Fall Apart* or *Arrow of God*. This is mostly so in the idioms and proverbs they use.

The surprising thing in the comparison between Achebe and Nazi Boni is that while many critics have acclaimed Achebe as the foremost writer in Anglophone Africa, French critics have said that Nazi Boni is weak because of his style! Robert Pageard says of Nazi Boni's book:

> La faiblesse de *Crépuscule des Temps Anciens* réside dans le style, qui pèche par l'emploi de tournures argotiques ou vulgaries. Celles-ci choquent d'autant plus qu'elles servent parfois à traduire les paroles d'Africains n'ayant eu aucun contact avec les Européens.[35]

This critic says that Boni's style shocks the French audience even though it sometimes throws light on the African manner of speech. Mr. Pageard, with this judgment, makes one understand that Boni wrote his book solely for the French public and as such should have taken into consideration the sensitivity and the literary aesthetics of that audience. That Pageard condemns

Boni's style and language still points to the inflexibility of the French language as opposed to the English.

Like Achebe, Boni uses local expressions which he explains not in a glossary at the end, but in appositions. We have therefore names such as: Kôbô-le-Coq, Humu-la-Mort, M'Bwoa-Pihoun-la-Lune, DomBéni-Dieule-Grand, Yèré-le-Lïon.

His technique of verbatim translation of local expressions has already been cited in comparison with Cheik Hamidou Kane. Chapter three describes a village assembly as it is conducted in real life. Here the oldest man is addressing the assembly and he strews his speech with proverbs and idioms. One of the proverbs he uses to explain the new position of the hero, Terhé, is also used by Achebe to explain the status of Okonkwo in Umuofia. The speaker in Boni's book enumerates the achievements of the hero and concludes with the proverb: "Quand un enfant a les mains propres, il prend ses repas dans le cercle des Anciens" (Crépuscule, p. 81). Achebe approves Okonkwo's social reward by using the same proverb: "If a child washed his hands, he could eat with kings. Okonkwo had clearly washed his hands and so he ate with kings and elders." (Things Fall Apart, p. 12).

Another technique Boni shares with Achebe is the traditional narrative style which they both introduce in stories within the story. These stories which are told in the evenings, and mostly by the children, are set down in the book as they are told in the village. In Boni, the usual introduction to a story is given in the vernacular:

> "Han Han Han Léé"
> "Ououm!"
> (Crépuscule, p. 38).

In Achebe's No Longer at Ease, we find Obi who does not know any folk tales but knows the introduction, so he always stops at it: "Olulu ofu oge" (No Longer at Ease, p. 61).

It is interesting to note that Birago Diop in his collection of traditional tales, Les Contes d'Amadou-Koumba, omits this formal introduction as well as the formal endings. Senghor regrets this important omission and points out that Diop did it because it is contrary to French taste! "Birago Diop supprime les formules initiales et finales parce que contraires, sans doute, au gout français, et c'est dommage."[36] Senghor's comment shows also that the author was more concerned with his French audience than with his African audience. And so if a typically African narrative form is displeasing to the French audience, it has to be dropped! Here is the foreign audience which places an embargo on the creative genius of the writer not only with his language, but also with its own literary aesthetics.

When Nazi Boni describes ceremonies, he does not just report that people sang and danced. Everything is set down even the sounds of the various instruments are written down:

> Le ti'mbwoani rugit: Konkofla! ... Kônkofla! ... Konkofla! ...
> Le ziri nko mugit: Doudou ... roudou ... doum! ...
> Le kere-nko aboie: Paon! ... Paon! ... boumpa! ... boum-
>   boum ...
>   Kônkôn! ... Kônkôn ... Kônkôn. ...
>   (*Crépuscule*, p. 87)

We find the same thing in Achebe's novels:

> The ekwe talks: Di-go-di-di-go-go-di-go
> the ogene sounds: gom-gom-gom-gom
> the cannons boom: Dim-diim--diim. ...
>   (*Things Fall Apart*, p. 113)

These parallels are being drawn to show how the same technique used by two authors strengthens one and weakens the other in the eyes of European critics. If the French critics and publishers frown on innovations such as Nazi Boni's, how would one expect the French-African writers to develop their literary talents to their fullest? Mr. Pageard makes a list of things he considers vulgar and shocking in Nazi Boni's language: "*J'en ai marre*" (p. 68), "*Ils encassaient mal la vacherie* (p. 128), "*La pauvre Hagni'nlé toute baba prenait en particulier une impitoyable raclée*" (p. 143), "*Bouffé*" *dans le sens de mangé.*[37]

If *"J'en ai marre"*—(I am fed up), is considered popular in French, what is more natural than the fact that an angry husband says that to his wife? In Boni's books, the phrase is in quotation marks because the author was quoting a villager; therefore, he used the villager's language. It is even likely that Boni consciously used the expression because it would be familiar to the French public! That is, they would expect their own village folks or peasants to use such expressions. One wonders what Pageard would do if he read, "Go and eat shit," which appears several times in Achebe's *Arrow of God*. These expressions may be vulgar but they would rather amuse than shock an African reader because they are used frequently by the village folks. Yet an African writer is condemned on the basis of language carried over to the foreign language from the mother tongue.

Furthermore, Nazi Boni is condemned for introducing elements of modernism "which destroy a historical fiction," because he uses words like *short* (p. 78), *Radio brousse* (p. 71). If Pageard condemns elements of modernism in what is a historical fiction, he would definitely throw Tutuola's *Palm Wine Drinkard* into the trash, for there he would find words like: *aeroplane, bomb, tank,* and many others, in a story based on Yoruba mythology. Yet Tutuola's language has been praised by eminent British critics who have indirectly encouraged him to continue.

What is hard to understand is that the French critic leaves no room for Nazi Boni, for he condemns his *argotique ou vulgaire* language and also condemns what he considers a "tendency toward the *précieux*":

> Ces tendances précieuses . . . ne nous semble pas devoir être encouragées en Afrique, bien qu'elles aient le mérite de rappeler des terms exactes et utiles, tels, dans l'ouvrage de Nazi Boni "spumeux," "vermiller," "pintades halbrenées," "venusté."[38]

If the influence of the writer's mother tongue on his French is discouraged, if his own invention is condemned and "preciosity should not be encouraged in Africa," what then is left for the writer? The only way he could escape these restrictions is to do one of two things—to invent his own peculiar form within the framework of the foreign language without paying any attention to what the owners of that language will say; or to write in his mother tongue where he could give reins to his creative genius.

Ahmadou Kourouma

Ahmadou Kourouma chooses to introduce his own innovations within the framework of the French language without regard to what the reaction of the French critics and publishers might be. His novel, *Les Soleils des Indépendances*, could be taken as the most recent attempt by an African writer to Africanize the French language. It has already been shown, in the section on publication, the difficulties he ran into before he got his book published. The main criticism is that he allowed his mother tongue to influence his French.

The review on the back cover of his book speaks of Kourouma's particular form in these terms:

> Au récit de cette fund'un "soleil" se mêlent librement contes et proverbes malinkés, transcrits dans une langue qui doit peu à l'académisme. Mais si Ahmadou Kourouma renouvelle en les violentant parfois, certains usages litéraires c'est pour créer une oeuvre originale et qui doit, pour exister, inventer sa propre forme.[39]

As the critic pointed out, Kourouma did invent his own peculiar form and it was that which made French publishers reject his book, for they said that "the French audience would not understand all those proverbs and nuances," as Kane put it. Although it is hard sometimes to detect the influence of an author's mother tongue on his writing, unless the reader speaks the same language as the author, one can easily notice certain elements in the structure of Kourouma's French which appear to have been carried over from the mother tongue. There is for example this constant use of *disons-le, précisons-le, avouons-le* to appeal to the reader's judgment, or to invite the reader to share the author's opinion.

When he describes a scene in which the Marabout tries to rape Salimata, he says: "A force de tordre les reins, de peiner, de piroutter, Salimata s'était stabilisée, *disons-le*, dans une position carrement provocante" (*Les Soleils des Indépendances*, p. 73). Each morning when Fama and Diamourou go to the Mosque, they stop to greet the widows and "Mariam les attendait. *Disons-le* parce qu'Allah aime le vrai" (*Les Soleils*, p. 134).

Kourouma also uses certain intransitive verbs in transitive form, thus instead of: "Fama sleeps with his favorite wife," we have "Fama sleeps his favorite wife." Fama has the right to "coucher sa favorite parmi cent épouses" (*Les Soleils*, p. 10). The word *nuit* (night) is also used as a verb, and we find: "Nuitez-en paix" (*Les Soleils*, p. 98); this could have been *bonne nuit*, or *passez-la nuit en paix*; the word *viande* (meat) is coined into an adjective *viandé*, this would literally be "meaty," "Les deux plus viandés et gras morceaux des Indépendances sont sûrement le secrétariat général et la direction d'une coopérative" (*Les Soleils*, p. 23). The subordinate pronoun *celui qui* is replaced by *Le*—"Le ci-devant caquetant ne savait ni chanter ni parler ni écouter" (*Les Soleils*, p. 16).

Speaking of these innovations, Pageard said they could not be approved. Not only does Kourouma invent new forms, he uses more idioms and proverbs than other French writers and his images are strictly African. The most recurrent image in his book is *une nuée de sauterelles*, followed by *une volée de mange-mil*. The harmattan is used frequently—"un ciel hanté par le soleil d'harmattan" (*Les Soleils*, p. 106), and there are such unusual similes as "aussi claire que la paume de la grenouille" (*Les Soleils*, p. 175).

There is one aspect of Kourouma's narrative style which reminds one of Amos Tutuola's. This is the repetition in parentheses of the person or thing already mentioned for fear that the reader may confuse the pronouns.

For instance, in a quarrel between Fama and a griot, Fama is repeated in parentheses several times:

"Des descendants de grands gueriers
(C'était Fama)
Vivaient de mensonges et de mendicité
(C'était encore Fama),
D'authentiques descendants de grands Chefs
(Toujours Fama)."
(*Les Soleils*, p. 16)

The resemblance is striking when one compares the above passage with one from Tutuola:

Then I began to travel on Death's road . . .
When I reached his (Death) house, . . . he was not at home
. . .
But when he (Death) heard the sound of the drum . . .
So when he (Death) saw that these stakes were beating him
He (Death) asked me from where I did come.
(*Palm Wine Drinkard*, p. 12)

Later on, the author talks about certain aspects of modernism that have changed the life in the town, and he uses the technique of authorian intervention throughout an entire paragraph:

Un homme stérile vivant d'aumônes dans une ville ou le soleil ne se couch pas (Les lampes électriques éclairant toute la nuit dans la capitale), ou les filles d'esclaves et les bâtards commandent, triomphe, en liant les provinces par des fils (le téléphone). des bandes (les routes) et le vent (les discours et la radio). (*Les Soleils*, p. 102)

The aspect of Kourouma's book that stands out more than the rest is the violent tone and the very crude expressions that one finds from the beginning to the end of the book. The hero's vocabulary seems to be made up of nothing other than cursing and swearing. Fama is a very disgruntled man who is disillusioned by the politics of his country after independence. He is much more disappointed with the town because he abandoned his inheritance in the ancestral home, hoping to find a more rewarding life in the town. Independence has betrayed his ambitions because the country is now run by bastards, tramps, and thieves!

Bâtard de bâtardise! Gnamokodé! Le soleil! Le soleil! Le soleil
des Indépendances maléfiques remplissait tout un côté du ciel,
grillait, assoiffait l'univers pour justifier les malsains orages des
fins d'après-midi. Les badauds! les bâtards de badauds plantés
en plein trottoir comme dans la case de leur papa. (*Les Soleils*,
pp. 9-10)

The book continues in this tone with the result that Fama's
cursing becomes the leitmotif of the story. Fama the only "clean"
person is trying to exist in a society of bastards, where independence brought nothing but "La carte d'identité nationale et
celle du parti unique" (p. 23).

After reading the book one would not be surprised that the
French publishers refused to publish it. For the author was not
only lamenting in very abusive and vulgar language the corruption and exploitation in his country, but he was abusing
France to her very face. The author comments that Fama: "s'était
debarrasse de tout: négoce. amitiés, femmes pour user les nuits,
les jours, l'argent et la colère à injurier la France, le père la mère
de la France" (p. 56). Fama felt it was his duty to abuse France
because "un fils légitime des chefs devait de tout son être par-
ticiper à la'expulsion des Français!" (p. 56).

One significant fact about Kourouma's book is that his innovations and inventions prove that the French language can indeed
be made to respond to the individual writer's needs, if only the
French critics and editors would give their blessing to such
experiments. But his rejection by the publishers and the con-
demnation of his innovations by the critics is one other case
against a French-African writer who tries to communicate his
particular message and sentiment by somehow dislocating the
traditional structure of the French language.

Again, it is President Senghor who pronounces the final statement on the dilemma of the African writer who is forced by
circumstances to express his cultural experience in a foreign
language. He is of the opinion that no matter how an African
uses the foreign language, he can only express the "Negro Soul"
by writing in his native language; thus he concludes:

Une littérature noire de langue française me paraît possible, il
est vrai. . . . Pour dire toute ma pensée, je la jugerais un peu
prématurée. Enfin une telle littérature ne saurait exprimer toute
notre âme. Il y a une certaine saveur, une certaine odeur, un
certain accent, un certain timbre noir inexprimable à des instruments européens. On se servirait de de la langue indigène dans
les genre littéraires qui exprime le génie de la race: poésie,
théâtre, conte.[40]

ENGLISH-AFRICAN WRITERS: THE FLEXIBILITY OF ENGLISH AND ITS ADVANTAGES TO THE AFRICAN WRITER

It has already been pointed out that a move from the foreign
to the African languages will take a long time. At the moment
the African writer is to make the best he can of what is available
—to experiment and bend the foreign language to meet his own
Negro aesthetics. Fortunately the English language has made
such experiment possible for the overseas Commonwealth writers.

It is the Indian writer R. K. Narayan who, in talking about
his use of English, summarizes what the English language means
to most Commonwealth writers:

> English has proved that if a language has flexibility, any ex-
> perience can be communicated through it. . . . We are not
> attempting to write Anglo-Saxon English. The English language
> through sheer resilience and mobility is now undergoing a process
> of Indianization. I cannot say whether this process of transmuta-
> tion is to be reviewed as an enrichment of the English language
> or a debasement of it. All that I am able to confirm after nearly
> thirty years of writing is that it has served my purpose admirably
> of conveying unambiguously the thoughts and acts of a set of
> personalities who flourish in a small town located in a corner of
> South India.[41]

Narayan's "we are not attempting to write Anglo-Saxon English" recalls Mphahlele's "we shan't be writing Oxford English,"
said in a different mood. Both point to the fact that English
tries to accommodate changes and innovations arising from efforts
by non-British users of English to express their cultural experi-

ence in English. What is important in Narayan's observation is that English is already accepting experiments within its framework and is thus serving the need of the nonnative speaker. Many African writers would indeed agree, and those I interviewed agree with Narayan, that English serves them well enough to "convey the thoughts and acts of a set of personalities," who live in different corners of Africa.

The answers of those interviewed show an interesting contrast with their Francophone counterparts. While the majority of Francophone writers would prefer to use their mother tongue if they had the opportunity, the Anglophone writers seem to have no regrets about using English, though they agree that certain moods or expressions would come out better in one language over another, depending upon the situation.

Ezekiel Mphahlele has often been very outspoken on the question of using English to write African literature. Below is what he has to say:

QUESTION: If you were writing exclusively for the Black people of South Africa whose mother tongue is not English, would you still have written in English?

MPHAHLELE: I would have continued to use the English language because there are two things which I consider: first, that if you are writing about your people's experiences and you are writing primarily and initially in response to oppression, you are going to be talking about ideas that operate in English which do not necessarily interpret in the same abstraction in an African language. What I mean is that when you first come in contact with the word *Liberty* or *Freedom* or *Oppression*, these are abstract things that we would never have spoken about in an African language; they come to us in English, so they have English connotations and they come heavily loaded with a culture and thought that come together with that language. So the most natural thing is, if I am going to talk about these abstractions, the easiest language to get hold of is English because they come to me in that language. Secondly, you want to reach a wider audience even for a local South African audience. In the urban areas they learn one another's languages to the extent that you could very well be understood but you can't take the chance; it's all a limited audience so you want to think of all the people in the reservations.

QUESTION: Now that you are basing your writing on your native experience in South Africa, don't you have a lot of difficulty transposing your ideas from, say, Sotho to English?

MPHAHLELE: No. I don't, but I never can tell each time I think in English and Sotho; it just goes back and forth and there are certain things that I'll say more easily in English, and there are certain things that resound in my mind in my mother tongue. I then have to stop and think how to put it across in English. I always have to do that.

QUESTION: So you have some conscious translation of one idea from one language to the other?

MPHAHLELE: Yes. It is conscious, because it rings more truly and more spontaneously in my mother tongue. I tend to think it's more natural so I work harder in finding the most appropriate translation which would not sound too English and at the same time would not be a literal translation.

QUESTIONS In which case it would have been easier to write such a thing in Sotho?

MPHAHLELE: Oh, yes, it may not have been easier but there probably would have been a better unity of feeling in it. Because here you are using your mother tongue and you are infusing a feeling that goes with that language. So when you write the same in English sometimes you fall into the trap of infusing a feeling that will not be typical of the language that your people speak from day to day but rather a feeling that comes with the English language. So one must always be on the alert and try to sound as authentic as one possibly can.

QUESTION: Is it justifiable to speak of "African Literature" when the writers are using the language, genre, and technique of a foreign audience?

MPHAHLELE: I would call it African in the sense that I talk of

European literature in different languages and coming from different cultures. The use of "African" is a convenient geographical boundary without necessarily attaching a certain quality that is distinctly African to it, in the sense that we don't have a unified quality to our writing. Apart from the geographical boundary, there is also the fact that this writing is done by Africans.

QUESTION: Do you think it is necessary to have an African literature written in African languages?

MPHAHLELE: I don't think we need it to the exclusion of English or French. I think we need it if only because there are a number of people who want to express themselves in languages other than the European ones, and people like that should not be discouraged from expressing themselves in their mother tongue.

QUESTION: I have no doubt that some traditional literature does exist in your mother tongue. Is there a link between your writing and the traditional literature of your people?

MPHAHLELE: In my own particular case it is more of the wisdom that comes from my tradition in terms of proverbs, epigrams, aphorisms, etc. I draw these from African speech. . . . This comes every time I want to express something which I want to symbolize. I must select a symbol that is from among my people and the way I create my symbols is very much influenced by the traditional oral literature. . . .[42]

Mphahlele gives almost identical answers as President Senghor as far as the abundance of abstract symbols in the foreign languages is concerned. Mphahlele would still use English even if he could write in his mother tongue. This is mainly because the substance of his writing comes from the situation in South Africa and in this situation which is identified as "Oppression," the ideas such as Freedom and Liberty are abstractions which do not find appropriate equivalents in the mother tongue. And even when the writer conceives an idea in his mother tongue, he still has to "work very hard and consciously" to render it into English for the benefit of other Africans whose mother tongue

is not the same as the writer's. Here we run again into the same
problem of limiting the artist's scope, because by the time he
finishes switching from one language to the other, he could
have spent that time improving his style.

Thus, even though English serves the nonnative speaker well
enough to express his native experience, one still finds a certain
limitation—that no matter how one tries to "sound as authentic
as one possibly can" one always loses something in transposition.

Ngugi Wa Thiong'O, when questioned about using the mother
tongue, replied as follows:

QUESTION: Since you are writing mainly for an East African
    audience, I would imagine that Swahili would have been a
    more appropriate language than English which you have been
    using?

THIONG'O: There are two problems here. In a sense one does
    not choose one's language because when one talks of language
    there is an assumption that one can in fact consciously choose
    the linguistic medium in which one is going to write. To
    those of us who are educated through English as a linguistic
    medium, even the very attempt to conceptualize is through
    English as a medium. One is already conditioned by his
    history and context in which he is writing, by the time, etc.,
    to use a particular language first of all. The question of con-
    scious choice comes afterwards. At the moment in which
    one is writing the question of choice does not arise.

    The other aspect is readership. By the time we were
    writing, most publishers would have shied away from pub-
    lishing a book in Swahili, for instance. They think it wouldn't
    have an adequate buying public. Even today this is true;
    those books which have been published in Swahili, not many
    people buy them. And Swahili is not yet a medium for
    education in East Africa.

    Also there is the facility with which you could use one
    language as opposed to the other. Most of us can't effectively

use Swahili as a medium of writing. Again it is the question of conditioning. It is not because it is incapable of handling this kind of raw material or ideas, it is rather the writer's limitation and not that of Swahili. One is writing with certain definite limitations which interfere with one's freedom of choice.

QUESTION: Personally do you find it easier to write in English?

THIONG'O: I wouldn't say it's easier, but, comparatively, with Swahili, yes, as a result of history.

QUESTION: How about your mother tongue Kikuyu?

THIONG'O: My mother tongue I have not tried yet, but I hope to when I finish my coming novel. I want to do some experimenting in writing in Kikuyu just to see how it works. To see if I can be meaningful.

QUESTION: Do you have any difficulty transposing your thoughts from Kikuyu or Swahili to English?

THIONG'O: No. Again this is a mental thing if you are trying to make linguistic terms conform to a certain rhythm, a certain way of feeling. . . . As one of my colleagues said, most African writers do not really write in English, all they do is to translate from their mother tongue; they do it in the very course of writing, and I think to some extent he is right.

QUESTION: I imagine there could be some obstacle in transposing an idea conceived in your mother tongue into another language?

THIONG'O: This is natural and only to be expected.

QUESTION: Apart from the fact that we have been conditioned to think and conceptualize in English, don't you think that the desire to reach a wider audience motivates the writer to use this foreign language?

THIONG'O: No, the question of a wider audience doesn't arise very much with me except, of course, that I like to reach a cross-section of Kenyan readers. I like to feel that my writing was being read by national communities in Kenya, in East Africa, in Africa as a whole. I would like to feel that I am reaching a basically African audience at the continental level or international level. I would like to feel I am reaching the Black community of third world communities.

QUESTION: Since the African reading public is a very minute one, I don't know how far you people are getting to the "people" for whom you claim to be writing?

THIONG'O: Actually it's true we are not reaching the people, but then writing itself is a minority occupation by its very nature. It is not a public art form. It's very elitist in itself. In Africa to be able to read is still a minority preoccupation. I see it as a wider structural problem. And this is a problem which will continue even if one is writing in one's own mother tongue.

There is need for a structural change; e.g., if illiteracy is abolished more people will have the opportunity for education, and books and reading will no longer be a privilege but a right. This will change the whole relationship between writer and audience.[43]

As far as Ngugi Wa Thiong'O is concerned, the question of choosing one's language does not arise because it is predetermined by one's history. And for the African it is both dependent on history and conditioning. There is actually no turning back for the writers at this point. The best any of them can do is to try to "experiment" with his mother tongue and see how it comes out. However, though the writer finds it more handy to write in English, he is still confronted with the problem of transposing his native experience into the foreign language. But worse than that is the fact that even if the writers were to change suddenly and write in their mother tongues, they would still be faced with the problem of a very limited audience, because they will not reach the people who, for the most part, are illiterate. Until this problem of illiteracy is solved, the writer has no choice but to continue writing for the "privileged," minute audience who, like himself, has been educated through foreign linguistic media. In addition to his local, "privileged" audience, he will still be writing for the larger, external audience whose language he has been conditioned to use.

Chinua Achebe

Chinua Achebe, more than any other African writer in English has made most of the suppleness of the English language to "convey the thoughts and acts of Ibo people in his writings." Like the rest of the writers, he explains his use of English by the inevitable colonial legacy, but does not show any great enthusiasm to write in his mother tongue. Below is what he has to say on the question of foreign language in African literature.

QUESTION: How would you justify the use of English to write a literature which is richly African?

ACHEBE: I don't know. The answer to that is: that is the way our world is. When I talk of a literate audience in Nigeria, it is also an English-speaking audience, and that is the way our continent is structured. There is really no answer as far as language is concerned. Inasmuch as I understand the reality of English, French, or Portuguese in Africa, I also understand the need for keeping the indigenous languages of Africa alive, at least those that are able to survive. In other words there is a double need; while you recognize the presence of an English-speaking audience that is Nigerian and not foreign to Nigeria, there is also this other need to recognize these other languages.

QUESTION: The fact that you are basing all your novels in your traditional society, and you are using the proverbs, idioms, etc., in that society, how do you manage to get your ideas across in English without losing much of the African flavor?

ACHEBE: It's really a question of looking around and deciding whether you can tell a story using English words and still keep the meaning of the story. To me it seems you can; you play around and see whether you can do it. I don't mean that you sit down and do it consciously, but you know it by the time you have written one sentence that you can do it.

QUESTION: I was of the opinion that it takes you a very long time to arrive at such expressions as you use in your novels?

ACHEBE: Not really. From the moment I decide to tell a story I play around with the forms of words to use. I come up quickly from the use of a different kind of English, different from the kind which a British or American writer would use. And I think the beginning of this English was already there in our society, in popular speech. There was already a development of a Nigerian English, the English language is capable of this kind of extension.

QUESTION: Are you saying that a Nigerian English exists?

ACHEBE: Oh, yes, though it's not something you can define, you can sense its presence. You may not find words or phrases that are Nigerian or African, but you find uses which ultimately will have a flavor that is recognizable.

QUESTION: There seems to be no possibility of Africans having an African literature in African languages. Do you think you can write a book in Ibo as you write in English?

ACHEBE: It doesn't have to be me. There's no reason why it has to be the same person. It is quite possible for this to be from other people. Fagunwa, for instance, writes in Yoruba while Tutuola writes in English. For one thing Fagunwa knows English better than Tutuola, so it becomes a matter of individual preference. But I think this can also be helped by definite conscious effort.

QUESTION: The reason I think it is impossible is that people of your generation and mine seem to know more Ibo than the later generations. I don't see how they can pick it up to the extent that they would be able to express themselves more adequately in Ibo than in English.

ACHEBE: I am not so sure about that. I think it is possible to have the situation alter. Mark you, I am not ruling out the possibility of writing in Ibo. But I think that given a little more time and formal encouragement things might begin to change. But if you say you don't think Ibo or Yoruba or Hausa will supplant English in Nigeria, I agree with you.

If we were to have an Ibo nation, a Yoruba nation, etc., and not a Nigerian nation, that is, to change the political realities, we might have a different situation but as things stand today, English is the thing that makes the idea of Nigeria possible. So the language is deeply entrenched, but that is no reason why you cannot develop a literature in Hausa, Ibo, or Yoruba.

QUESTION: In other words you don't think that English is easier to handle than Ibo for instance?

ACHEBE: No, not really. I think it's a matter of preference. There are things I can conceive of doing better in Ibo. For me at this time it's a question of time; for instance, there's a fairly important poem I wrote in Ibo . . . not finished, and it seems to me there are things I say in it which I can't say in English; similarly, there are things I say in English which I can't say in Ibo. There are things that come more easily because they belong to an Ibo way of thinking and if you want to convey these ideas it is easier in Ibo, for instance, *Ume Omumu*, which conveys the whole meaning of succession of deaths of infants. It's not infant mortality; there's no word in English or phrase to express it, whereas *Ume* simply says it all. It depends on where a language emphases are. This is why it is impossible to say that one language is better than another; it depends on what you are talking about.

QUESTION: In most of your works, a lot of traditional literature is inserted; what is your link with traditional literature? What is your main source of inspiration?

ACHEBE: I would say my main source is the Ibo civilization, which includes oral literature. I have often said that one of the most important genres in Ibo is oratory and this is not preserved in the same way as proverbs, anecdotes, stories, etc.; this is a matter of individual excellence. It's part of Ibo culture, all that is part of the inheritance I feel I am working with; proverb is just a portion of this inheritance; the whole way of looking at the world, the cosmology of the Ibo people is something deep and profound. For instance, the concept of *Chi* is one form of humanity that is non-

Western, and I don't think the world knows about it and
I think I should work from it.

QUESTION: The African writer writes in a foreign language, uses
foreign genre, tradition, and publishers; yet he is called an
African writer. It is by reason of your origin that you are
called an African writer. Don't you think it would be more
appropriate to include you among English writers as they
do with Conrad, Eliot, etc?

ACHEBE: Well, you can if you want to. I think there's more to
it, but I think you are insisting on a neatness and a kind
of simplicity that does not exist in our situation. I think
you can group my novels with writing in English, as long
as you define what you are doing. And it's been done.

It's not just the language that determines what the literature is; it's important, but it's not the main issue. If you
have a place called Nigeria in which education is in English,
then there is a certain way in which English becomes part
of that reality. Literature is just one way in which this
reality demonstrates itself.[44]

Achebe chooses to dismiss his almost perfect simulation of
Ibo expressions into English as merely the result of "playing
around with words," that he does not sit down consciously to
work out his expressions. He denies that it takes him time to
come out with his simulated phrases, yet there is no amount of
"playing around" which is not time consuming. At least by the
time he finishes his play with words he could have got something extra done and perhaps more meaningfully rendered in
his mother tongue. For he admits that certain things would
have been easier and better rendered in Ibo than in English
depending on the context. But because he is writing in English
he is forced to spend time looking for adequate equivalents in
English so as to be intelligible to his English-speaking audience.

He claims that he does not sit down consciously to work out
his phrases from Ibo to English, but, ironically, in his appraisal
of Fagunwa's writings in Yoruba, Achebe concedes that one
requires a definite, conscious effort to write in African languages

because we have not been conditioned in our colonial educational system to think and conceptualize in our mother tongues.

As far as supplanting English by African languages is concerned, Achebe does not see any hope of its taking place in the near future. What he, like Thiong'O, suggests is that the writer can also experiment with his mother tongue, maybe, then, we shall come out with African literature in African languages existing side by side with African literature in foreign languages.

It is true that Achebe claims that he only plays with words to arrive at his unique type of English, but anyone who takes time to study his language will realize that nothing could have been more consciously worked out. And as a result of this conscious exercise Achebe has successfully disproved Gerald Moore's assertion that "an African writer cannot write English and simultaneously preserve the linguistic structure of the vernacular," because Achebe is a perfect example of an African writer who can write in good English and still preserve the structure of his native language. Donald Stuart, who talked about the standard for measuring African writing, feels that Achebe is "the most literary in the full and right sense of all present African authors writing in English, because he above all has cared to give complete meaning to all that he writes about. His English is masterly, but it is also, in all its inner texture, most richly African."[45]

Examples will be taken from Achebe's works to show some "Africanized English" which the writer himself would not use in normal English conversation. For instance among his peers, Achebe would not speak like Ezeulu: "Ofoedu did not contain the smallest drop of human presence inside his body" (*Arrow of God* p. 99), instead of, "Ofoedu is very stupid"; neither would he say: "If you have any grain of sense in your belly" (*Arrow of God*, p. 170), instead of "If you have any common sense"; nor would he call a person a "beast of the bush" (*Arrow of God*, p. 104), instead of "foolish person."

But Achebe puts these expressions into the mouths of his Ibo characters in order to bring out those "swift and subtle turns of mind, and those little catch-phrases that are peculiarly Igbo."

There are so many of these "Igboisms" in Achebe that one could write volumes picking them out. It is not that Achebe could not find appropriate English equivalents to expressions like, "put their fathers into the earth"—bury their fathers—(*Arrow of God,* p. 7); "shining white like the nut of the water of heaven" —as white as hailstone—(*Arrow of God,* p. 236); "Don't put your mouth in this—Don't interfere—(*Arrow of God,* p. 255); "He was at the mouth of death"—His condition was critical (*Arrow of God,* p. 202).

Achebe is doing what E. C. Okwu terms "squeezing out of it [English]" the color of African thought. When Achebe was asked why he chooses to make his characters speak in this peculiar way when he could make them speak "official" English, he selected a passage from *Arrow of God* to show how African beliefs and attitudes could be lost to the readers if the character spoke orthodox English. Thus Ezeulu explains his reason for sending his son to church-school:

> I want one of my sons to join these people and be my eye there. If there is nothing in it you will come back. But if there is some-thing there you will bring home my share. The world is like a mask dancing. If you want to see it well you do not stand in one place. My spirit tells me that those who do not befriend the white man today will be saying "had we known" tomorrow. (p. 55)

And Achebe asks, "supposing I had put it in another way, for example":

> I am sending you as my representative among those people, just to be on the safe side in case the new religion develops. One has to move with the times or else one is left behind. I have a hunch that those who fail to come to terms with the white man may well regret their lack of foresight.[46]

In Ezeulu's rendering, the general simplicity of the phrasing and the figures of speech distinguish the African turn of thought from the more Western turn, found in the second rendering of the same speech. The word representative is rendered by "be my eye there," and "have a hunch," by "my spirit tells me." In this example, Achebe shows how he has consciously worked out his own mode of artistic expression by getting away from normal English usage, which tends to block out all traces of Africanness from an indigenous African expression.

It is in his weaving of Igbo proverbs into the narrative that Achebe succeeds most in communicating to the reader the quality and complexity of Igbo thought.

The proverbs are mostly found in speeches or in dialogues among the African characters. For instance, in two short paragraphs we have three proverbs: "The lizard that jumped from the high iroko tree to the ground said he would praise himself if no one else did," "Eneke the bird says that since men have learned to shoot without missing, he has learned to fly without perching," and "As our fathers said, you can tell a ripe corn by its look" (*Things Fall Apart*, p. 24).

The most striking example of this abundant use of proverbs is in *Arrow of God*, in the scene where Obika is doing the Ogbazuluobodo traditional running. In fact, the author seemed to be beyond himself, for he just pours out three paragraphs of idioms and proverbs which do not seem to be connected with the action, but they actually convey very vividly to an Igbo speaker from the state of Obika. It is also quite in keeping with the kind of monologue one would expect to hear from Obika's father and Obika's admirers. Thus, as soon as Obika "vanished like the wind in the direction of Nkwo," the proverbs and idioms begin to flow:

The fly that struts around on a mound of excrement wastes his time; the mound will always be greater than the fly. The thing that beats the drum for Ngwesi is inside the ground. Darkness is so great it gives horns to a dog. He who built a homestead before another can boast of more broken pots. It is *ofo* that gives rainwater power to cut dry earth. The man who walks ahead of his fellows spots spirits on the way. Bat said he knew his ugliness and chose to fly by night. When air is fouled by a man on top of a palm tree the fly is confused. An ill-fated man drinks water and it catches in his teeth . . . (p. 282).

At the end of the paragraph, the author takes a break from proverbs, switches to antithesis to explain Obika's mental state:

> He was at once blind and full of sight. He did not see any of the landmarks—but his feet knew where they were going. He did not leave out even one small path from the accustomed route. He knew it without the use of his eyes. He only stopped once when he smelt light (p. 282).

Then the proverbs start flowing again till the end of the paragraph, and the break explaining Obika's state follows:

> A fire began to rage inside his chest and to push a dry bitterness up his mouth. But he tasted it from a distance or from a mouth within his mouth. He felt like two separate persons, one running above the other (p. 282).

Finally, the third paragraph begins and ends with a proverb.

A short paragraph shows the eight men waiting for Obika's return and before they could realize it, Obika was already back, only to collapse and die from exhaustion.

To a Western reader, these three paragraphs do not add anything to the story. And to a critic like Ronald Christ, "One must go back as far as Cervantes to find anyone else as meaninglessly proverbial.[47]

But by resorting to proverbs, Achebe creates the right traditional atmosphere for the mystical run. He had no need to justify their use for they create a background against which local situations are enacted. And there is no way he could have captured the scene in plain English. Yet, the interesting thing is that the proverbs are so well rendered in English that they really make English do what the African language does.

Judging from the people who use the proverb, we notice that Achebe makes it fulfill one other function that the English language fulfills—it creates a social distinction among the people.

Just as elegant speech in English is associated with the upper class, so are proverbs associated with the elders in the society.

This division of the society into elders and nonelders was about the only visible social division in animist African societies before the colonial period.

With the coming of Western education, other divisions came in. We now have well-educated people, semieducated people, and illiterate people. But as far as the African language is concerned, everybody speaks the same language. This means that no one could tell whether a person is educated or illiterate by the way he speaks Igbo or Yoruba, for instance, but one could recognize the speech of an elder from that of a young person because the former adorns his speech with proverbs while the latter normally does not.

To portray these new social hierarchies, Achebe and many other Nigerian writers make a kind of character differentiation in language that one finds in English. They do this by making their characters speak the type of English that is representative of their academic level. This new division is just starting in *Arrow of God*, where the semieducated interpreters mix good English with Pidgin English and sometimes add their own special local flavors in the translation. Such is the scene in which Unachukwu is translating for Mr. Wright, the Road Overseer:

> "Tell them this bloody work must be finished by June."
> "The whiteman says that unless you finish this work in time you will know the kind of man he is."
> "No more lateness."
> "Pardin?"
> "Pardon what? Can't you understand plain, simple English? I said there will be no more late-coming."
> "Oho. He says everybody must work hard and stop all this shit-eating."
> "I have one question, I want the whiteman to answer." This was Nweke Ukpaka.
> "What's that?"
> "Dat man wan axe master qeshan."
> "No questions."
> "Yessah." He turned to Nweke. "The whiteman says he did not leave his house this morning to come and answer your questions" (p. 102).

Here we have the Englishman speaking English correctly, and the interpreter who vacillates between Pidgin English and the vernacular. Nweke Ukpaka's question is put in correct English because he normally would speak correct Igbo.

With his faulty English, Unachukwu's position in the village has risen because he could speak the white man's language. And even when the African can only speak pidgin, he is still admired by the villagers who cannot. For instance, the two policemen who came to summon Ezeulu to Okeperi "conferred in the whiteman's tongue to the great admiration of the villagers." But the author recorded their conversation, which is only in Pidgin English:

> "Sometimes na dat two parson we cross for road."
> "Sometimes na dem."
> "But we no go return back just like dat. All this waka wey we waka come here no fit go for nothing."
>
> "Sometime na lie dem de lie. I no wan make dem put trouble for we head" (pp. 189-90).

The character differentiation in language is more elaborate in *No Longer at Ease*, a novel situated in modern Nigeria. There we have Obi and Clara who have just returned from England and speak the "been-to" English—the queen's English. Then there is the average educated secretary of Umuofia Progressive Union. The welcome address he reads at Obi's reception is very typical of the English spoken by people of his academic rank:

> Sir, we the officers and members of the above-named Union present with humility and gratitude this token of our appreciation of your unprecedented academic brilliance. The importance of having one of our sons in the vanguard of this march of progress is nothing short of axiomatic. (pp. 36-37)

The secretary referred to the arrangement whereby every beneficiary of Umuofia Union Scholarship was expected to repay his debt so that "an endless stream of students will be enabled to drink at the Pierian Spring of knowledge" (p. 37).

At the end of the speech, the audience cheered and clapped their hands. The author comments on the peoples' reaction to the Secretary's English:

> He deserved to go to England himself. He wrote the kind of English they admired if not understood: the kind that filled the mouth, like the proverbial dry meat. (p. 37)

Obi later replied to the speech in plain, simple English to the disappointment of the audience. "Obi's English was most unimpressive. He spoke 'is' and 'was.' That was his 'Mistake Number Two.'" (*No Longer at Ease*, p. 37). (His 'Mistake Number One' was that he showed up in shirt sleeves instead of in a suit as was expected of a young man from England.)

Achebe probably inserted the average educated man's English to show the mentality of the semieducated or uneducated Africans. To a "been to" like Obi, the English of the Secretary may sound forced and pompous, but to the audience it is eloquent and dignified; it is the sign of higher learning. One finds a lot of this bombastic English in Aluko's *One Man, One Matchet*, used especially by the picaresque hero Benjamin, whose "reports were full of long words and flourishes, the sort of style that newspaper readers lap up" (*One Man, One Matchet*, p. 11).

Later we find Obi with the semiliterate driver who only speaks Pidgin English. Obi's presence in the lorry prevents the driver from giving the police the now customary bribe of two shillings. The driver is angry with Obi and he asks him:

> Driver: Why you look the man for face when we want give um him two shillings?
> Obi: Because he has no right to take two shillings from you.
> Driver: Na him make I no de want carry you book people. Too too know na him de worry una. Why you put your nose for matter way no concern you? Now that policemen go charge me like ten shillings? (*No Longer at Ease*, P. 47)

In his statement, the driver refers to Obi's social rank, he belongs to the "Book People," the "too-know."

Finally, Obi goes to the village and in his conversation with the villagers he speaks Igbo, uses their pattern of speech; he tells them of his journey home:

> It is not something that can be told. It took the whiteman's ship sixteen days—four market weeks—to do the journey. Sometimes for a whole market week there is no land in front, behind, to the right, and to the left. Only water." (p. 54)

In *The Interpreters*, Wole Soyinka makes a more elaborate use of language for character differentiation. For, in addition to the different classes already mentioned in Achebe's novels, we find a class of university graduates working in different fields, foreign expatriates, professors and doctors. But among the university-educated Africans, there is a sector that is notorious for its very affected English. In this group we find Professor Oguazar. He is looking for his wife Caroline:

> "I thought Ceroline was here."
> "She was here a moment ago."
> "Oh der, end the ledies are wetting for her."
> "Ceroline der, the ledies herv been waiting for you."
> "I know—will you handle things at this end?"
> "Ef cerse der."
> "Cem en der, we mesn't keep the ledies wetting?" (*The Interpreters*, p. 153).

Then there is the class of influential but not highly educated politicians and foremen, unsure of their grammar and tense. This class is represented by Winsola who traces Sagoe to his hotel Excelsior to ask for a bribe. Sagoe does not remember him and he reminds him:

> "You were our interviewee the day before yesterday morning."
> "Your what did you say?"
> "Our interviewee. I am a member of the board to which you came to answer our advertisement."
> "You are a bad boy the other morning."

He then proceeded to tell Sagoe that a degree was no longer a guarantee for getting jobs, because, "Before, degree is something, but now everyone is having a degree. Degree is two for penny—No more degree passport." (*The Interpreters*, pp. 87-88).

By thus using different kinds of English to portray the new social hierarchy, the African writers are consciously imitating an English tradition which does not exist in the African language.

Apart from using language to show the social hierarchy, the writers also use it in another Western sense, that is, using it on another level of character differentiation, that of individualizing a character by his utterances. The use of language in this way is very important because it is rarely used in that sense in Africa. The maxim "Action speaks louder than words" exists in many African languages. In Owerri dialect they say *Eji onu ele?* literally, "Do we judge by the mouth?"—the implication being, "You do not judge by words of mouth but by action."

As far as character portrayal is concerned in Africa, it is done through the actions of the charatcer rather than his words. It is this method that Achebe uses mostly in his portrayal of Okonkwo in *Things Fall Apart*. "Okonkwo was a man of action, a man of war" (p. 14). Okonkwo says very little and does not engage in long conversations and dialogues. But he is seen more often in action—he rules his family with a heavy hand; he beats his wife during the week of peace; he nearly killed one of them by firing his rusty gun at her; he deals the blow that killed Ikemefuna; his gun explodes accidentally and kills a boy. Finally he kills the whiteman's messenger and hangs himself. Through his actions Okonkwo is seen as a man with an inordinate desire to prove his strength. He does it without regard to the will of the gods or that of the people.

On the other hand, Obierika is characterized in a typically Western method. We know him through his utterances. He is Okonkwo's opposite. "Obierika was a man who thought about things" (p. 117). He blamed his friend Okonkwo for his excessive zeal and lack of compromise. After Ikemefuna had been killed, Okonkwo goes to his friend to find out why he did not join the party to kill the boy. Both men engage in an argument on the justification of the act:

> "I cannot understand why you refused to come with us to kill that boy."
> "Because I did not want to. I had something better to do."
> "You sound as if you question the authority and the decision of the oracle, who said he should die."
> "I do not, why should I? But the oracle did not ask me to carry out its decision."
> "But someone had to do it. If I were afraid of blood, it would not be done."
> "You know very well, Okonkwo, that I am not afraid of blood. . . . And let me tell you one thing my friend, if I were you I would have stayed at home. What you have done will not please the earth. It is the kind of action for which the goddess wipes out whole 'families.' The earth cannot punish me for obeying her messenger. A child's fingers are not scalded by a piece of hot yam which its mother put into its palm."
> "That is true. But if the oracle said that my son should be killed I would neither dispute it nor be the one to do it." (pp. 64-65).

In this dialogue, the difference in character of both men is clearly shown. Okonkwo will go to any length to carry out an objective even if it involves his killing a child who has lived in his household for three years. On the other hand, we have Obierika, a thoughtful man who knows when to make compromises. Surely he would give his son to be killed but he would not be the one to do it.

Obierika shows himself a man of thought and foresight when he warns Okonkwo that to fight the white man would be like committing suicide. He told him the story of Abame which was destroyed by the white man on account of one white man whom they killed. Moreover, to fight the white man would mean fighting against some of their clansmen who had already joined the white man's religion. He says to Okonkwo:

> It is already too late, our own men and our own sons have joined his religion and they help to uphold his government. If we

should try to drive out the whitemen in Umuofia we should find it easy. There are only two of them. But what of our own people who are following their way and have been given power? They would go to Umuru and bring the soldiers, and we would be like Abame. (p. 161)

It is Obierika who summarizes the tragedy that has befallen the clan. Through his utterances we get the title of the book. Okonkwo asks him if the white man understood the custom about land to judge land cases. Obierika replies:

How can he when he does not even speak our tongue? But he says that our customs are bad, and our own brothers who have taken up his religion also say that our customs are bad. How do you think we can fight when our own brothers have turned against us? The whiteman is clever. He came quietly and peaceably with his religion. We were amused at his foolishness and allowed him to stay. Now he has won our brothers, and our clan can no longer act like one. He has put a knife in the things that held us together and we have fallen apart. (p. 162)

It is also through the words and manner of speech of the European characters that Achebe lets the reader judge their character. He imitates the kind of language used by the British administrators. Thus the District Commissioner says to the delegates of Umuofia whom he had imprisoned:

We shall not do you any harm if only you agree to cooperate with us. We have brought a peaceful administration to you and your people so that you may be happy. If any man ill-treats you we shall come to your rescue. But we will not allow you to ill-treat others. We have a court of law where we judge cases and administer justice as it is done in my own country under a great queen. (p. 178)

In the Commissioner's statement the holier-than-thou attitude of the colonizers is manifested, while the message of Pax Britannica is preached.

In *No Longer at Ease,* the British councilman does not under-

stand why a man like Obi should take bribes. But Mr. Green
says he can understand and he gives the reason as follows:

> The African is corrupt through and through. They are all corrupt.
> I'm all for equality and all that. I for one would hate to live
> in South Africa. But equality won't alter facts. . . . The fact is
> that over countless centuries the African has been victims of the
> worst climate in the world and of every imaginable disease. Hardly
> his fault. But he has been sapped mentally and physically. We
> have brought him Western education. But what use is it to him?
> (p. 11)

Here Mr. Green refuses to see the pressures that lead to
Obi's corruption. He does not even imagine that "white men
eat more bribe than black men nowadays" (p. 38). Achebe
thus exposes the wide gap of social and cultural misunderstand-
ing between the two groups by differentiating their style of speech.
In this differentiation of characters through their manners of
speech, one notes the influence of Western literary conventions
on the African writers.

Achebe is particularly noted for his ability to capture the
rhythm of Igbo speech. This is often found in the dialogues or
in the formal speech by the elders. The characters speak simulated
English. But there are certain aspects of the sentence structure
that are carried over from Igbo language. The most outstanding
of these is repetition; this does not mean saying one thing over
and over again, but it is a kind of enumeration in which a verb
or a group of words are repeated in a pattern that makes them
sound like a refrain. An example of this is the speech by Okika
in *Things Fall Apart*:

> You all know why we are here, when we ought to be building
> our barns or mending our huts, when we should be putting our
> compounds in order. My father used to say to me: "Whenever
> you see a toad jumping in broad daylight, then you know that
> something is after its life." When I saw you all pouring into
> this meeting from all the quarters of our clan so early in the
> morning, I knew that something was after our life. . . . All our
> gods are weeping. Idemili is weeping. Ogwugwu is weeping,

Agbala is weeping, and all the others. Our fathers are weeping because of the shameful sacrilege they are suffering and the abomination we have all seen with our eyes. (pp. 186-87)

This kind of repetition is also found in *Arrow of God*, when Ezeulu re-enacted the first coming of Ulu and how each of the four market days put obstacles in his way(pp. 87-88).

Very often the African flavor is heightened by the use of images and similes which are indicative of cultural milieu. The images and similes in *Things Fall Apart* and *Arrow of God*, are strictly drawn from the life and activities in the village. In *Things Fall Apart* we have:

Okonkwo's fame had grown like bush-fire in the harmattan. . . . (p. 7)

He grew rapidly like a yam tendril in the rainy season. (p. 51)

Something seemed to give way inside him like the snapping of a tightened bow. . . . (p. 59)

I am Evil Forest; I am Dry-meat-that-fills-the-mouth; I am Fire-that-burns-without-faggots. (p. 89)

Obierika's compound was as busy as an ant hill. . . . (p. 106)

The white men were like locusts. (p. 128)

A fire that burned like palm oil. (p. 135)

Living fire begets cold impotent ash. (p. 143)

From *Arrow of God*:

Like the walk of an Ijele Mask lifting and lowering each foot with weighty ceremony. . . . (p. 84)

Like the lizard who fell down from a high iroko tree. . . . (p. 143)

I shall beat okro seeds out of your mouth. . . . (p. 158)

He is as tall as an iroko tree and his skin is white like the sun. . . . (p. 189)

Like the blue, quiet, razor-edge flame of burning palm nut shells. . . . (p. 274)

In the novels set in the towns the similes are appropriately drawn from urban surroundings, but sometimes one finds some images drawn from the village. Perhaps this is because the characters in the urban-set novels had lived in the village before moving to the towns, whereas those in the villages had never left it.

In *No Longer at Ease*:

> He fixed him with his gaze as a collector fixes his insect with formalin. . . . (p. 9)

> Like a giant tarmac from which God's aeroplane might take off. . . . (p. 30)

> The white walls and red tiles looked like an enchanted isle. . . . (p. 33)

> Like a brand new snake just emerged from its slough. . . . (p. 154)

> Like a palm tree bearing fruit at the end of its leaf. . . . (p. 156)

> Like a bird that flies off the earth and lands on an ant hill. . . . (p. 150)

Achebe has various techniques of making a distinction between the village and the urban dwellers. The most outstanding of these is the time concept he uses in village and urban-set novels. In the village there is neither clock nor dial for timekeeping. The hours are reckoned in blocks by "cock crows:" In *Things Fall Apart*:

> During the planting season Okonkwo worked daily on his farms from cock crow until the chickens go to roost. (p. 17)

> And whenever the moon forsook evening and rose at cock crow the nights were as black as charcoal. . . . (p. 90)

> The first cock had not crowed and Umuofia was swallowed up in sleep. . . . (p. 113)

> We had meant to set out from house before cock crow . . . (p. 131)

The week is made up of four market days: Eke, Orie, Afo and Nkwo. The market week is used to measure longer periods:

The drought continued for eight market weeks. . . . (p. 26)

He was ill for three four market weeks. . . . (p. 29)

For many market weeks nothing else happened. . . . (p. 129)

In *Arrow of God*:

During the four market weeks he had been locked up . . . (p. 220)

On the eighth Eke market since his arrest he was free . . . (p. 220)

To refer to a very long time in history we find the recurrent phrase:

When lizards were still in ones and twos. . . . (p. 87)

In the novels set in the urban area the time concept changes to Western time usage. In *No Longer at Ease* we find:

This court begins at nine o'clock. . . . (p. 9)

At ten they rose to go because their ship would sail at eleven. . . . (p. 34)

Obi brought a Morris Oxford a week after. . . . (p. 67)

Four months is a short time. . . . (p. 81)

Like the new social hierarchy, the Western time usage shows the distinction between "new" and traditional Africa. This distinction is made possible by the foreign language.

In these examples, we see that Achebe's Africanization of English does not stop at weaving of proverbs and idioms into the narrative. It also does not stop at dialogues in which the Igbo rhythm of speech is demonstrated. He extends it to images and similes drawn from local scenes and applied to the appropriate milieu in which each novel is set.

Achebe's ability to create his particular mode of expression within the framework of the English language makes his style very authentic. In his innovations he does not in any way distort the English language. B. Lindfors has very correctly observed that "Achebe does not violate natural English syntax or reduplicate words in order to simulate African expression. He manages to achieve a different kind of African vernacular style in English and limits his use of it to dialogues."[48]

This capacity to adapt English to his need shows the author's mastery of that language. Yet many critics say that "Africans can only write like Africans." This implies that they cannot write "normal" English. John Povey said in his article in *Books Abroad*, No. 40, 1966: "But the English of these writers is rarely official British. It is not static but derives a new resilience and color from local usage."[49] And John Ferguson said: "They [Nigerian writers] write as Africans of course."[50]

Opinions such as the above sent me looking for a definition and examples of standard African English. In an article, "Standard Nigerian English," Adebisi Salami said: "Some of the speakers or writers on the subject are themselves doubtful of the existence of such a thing as Nigerian English."[51] Mr. Salami cited a few grammatical mistakes and such local usages as "motor park" which critics label Nigerian English. He then warns that "to collect solecisms made by candidates for a concessional entrance examination into what is more appropriately a sixth-form class, and to use such mistakes as appropriate examples of 'Nigerian English,' is indeed, looking in the wrong place for the right thing."[52] The African writers themselves show that various kinds of English exist in Africa, by the way their different characters speak. But a standard African English has not been established. And as far as Nigeria is concerned, Mr. Salami concludes: "It is, in my opinion, improper to assert that a 'legitimate' Nigerian English already exists. It is also necessary to make first of all a proper linguistic analysis of the different types of English spoken in

Nigeria and to distinguish clearly between 'simple mistakes' and
'legitimate' Nigerian usage."[53]

Since there is yet no definition or examples of standard
Nigerian English in books, I had to ask some Nigerian students
and professors for some examples, but they all ended up citing
a few expressions from Achebe's books! And the funny thing is
that neither Achebe nor these professors use such expressions as
"three moons ago" in their own circle. Yet they are Nigerians!
Finally I had to ask John Ferguson, an Englishman who taught
classics in the University of Ibadan, Nigeria, for ten years, to
give me examples of Nigerian or African English and to explain
what he meant by saying that Nigerian writers "write as Africans." Ferguson did not give me any examples of Nigerian or
African English. And to explain what he meant in his article
he said:

> I was not there referring to style but to content and attitude.
> I mean that they see the world as Africans. Of course there are
> elements of indigenous language patterns which have been used
> in writing, for example, the use of proverbs, which easily de-
> generates into cliché. There has been some use of pidgin. But in
> general I agree with you. There is nothing in *Things Fall Apart*,
> or for that matter *Jagua Nana* which couldn't stylistically have
> been written by an Englishman except that I think Achebe has
> a better style than most contemporary English novelists.[54]

Until Ferguson's clarification, what I understood from the
critics is that African writers are incapable of writing "official"
British English. But from what Ferguson said it is most likely
that other critics are also referring to content and attitude rather
than to style. Achebe himself has even indicated that what is
now considered his particular African English is the result of
"playing around with words" made possible by his mastery of
English. In his article "The Role of the Writer in a New
Nation" Achebe states:

> I submit that those who can do the work of extending the
> frontiers of English so as to accommodate African thought-pat-
> terns must do it through their mastery of English and not out
> of innocence.[55]

Perhaps the fact that the texture of Achebe's English "is most richly African" makes critics think that "African writers can only write as Africans." A critic can hardly make such a statement about Wole Soyinka after reading *The Interpreters*. It will equally be unwise to say that Okara's *The Voice* or Tutuola's *The Palm Wine Drinkard*, are typical examples of African English. The most important observation which one makes from reading the various works is that the African writer is capable of saying what he wants to say "within the limits of conventional English," but "when he finds himself describing situations and modes of thought which have no direct equivalent in English, he is equally capable of 'pushing back those limits to accommodate his idea.' "[56]

One has to point out that it is the flexibility of the English language that makes it possible for the African writer to "push back the limits of conventional English to accommodate his idea." Equally important is the encouragement and often favorable criticisms they receive from English critics and publishers. The French-African writers are denied these two important factors, hence their complaint against the exigency of French and the resultant classic French in most Francophone writing.

Gabriel Okara

The extent to which English could be bent to suit each author's need is shown in the way in which Okara uses English in *The Voice*. In an article "African Speech . . . English Words," Okara mentions one school of thought which said, "Once an African, always an African, it will show in whatever you write."[57] This implies that an African writer does not need to exert a conscious effort to make his writing sound "African" through the use of certain words or the pattern of his sentence construction. Okara made this statement in an effort to explain and justify the bizarre linguistic experiment he carried out in *The Voice*.

In the same article he makes a statement that seems to contradict his first idea:

In order to capture the vivid images of African speech, I had to eschew the habit of expressing my thoughts first in English. It was difficult at first, but I had to learn.[58]

If Okara claims that "an African writer" does not have to exert a conscious effort to make his writing "African," how does he explain the fact that he himself found it difficult in his "fascinating exercise" of studying Ijaw expressions and discovering "the probable situation in which it was used in order to bring out the nearest meaning in English"? Okara may have found the "exercise fascinating," but the result, as far as the African English novel is concerned is not that fascinating, if anything, it appears absurd.

It is unfortunate that the readiness of English to accommodate different kinds of local usage can easily be misused if not abused. Okara in *The Voice* appears to have taken undue liberty with English and his unusual use of language led him several times to commit what Arthur Ravenscroft called "linguistic perversity."[59] Among these "perversities" Ravenscroft stresses his use of "a too medically-technical term" in sentences. For instance, "since Okolo came nothing but troubles and difficulties which [Izongo] had to place his eyes on his occiput to overcome . . ." (p. 126); "We did it with our eyes on our occiput" (p. 72). Unlike Achebe who achieved his African texture within the framework of English, Okara violates the normal English sentence pattern and even the syntax deliberately in order to achieve an exotic effect which his foreign audienec likes. Here are some examples from *The Voice*:

This man a big man be. . . . (p. 79)

You are an intelligent man be. . . . (p. 79)

This time girls are not like us be. . . . (p. 102)

We are from the same womb be and we are of the same father be. . . . (p. 103)

I tell you, yourself hold before this thing a big thing turns. . . . (p. 125)

There is a frequent use of physical terms to describe the mental state and inner feelings of his characters:

> Okolo had no chest [He is a Coward]. (p. 23)
>
> Doesn't shame fall on your head, you man without a chest? (p. 36)
>
> . . . her inside smelling with anger (p. 36)
>
> His breath reached the floor (p. 53)
>
> Your head is not correct [You are insane]. (p. 38)
>
> Okolo entered the laughter and laughed. (p. 64)
>
> His inside was a room with chairs, cushions, papers scattered all over the floor by thieves [His mind was in confusion]. (p. 76)

Another exasperating technique of Okara is his repetition which is carried over from Ijaw. Okolo who has a clean "inside" is looking for "it," and the words "inside" and "it" are repeated to the point of absurdity. Here are passages showing their repetition:

> Why should Okolo look for it . . . ?
>
> No one in the past has asked for it
>
> Why should Okolo expect to find it . . . ?
>
> They sent messengers to Okolo to ask him to cease forthwith his search for it. (p. 24)
>
> If the masses haven't got it. . . .
>
> He will create it in their insides.
>
> He will plant it make it grow in spite of Izongo's destroying words.
>
> He will uproot the fear in their insides, kill the fear in their insides and plant it. . . . (p. 90)
>
> Izongo spoke with his inside and agreed with his inside to celebrate his freedom from Okolo. So he agreed with his inside; but he also with his inside became free of the voice of Okolo. . . . So Chief Izongo sent his messengers to the elders who willingly or unwillingly had their insides put in his inside. (p. 91)

Okara's repetition is not limited to "it" and "inside." It is even more sustained in his strange parallel, similes, adverbs and adjectives. Here are some of his unusual comparisons:

It rained more than rain. (p. 62)

The eye of the day is cleaner than cleanliness. (p. 71)

Soft as water, softer than softness. . . . (p. 72)

Silence, she was, itself. No she was silent more than silence. (p. 59)

A whole page is filled with the repetition and reduplication of "black" and "darkness":

"We are taking you to a place where you can find it." At this, two chunks of darkness detached themselves from the darkness and gripped Okolo's hands and pushed him through the black black night like the back of a cooking pot.

Through the black black night Okolo walked, stumbled, walked. . . . His eyes shut and opened, shut and opened, expecting to see a light in each opening, but none he saw in the black black night.

At last the black black night like the back of a cooking pot entered his inside and grabbing his thoughts, threw them out into the blacker than black night. And Okolo walked, stumbled, walked with an inside empty of thoughts except the black black night. (p. 76)

Boring and stale as these examples are, Ravenscroft praises them lavishly, saying: "The effects are produced in much the same way as the sharp, dramatic, but simple effects of the 'primitive' English medieval ballads."[60] It is also passages like the ones cited that led Lindfors to say:

The Voice is the most successful novel to come out of Nigeria so far. . . . As interesting as the story itself is the language in which it is told. He takes liberties with English syntax, reduplicates nouns, adjectives and adverbs and uses concrete metaphysical language to express abstract concepts. In Okara's hands, this experiment does not fail. Rather, he manages to achieve

with it new lyrical effects which turn passages of prose into
poetry.[61]

There are other critics who see *The Voice* the way Lindfors
sees it. John Ferguson says that "the strength of the book lies
in its poetry, which persuades us that we are meeting real people
in real situations."[62] M. Macmillan calls *The Voice*: "An interesting and imaginative piece of writing. . . . It has the simplicity
of parable and the poignancy of an epitaph."[63]

These lavish praises illustrate the readiness of English critics
and publishers to accept and encourage innovations in the English
language by foreign users of the language. Judging from the
harsh criticism on Nazi Boni's *Crépuscule des Temps Anciens*
and the rejection of Kourouma's *Les Soleils des Indépendances*
by French publishers, it is most unlikely that *The Voice* could
have been published if Okara were a French-African writer.

Africans tend to agree with Kolawole Ogungbsam who called
the book "an interesting freak" and concluded by saying that
"*The Voice* is not a successful novel, mainly because of its innovation of language."[64] Many Nigerian readers share the same
opinion as Ogungbsam; to them, *The Voice* is absurd and annoying in its strange language. Yet it is this strangeness of its language
which the bourgeois English readers admire. To them it is exotic
and this is exactly the effect that the author wants to produce
on his European audience.

On the whole, the language and style of *The Voice* show
once again how the African writer is often influenced by the
literary taste of his external audience.

Amos Tutuola

"Nowhere has the dependence on foreign readership influenced African writing more than its language."[65] Amos Tutuola
proved this by writing *The Palm Wine Drinkard* in English,
because there is no reason why he couldn't have written a much
better story in Yoruba. But Tutuola's intention was not to write
for a Yoruba audience. In a letter, he explained his reason for
writing in English:

I wrote *The Palm Wine Drinkard* for the people of the other countries to read the Yoruba folklores. . . . My purpose of writing is to make the other people to understand about Yoruba people and, in fact, they have already understood us more than ever before.[66]

Some Nigerian critics like Olawole Olumide attributed Tutuola's writing in English to "dare devilry," an "unflagging belief in himself."[67] Olumide also inferred that Tutuola must have been aware that he couldn't equal Fagunwa if he wrote in Yoruba. Babasola Johnson said, "The book ought to have been written in West African patois proper or in Yoruba, but then Tutuola's literary tactic would have been exposed."[68]

One sees from Tutuola's letter that these other critics are merely guessing at his decision to write in English. There is no need to doubt Tutuola's reason. He wanted to write for an English-speaking external audience, so he had to write in the language of that audience. Having made his decision, he did not let the exigencies of the English language deter him. He would write it as he understands and speaks it. Thus, Tutuola tore into English, breaking all the conceivable rules of grammar, syntax, punctuation, etc. John Ferguson says that Tutuola's "grammar, syntax, and use of words are eccentric."[69] Here are some excerpts from *The Palm Wine Drinkard* showing part of Tutuola's manipulation of English:

I lied down on the middle of the roads, I put my head to one of the roads, my left hand to one, right hand to another one, and my both feet to the rest, after that I pretended as I had slept there. But when all the market goers were returning from the market, they saw me lied down there and shouted thus: "who was the mother of this fine boy, he slept on the roads and put his head toward Death's road." (pp. 11-12)

I could not blame the lady for following the Skull as complete gentleman to his house at all. Besides if I were a lady, no doubt I would follow him to wherever he would go, and still as I was a man I would jealous him more than that because if this gentleman went to the battlefield, surely, enemy would not kill him or capture him and if bombers saw him in a town which was to be bombed, they would not throw bombs on his presence, and if

they did throw it the bomb itself would not explode until this
gentleman would leave that town, because of his beauty. . . .
(p. 25)

As we were travelling about in the bush my wife was feeling overloading of this baby and if we put him on a scale by that time,
he would weigh at least 28 pounds; when I saw that my wife
had tired of carrying him and she could not carry him any
longer, then I took over to carry him along, but before I could
carry him to a distance of about one quarter of a mile. I was
unable to move again and I was sweating as if I bath in water for
overloading, yet this half-bodied baby did not allow us to put
him down and rest. . . . (p. 37)

He told us that both white and black deads were living in the
Dead's town, not a single alive was there at all. Because everything that they were doing was incorrect to alives and everything
that all alives were doing was incorrect to Deads too. . . . (p. 100)

This then is Tutuola's "particular" English which provoked
"educated" Nigerians to anger and was "applauded with all
gusto"[70] by foreign critics.

To the Nigerians *The Palm Wine Drinkard* should not have
been published at all because it is "a long tale written in a
language we did not understand. It is bad enough to attempt an
African narrative in 'good English' but worse to attempt it in
Tutuola's strange lingo."[71] In short, Tutuola has revealed to
the outside world that Nigerians could not write "good English."
His book was therefore regarded as a letdown if not a calamity
to the national image abroad. Kolawole Ogungbsan has even
surmised that "the first crop of Nigerian writers were consciously
reacting against the Tutuola phenomenon by writing in standard
English. Ekwensi and Achebe are examples."[72]

The same *The Palm Wine Drinkard* is described by Dylan
Thomas as a "thronged, grisly and bewitching story, written in
young English by a West African. . . ."[73] Echoing Dylan Thomas's
"young English" idea, is Lee Rogow who called the book a
"fantastic primitive . . . written in English . . . but an English
with inflections and phrasings which make it seem like a newborn
language."[74]

It is hard to determine what these critics mean by "young

English" and "newborn language," yet one must admit that Tutuola's English is an *un je ne sais quoi de langage*, very amusing and entertaining to the foreign reader, but very irritating and embarrassing to many Nigerian readers who feel that Tutuola is showing the outside world that Nigerians cannot write "good" English. An enthusiastic critic sees Tutuola's book as "an emergence of a new, mad African writing, written by those who don't learn English, they don't study the rules or grammar, they just tear right into it and let the splinters fly."[75]

Unlike the university-educated Nigerian writers such as Okara, Tutuola's violation of normal English is quite unintentional because he writes the only English he knows. He does not see anything unusual in carrying modernity into mythology as long as it makes his story interesting. As a result, in *The Palm Wine Drinkard* we find numerous descriptive passages with vocabulary taken from modern technology. Here are some examples:

> At the same time that the red fish appeared out, its head was just like a tortoise's head, but it was as big as an elephant's head and it had over thirty horns and large eyes which surrounded the head. All these horns were spread out as an umbrella. It could not walk but only gliding on the ground like a snake and its body was just like a bat's body and covered with long red hair like strings. . . . All the eyes which surrounded its head were closing and opening at the same time as if a man was pressing a switch on and off . . . (pp. 79-80)

> There appeared a half-bodied baby, he was talking with a lower voice like a telephone. . . . (p. 35)

> He took the food and swallowed it as a man swallows a pill. . . . (p. 36)

> As their king was talking, a hot steam was rushing out of his mouth as a big boiler. . . . (p. 46)

> He looked at us with his eyes which brought out a floodlight like mercury in colour. . . . (p. 54)

> All the lights in this hall were in technicolour and they were changing colours at five minutes intervals. . . . (pp. 68-69)

In Tutuola's mythical world, time is kept by the clock, space was measured in inches, feet, yards, and miles. Weights are in pounds and currency was the British sterling! Thus, "We left by two o'clock in the midnight" (p. 39); "The wonderful baby grew to a height of about three feet and some inches within the hour" (p. 31), and weighed "at least twenty-eight pounds" (p. 37). Death was sold "for the sum of £70:18:6 and fear was rented "on the interest of £3:10:0 per month" (p. 67).

One thing that links Tutuola to some African writers is that the influence of the mother tongue is easily perceived in his style. The difference is that Tutuola's carry-over from the mother tongue is not forced. The way he writes is the way he speaks, and this is the only way he knows; otherwise, he would not have written the way he did. On the other hand, the English that Achebe makes his African characters speak is not the type of English that he himself speaks in normal circumstances. Thus Achebe's carry-over from the mother tongue is forced and cultivated.

Among the noticeable influences of the mother tongue in Tutuola is the expression "more than to," which takes the place of "except." We find that at the very beginning of the narrative:

> I was a palm wine drinkard since I was a boy of ten years of age. I had no other work more than to drink palm wine in my life. . . . I was drinking palm wine from morning till night and from night till morning. By that time I could not drink ordinary water at all except palm wine. But when my father noticed that I could not do any work more than to drink, he engaged an expert palm-wine tapster for me; he had no other work more than to tap palm wine every day. (p. 7)

There is also a significant influence of the traditional oral narrative; that is the tying up of the tales in a set pattern of, "so. . . ."

> So, I saved the lady from the complete gentleman in the market who afterwards reduced to a "Skull" and the lady became my wife since that day. This was how I got my wife. . . . (p. 31)

> So that since that day that I had brought Death out from his house, he has no permanent place to dwell or stay, and we are hearing his name about in the world. (p. 16)

So when these three fellows (Drum, Song and Dance) disappeared the people of the new town went back to their houses. Since that day nobody could see the three fellows personally, but we are hearing their names about in the world and nobody could do in these days what they did. (p. 85)

It is interesting to note that Achebe uses similar end units in the substories in *Things Fall Apart*, for example:

And that was how he came to look after the doomed lad who was sacrificed to the village of Umuofia. . . . The ill-fated lad was called Ikemefuna. (p. 12)

And so for three years Ikemefuna lived in Okonkwo's household. . . . (p. 16)

It is this traditional aspect of Tutuola's style that makes *The Palm Wine Drinkard* more of a recorded, traditional, oral folklore than a novel. It is much closer to Birago Diop's *Les Contes d'Amadou Koumba*, and other collected oral tales, than to any other literary pieces in West Africa. But while Birago Diop wrote in very good French, and also suppresses the traditional introductions and endings of the tales, to suit the taste of his French audience, Tutuola wrote in what Povey called a "broken idiom," and thus he received more attention on his language than on the depth and quality of his work. Charles R. Larson, has commented that apart from praises showered on Tutuola's language, many critics say very little about his writing abilities as a novelist.[76] But one couldn't really say very much about an oral tale except that it is "well told or poorly told." Tutuola is admired by Europeans for his ability to tell a lively and bewitching story in a kind of English which Nigerians "do not understand," and which the British audience understands! To the Nigerian critics who said that anyone could write these "compilations of folklore," John Ferguson said:

The fact remains that no one else has done so as vividly and compellingly. The great virtue of the story is its economy: it is told directly and vigorously. . . . Tutuola is entranced by language even when he abuses it. . . .[77]

In the same vein, Mable Jolaoso said, "The very imperfections of Tutuola's English have made him the perfect African storyteller."[78]

The popularity of Tutuola's works with foreign readers emphasizes the advantage that the African writer gains by writing in English. Judging from the reaction of Nigerian and European readers, it has been shown that it is the latter that has encouraged Tutuola, that if Tutuola had intended his book solely for the Nigerian audience, it is most unlikely that he could have published any other works after *The Palm Wine Drinkard*. One could therefore say that Tutuola's success came from the initial approval he received from his external audience.

From the preceding survey of some of the outstanding works in African literature, we see that both the French and English African writers are controlled in one way or the other by the foreign languages which they use and, by extension, their foreign audience.

Several Francophone writers like Senghor, Kane, and Camara write classical French, but they complain that the exigencies of French make it very difficult for the African writer to adequately express his "Africanity." Some of them like Nazi Boni, Sembène, and Kourouma, who have tried to introduce some form of "Africanized" or popular French into their writing, have either been condemned outright or called "poor" writers. In this way the Francophone writer is very conscious of the watchful eyes of his French critics and publishers who select what the French audience reads. The writer is thus compelled to respect the demands of the foreign audience whose language he is using. This is then the way in which his writing is inevitably controlled by his external audience.

In the English sector, the writers' experiment and innovations within the English language have received wide approval and encouragement by the English critics, publishers, and readers. This gives the African writer a greater scope in his literary creativity. However, in spite of this favorable reaction from the British audience, the African-English writer is more or less in the same position as his Francophone counterpart, because both of them depend on the approval of their European audience.

One therefore sees that as long as the African writers write in European languages and also depend on foreign publishers, their writing will very much be controlled by the sensitivity and literary tastes of their foreign audience.

NOTES

1. Christina Aidoo, Introduction to Armah's *The Beautiful Ones Are Not Yet Born*, p. vii.
2. Obi Wali, "Dead End of African Literature", *Transition*, IV, (September, 1963), p. 14.
3. Robert G. Armstrong, "Language Policies and Language Practice in West Africa," *Language Problems of Developing Nations*, ed. J. A. Fishman *et al*, (New York, 1968), p. 232.
4. L. S. Senghor, *Liberté I: Négritude et Humanisme*, (Paris: Seuil, 1964), p. 399.
5. *Ibid.*, p. 231.
6. *Ibid.*, p. 359.
7. Obi Wali, "Dead End of African Literature," *Transition*, IV (September, 1963), p. 14.
8. L. S. Senghor, Postface to "Ethiopiques," *Poèmes* (Paris: Seuil, 1964), pp. 166-167.
9. Herbert Passin, "Writer and Journalist in the Transitional Society," *Language Problems of Developing Nations*, ed. J. A. Fishman, *et al.* (New York, 1968), p. 446.
10. L. S. Senghor, *Liberté I: Négritude et Humanisme*, p. 360.
11. *Ibid.*, p. 228.
12. *Ibid.*
13. Janheinz Jahn, *Muntu: The New African Culture* Trans. Majorie Greene (New York, 1961), p. 195.
14. E. C. Okwu, "A Language of Expression for Nigerian Literature," *Nigeria Magazine*, no. 91 (December, 1960), p. 314.
15. Renato Berger, "A Review of Négritude et Humanisme," *Nigeria Magazine*, no. 95, (September, 1963), p. 14.

16. Interview with Senghor by the author, Dakar, December, 1972.
17. *Ibid.*
18. Ivor Case Frederick, "The Cultural Predicament of L. S. Senghor," *Literary Studies*, vol. 1, no. 4. (Fall, 1970), p. 22.
19. Information by Professor El Nouty, based on his conversation with a Senegalese woman.
20. L. S. Senghor, Postface to "Etiopiques," *Poèmes*, p. 159.
21. Interview with Senghor by author.
22. *Ibid.*
23. *See* note 18.
24. Interview with Senghor by author.
25. Cyprian Ekwensi, "African Literature," *Nigerian Magazine*, no. 83, (December, 1964), p. 296.
26. Interview with Cheik Hamidon Kane by author, Abidjan, December, 1972.
27. L. S. Senghor, *Liberté I: Négritude et Humanisme*, p. 174.
28. Martin Banttam, "Nigerian Dramatists in English and the Traditional Nigerian Theatre," *Journal of Commonwealth Literature*, no. 3, 1967, p. 102.
29. Robert Pageard, *Littérature Negro-Africaine* (Paris, 1966), p. 74.
30. Lilyan Kesteloot, *Authologie Negro Africaine* (Verviers, Belgique, 1967), p. 193.
31. L. S. Senghor, *Liberté I: Négritude et Humanisme*, p. 173.
32. Interview with Laye Camara by author, I.F.A.N., Dakar, December, 1972.
33. Interview with Ousmane Sembène by author, Dakar, December, 1972.
34. *Ibid.*
35. Robert Pageard, *Litterature Negro-Africaine* (Paris, 1966), p. 74.
36. L. S. Senghor, "D'Amadou Koumba a Birago Diop," *Negritude et Humanisme*, p. 243.
37. Robert Pageard, *Litterature Negro-Africaine* (Paris, 1966), p. 74.

38. *Ibid.*
39. Ahmadou Kourouma, *Les Soleils des Independances*, cover blurb.
40. L. S. Senghor, *Negritude et Humanisme*, p. 19.
41. Norman Jeffares, "The Author in the Commonwealth," *Nigeria Magazine*, no. 95, (December, 1967), pp. 351-53.
42. Interview with Ezekiel Mphahlele by author, Philadelphia, September, 1974.
43. Interview with Ngugi Wa Thiong'O by author, Nairobi, December, 1974.
44. Interview with Chinua Achebe by author, Amherst, September, 1974.
45. Donald Stuart, "The Modern Writer in His Context," *Journal of Commonwealth Literature*, no. 4 (1967), p. 128.
46. Chinua Achebe, "A Language of Expression for Nigerian Literature," *Nigeria Magazine*, no. 91, (December, 1968), p. 314.
47. Ronald Christ, "Among the Ibo," *New York Times Book Review*, (December 12, 1967), p. 22.
48. Bernth Lindfors, "Five Nigerian Novels," *Book Abroad*, vol. 39 (1965), p. 412.
49. John Povey, "Contemporary West African Writing in English," *Books Abroad*, no. 40 (Summer, 1966), p. 253.
50. John Ferguson, "Nigerian Poetry in English," *Insight* (July-September, 1966), p. 231.
51. Adebisi Salami, "Defining a Standard English for Nigeria," *Nigerian English Studies Association* (November, 1967), p. 99.
52. *Ibid.*, p. 100-101.
53. *Ibid.*, p. 105.
54. John Ferguson, letter to author, March 30, 1973.
55. Chinua Achebe, "The Role of the Writer in a New Nation," *Nigeria Magazine*, no. 81, (June, 1964), p. 160.
56. *Ibid.*
57. Gabriel Okara, "African Speech . . . English," *Transition*, III, 10, (September, 1963), p. 15.

58. *Ibid.*
59. Arthur Ravenscroft, Introduction to Okara's *The Voice* (New York: Africana Publishing Corporation, 1970), p. 19.
60. *Ibid.*, p. 18.
61. Bernth Lindfors, "Five Nigerian Novels," *Books Abroad*, vol. 39, p. 411.
62. John Ferguson, "Nigerian Prose Literature," *English Studies in Africa* (9:1:1966), p. 58.
63. M. Macmillan, "Language and Change," *Journal of Commonwealth Literature*, no. 1. (1965), p. 174.
64. Kolawole Ogungbsan, "Literature and Society in West Africa," *African Quarterly*, vol. XI, no. 3, (December, 1971), p. 220.
65. *Ibid.*
66. Amos Tutuola, in a letter to Bernth Lindfors, May 16, 1968.
67. Olawole Olumide, "Amos Tutuola's Reviewers and Educated Africans," *New Nigeria Forum*, I (October, 1958), pp. 5-16.
68. Babasola Johnson, "The Books of Amos Tutuola," *West Africa*, (April 10, 1954), p. 322.
69. See note 59.
70. See note 61.
71. See note 65.
72. See note 61.
73. Dylan Thomas, "Blight Spirits," *London Observer*, (July 6, 1952), p. 7.
74. Lee Rogow, "African Primitive," *Saturday Review*, XXXVI (October 17, 1953), p. 30.
75. Tom Hopkinson, "Review of African Treasury", ed. Langston Hughes, *London Observer*, (September 17, 1961), p. 28.
76. Charles Larson, *The Emergence of African Fiction* (Bloomington: University of Indiana Press, 1971), p. 10.
77. John Ferguson, "Nigerian Prose Literature in English," *English Studies in Africa* (January 9, 1966), p. 46.
78. Mabel Jolaso, "Review of Tutuola's Books," *Odu*, no. 1 (January, 1965), p. 43.

4

SUBJECT MATTER

Up to the moment, the subject matter of African literature is Africa. Every African novel draws upon the culture and upon the experience of Africa since her contact with the Western world. Naturally the more a writer draws upon his society, the more he is supposed to be addressing his own people. But in African literature, this is only partially true because the aspect of Africa which the writers choose and the way they present these aspects show that they often have some non-African audience in mind.

In my interview with Cheik Hamidou Kane, I asked him why African writers tended to dwell on Africa and particularly her past. Mr. Kane explained it by the colonial factor:

> It is because we have been subjected and colonized. Africa has been presented to the world as devoid of culture and history, as being inhabited by intellectually inferior beings; therefore, the first problem for the African writer is to explain and translate Africa to the Western world and to the entire cultural world.[1]

Mr. Kane made it clear that the African writer is "engaged" in the recovery of Africa's cultural identity as well as her lost dignity. Chinua Achebe, "the foremost African novelist writing in English today,"[2] expresses the same opinion as Kane. In his article "The Role of the Writer in a New Nation," Achebe also made it clear that it is the duty of the writer to explain to the world that

African people did not hear of culture for the first time from Europeans. Their societies were not mindless, they had a philosophy of great depth and value and beauty, they had poetry and above all, they had dignity.[3]

This idea of presenting Africa to the external audience is shared by many African writers, and they justify it by the colonial factor. If we look into American literature for instance, we do not get any impression that the writers are writing for a double audience made up of Americans and non-Americans (Europeans). Yet America was once colonized by European powers. When a writer like Hawthorne presents the Puritan society of New England, he does not do it with the intention to show a non-American reader what that society was like in the olden days. But when an Achebe presents the traditional Ibo village, he dwells on, and explains most aspects of the custom which should be taken for granted with a local audience. Achebe could argue very rightly that even with a Nigerian audience he still has to explain some aspects of Ibo culture since these could be different from the Yoruba or Hausa or some other tribe's customs. But what of when he explains practices that are common to all these tribes and in fact to all Africa? For example, why should he explain *kola* and *bride price* to an African audience? He must therefore have some non-African audience in mind when he explains certain things that an African reader is supposed to know.

In Sadji's *Maimouna*, one finds sentences like the following:

La musique se transmet et se conserve merveilleusement chez le nègre. La petite fille noire n'apprend pas les airs qu'elle chantera plus tard. Elle en porte la gamme en naissant . . . il faut qu'elle chante la gloire des ancêtres. (p. 18)

Sadji has no need to explain these things to any African reader, but the fact that he does explain them shows that he must be thinking of a non-African reader who would not understand everything without some help from the author.

This general tendency to explain what should be taken for granted by a local audience and the attachment of a glossary are among the outstanding facts that give away the African writer who claims to be writing solely for an African audience. As it will be shown in the analysis of chosen works, we find in African literature that the presentation of a subject matter is determined by the extent to which the novel is to be read by a particular audience.

In addition to presenting Africa to the external world, Achebe also maintains that the African people have to be reeducated on those aspects of their culture that they have been forced by historical circumstances to neglect or despise. In his article "The Novelist as a Teacher," Achebe points out the obligations of a writer to his people:

> The writer cannot expect to be excused from the task of reeducating and regeneration that must be done. In fact he should march right in front. . . . Art is important but so is the education of the kind I have in mind. And I don't see that the two need be mutually exclusive.[4]

Achebe may be right in talking of reeducating the people on their culture. But the truth is that the majority of African people do not need this kind of cultural reeducation because they were not culturally colonized in the first place. Speaking of this cultural decolonization Janheinz Jahn says:

> The problems for the African masses are not those of decolonization, because, let's face it, they have never been colonized. Their spirit has not been colonized, never even been touched! . . . Decolonization is necessary for those Africans educated overseas and by missionaries. Those who have not been educated in this sense, and who have remained faithful to their traditions, need no decolonization, simply because, in keeping with their own values system, they have consistently considered all European ways of doing things wrong.[5]

It is only the culturally alienated elite who need this kind of education and incidentally they have the same literary taste as their European bourgeois counterpart. Both of them want to see Africa other than what she is. The European bourgeois wants to read of Africa, the land of strange people with bizarre customs; and the African elite wants to read of Africa with a glorious past and with rich culture quite different from other cultures in the world.

The quotations from Kane and Achebe together refer to one important aspect of African literature—the double audience, comprising the European bourgeois and the Western-educated African elite. Here we find the African writer faced with the problem of satisfying an audience partially African and partially European. This problem of double audience is quite unique in literature. We shall find therefore that the African writer's effort to satisfy the literary tastes of his two audiences will very much influence his choice of subject matter and the way he handles it.

A cross section of African novels shows three major areas from which the writers choose their subject matter:

   I. Traditional Africa and her cultural institutions
  II. The colonial experience
 III. Independent Africa

TRADITIONAL AFRICA AND HER CULTURAL INSTITUTIONS

The foremost concern of the novels in this division is to present some aspects of African culture that are unfamiliar to the non-African readers and to correct the distorted images that these readers may already have about Africa. These novels, according to Achebe and Nazi Boni, are also meant to reeducate the African elite who has been alienated from his culture as a result of his Western education.

Several novels are situated in traditional African societies, but selection of those to be studied will be based on works in which the author's handling of his subject matter helps to indicate which of his two audiences is controlling his writing.

A brief study will be made of each of the following novels:
L'Enfant Noir and *Le Regard du Roi* by Laye Camara.
L'Aventure Ambiguë by Cheik Hamidou Kane.

Things Fall Apart by Chinua Achebe.
Wand of Noble Wood by Onuora Nzekwu.
Le Devoir de Violence by Yambo Ouologuem.

Laye Camara: L'Enfant Noir

Camara has been severely criticized by his fellow Africans for the way he presented Africa in his first autobiographical novel, *L'Enfant Noir*. He is particularly accused of closing his eyes to the problems of Africa and romanticizing on a glorious past. A writer in *Presence Africaine* says of Camara:

> Laye resolutely shuts his eyes to the most crucial realities, those which we have always been careful to reveal to the public here. Has this Guinean, of my own race, who it seems was a very lively boy, really seen nothing but a beautiful, peaceful and maternal Africa? Is it possible that not once has Laye witnessed a single minor extortion by the colonial authorities?[6]

This critic is angry that Laye did not deal with the colonial problem "which we have been very careful to reveal to the public here," meaning the European public. In other words, Laye is not an "engaged" African writer who is expected to present the case of the colonized and suffering Africa before the European audience.

One could compare this critic's reaction to that expressed by Miss Aidoo in her introduction to Armah's *The Beautyful Ones Are Not Yet Born*. Laye's critic is angry that Laye has betrayed Africa by shutting his eyes to the pressing problem of colonialism. Miss Aidoo is angry that Armah has betrayed Africa by "washing her linen in public," for she complains,

> Certainly, writers like Armah and Ferdinand Oyono of *House-boy* deny a fellow African the opportunity to feel good, or the foreigner to smirk at the fact that they have managed to get into print at all. For both Oyono and Armah have betrayed themselves in *Houseboy* and *The Beautyful Ones Are Not Yet Born* to be in possession of that kind of creative genius—nearly always committed—which operates on the belief that if the

only way to get one's linen clean is to wash it in public, then one does exactly that, whether or not one's detractors are look-ing on and exchanging knowing glances.[7]

These two critics clearly demonstrate the kind of pressure put on the African author. Certainly he draws from Africa, but he must choose his subject matter carefully and present it in a way to make the African audience "feel good." Both critics pre-sume that the author has an external audience in addition to his local audience, and as such he should be careful in the light in which he presents any particular aspect of Africa to the external reader.

In the interview with Camara, I asked him how he felt about the reaction of several African intellectuals to his first novel. In his reply, he stated what his intentions in the novel were:

> When *L'Enfant Noir* was published, many African intellectuals did not agree with me on the subject matter. Many wanted me to talk of colonialism or colonization. I thought personally that the best way to attack colonialism was to talk of African civiliza-tion. My interest at that time was not colonialism which was staring me in the face, it was the African civilization which I wanted to present to the world since her existence is contested. Besides, colonization is ephermeral and if I had attacked a situation which no longer exists today, the work would have lost its value.[8]

In the above passage, Camara made it very clear that his purpose in writing *L'Enfant Noir*, was to present the African civilization to the world that has been doubting its existence. This "world" is that of his European bourgeois audience.

In his novel, Camara presents the peaceful and happy child-hood of the boy Laye. He traces the hero's life from about the age of six when he attended the Koranic school, to the time he passed out from the colonial technical college to finish his studies in France. The author lays special emphasis on love, respect, and concern for one another in the village community. He dwells on the communal nature of African societies in a way to show his European reader that African societies are very different from the individualistic societies of Europe. To an African reader, such details are not exciting because he knows all about them, but to the European reader, they are something new and exciting therefore the author dwells on them to please him.

Special emphasis is also laid on the family structure and the complimentary roles of husband and wife in the family. Again the author sees the need to present this aspect of African culture to the European reader who thinks of the African woman as a minor appendage to her husband. That Camara is specifically addressing a non-African audience is made clear in the following passage:

> I realize that my mother's authoritarian attitudes may appear surprising; generally the role of the African woman is thought to be a ridiculously humble one, and indeed there are parts of the continent where it is insignificant. . . . The woman's role in our country is one of fundamental independence, of greater inner pride. We despise only those who allow themselves to be despised, and our women very seldom give cause for that. (p. 69)

In the above passage the author is defending the position of the African woman before an audience that has either misunderstood that position or has been ignorant of it. Camara does not need to prove this to an African audience. Furthermore, the use of "our" and "we" shows that the author is distinguishing himself and his society from the foreign reader.

The greater portion of *L'Enfant Noir* deals with the mystery and magic world of Africa. In the opening paragraph of the novel we find the little Laye playing with a little black snake. The entire chapter is then devoted to the explanation of the role and the significance of the little black snake to Laye's race. Thus his father tells him:

> That snake is the guiding spirit of our race. . . . That snake has always been with us; he has always made himself known to one of us. In our time, it is to me that he has made himself known . . . My name is on everyone's tongue, and it is I who have authority over all the blacksmiths in the five cantons. If these

things are so, it is by virtue of this snake alone, who is the
guiding spirit of our race. It is to this snake that I owe everything, it is he who gives me warning of all that is to happen.
(p. 26)

Having enumerated all the things he could do with his power
from the snake and how he conducted himself in order to acquire
that power, Laye's father advised him to conduct himself in the
self-same manner, if he desired the little snake to appear to him
one day and confer the special powers of their race on him.

The story of the little snake is indeed a very interesting one
but it would not strike an African reader as something unusual
since it is a common practice for each group to have its own
guiding spirit. To the European reader, the story of the little
snake is exotic and part of the mystery world of Africa. The
author is very much aware of the interest of his non-African
audience and as such he devotes more time explaining such
aspects of African culture that help his European reader see
Africa as an exotic land with strange customs.

The whole of chapter five deals with the special powers of
Laye's mother. Several examples are given of the things she
does, such as making an obstinate horse walk, forestalling the
evil machinations of spell casters, foretelling the future, and so
on. Laye explains why his mother possesses these powers:

My mother was the next child born after my twin uncles in Tin-
dican. Now they say that twin brothers are wiser than other
children, and are practically magicians. As for the child that
follows them, and who receives the name sayon, . . . he too is
endowed with the gift of magic, and he is even considered to
be more powerful and more mysterious than the twins in whose
lives he plays a very important role. He is accredited with a
wisdom greater than that of the twins, and is given a superior
position. (p. 71)

The reader finds out from the above passage that Laye's
mother is endowed from birth with magical and occult powers
by virtue of being born after twins. Then the author goes on

to explain the special treatment given to twins: "It is the custom with us for twins to agree about everything. . . ." Again the author distinguishes himself from his audience by the use of "us." If he were writing for a Guinean or even an all-African audience, he would not need the distinction "us." He does not even need to explain the treatment of twins because what he says is basically true of many other African societies. But the explanation is interesting to the European reader in whose country twins are probably treated differently from those in Africa. Moreover, the special powers which the author attributes to the twins corroborate other stories of superstition and magic in Africa—all these things make his story very interesting for his foreign reader.

In the same chapter, we read of other supernatural powers which Laye's mother inherited from birth. Among her powers, most impressive is her capacity to draw water from the crocodile-infested river Niger. She alone is able to do it because

> she had inherited as a matter of course, my grandfather's totem which is the crocodile. This totem allowed all Damans to draw water from the Niger without running any danger of harm. . . . (p. 74)

For the rest of the chapter, the author explains totemism and the identification of a totem with its possessor. Here again the explanation will not be necessary for an African audience since every tribe has its totem or sacred animal, but it is interesting to a foreigner who is reading about it for the first time.

Up to this point, Camara's handling of his subject matter is largely controlled by his European audience. He is careful to talk about things which would be more exciting to the European reader than to the African. With his stories he is gradually making his external audience see Africa as a place quite different from their own environment.

What further proves that Camara had his external audience in mind is the statement he made before he ever started to tell his "unbelievable" stories. He feared that his reader may find his story incredible, thus he says:

I know that what I say will be greeted with skeptical smiles. . . .
They seem to be unbelievable, they are unbelievable. Nevertheless I can only tell you what I saw with my own eyes. . . . In
our country there were mysteries without number, and my mother
was familiar with them all. (pp. 69-70)

We find again the use of "our" to separate the author-nar-
rator from his audience. And one may ask, who is the "you"
in the passage, and why does the author need to emphasize
that he saw these things with his own eyes? One would imagine
that such a statement can only be directed to a reader whom
the author feels would be surprised and skeptical about what
he reads. It is very unlikely that the reader is an African because
he will not be discovering for the first time about totemism, spell
casters, diviners, and other mysteries and beliefs in Africa. The
"you," therefore, can only refer to a foreigner who is reading or
rather discovering about these things for the first time.

Leaving the magic world of Africa, Camara devotes chapters
seven and eight describing the initiation and circumcision rites.
Here he seems determined to unveil the mystery surrounding
the initiation ceremony. He actually explains that the roaring
of the "lions" was produced by waving a wooden instrument
which is like a sling. He tried desperately to figure out how
the white threads were hung on the sixty-feet-high bombax trees,
and there is no doubt that he would have disclosed the secret
if he knew.

If Camara had an African audience in mind, it would have
been sufficient to mention that the boys underwent initiation
and circumcision ceremonies; the rites that go with these ceremonies should be taken for granted by an average African reader
because initiation is one of the commonest customs in Africa.
Yet the author devotes two whole chapters explaining initiation
ceremony to his European reader whom he knows would be
intrigued by his story. One important fact that shows the extra
descriptions are deliberately done to make the story more interesting is that they could be easily detached from the story
without any damage to the main plot.

Several other customs are described, for instance, meal etiquette, celebration of planting and harvest seasons, etc. The manner in which Camara handles these topics shows that his intention, as he said, was "to present the African civilization to the world since her existence is contested."[9] The "world" is his European audience. It is his desire to satisfy the taste of this audience that determined what he included in his novel and the way he presented it.

Laye Camara: *Le Regard du Roi*

In this novel, one could argue that the author is writing for both the African and European audiences. On the one hand, his intention may be to make the African proud of his heritage, to make him realize that Africa has something to offer to Europe. On the other hand, his intention may be to satirize European ideas about Africa and to make the Europeans realize that, unless they learned to accept Africa as she really is, they would never understand her. Both of these assumptions could be right but when one carefully examines the presentation of subject matter in *Le Regard du Roi*, one is inclined to believe that Camara's preferred audience is certainly European.

Camara undertakes a deliberate but ironic presentation of those aspects of African customs which fascinate the European reader—Africa the land of music and dancing, of sensualism, of sorcery, and of all that is exotic and erotic! He portrays all this in a most dramatic way by making the hero, who is a European, actually participate in various African practices without ever understanding what he was doing. The author goes out of his way to portray an impenetrable and mysterious Africa just as his preferred audience wants to see it.

The form of the novel is allegorical. The adolescent African king embodies the impenetrable mysteries of the continent. The author idealizes the young king to a quasi-divine level. He is a Christlike figure with all his redeeming attributes. He is young and he is old, he is frail but he is strong; in short, he is eternal. His emblem is Gold, the symbol of his love for his people, but the hour of his coming is never known to his subjects who wait hopefully for him all their lives. When he comes he bestows his kindness on whom he chooses, irrespective of race, color, or worthiness.

In the context of the book, Camara's majestic African, adolescent king is the symbolic source of every man's desires. Because he stands for Africa, Africa is therefore presented as the hope of the world, and Europe is to humble herself and accept Africa as she is.

Clarence, the hero, represents Europe. He displays all the arrogance, prejudice, and superiority complex of his race. He has been rejected by his own kind and he comes to Africa, the land of opportunity where he hopes to make a new life for himself. Clarence is very sure that the African king will give him employment, just because he is a white man. He is made to understand that the king is no respector of persons and that he must first of all get rid of his prejudices and become one of the people. Clarence has no other choice and soon his education in the African way of life begins. In his ever sleep-walking state, he is taken through several incidents in which he observes African practices that to him appear contrary to common sense.

But Clarence will soon integrate into the system in spite of himself. Thus, in Aziana, the land of erotism, he is soaked in nocturnal debauchery because he is made to pay for his keep by sleeping with a different woman every night. He wonders why his woman, Akissi, changes so much every night! But Clarence will never know the truth, for he goes in to the women half conscious, drugged from the smell of the herbs that produced aphrodisiac effects. Within a short time the Naba's harem is filled with half-caste babies from Clarence. When Clarence sees them he cannot understand how they came to be there.

Most of the time Clarence spends his time daydreaming over his nightly activities. At the bank of the river he dreams of the fish-women thrusting their breasts at him and unable to resist them he slips into the river and gets carried away by them. When he wakes up he is so ashamed of his weakness for women that he decides to spend the rest of his life in the desert.

While Clarence is getting his African education, he waits for the king to come and employ him in his service. When he grows impatient he goes to consult a snake charmer soothsayer. He braves the session, with the snakes crawling all over his body. Finally he is put in a trance during which he witnesses the king's arrival before it ever takes place. By thus making Clarence actually take part in these "bizarre" practices, the author is ironically telling his European reader, "Here is Africa with all the things you imagine about her."

In several passages, the author makes it clear that Africa is the teacher while Europe is the pupil. Among the things that Clarence learns are the African notions of time and art.

Clarence is constantly asking for the exact day and hour of the king's arrival and the people keep telling him that only the king knows the time. Clarence is about to give up, and he believes it is too late for him to make himself worthy to serve the king. At this point he is given a lesson on African notion of time. Diallo the smith explains it to him:

> "Il est toujours trop tard. A peine sommes nous nés, qu'il est déjà trop tard. Mais le roi ne l'ignore pas, et c'est pourquoi aussi il est toujours temps."
> "Est-ce là ce que tu disais hier?"
> "Hier? Est-ce que hier compte encore? Ce jour seul et cette heure seule comptent. . . ." (p. 247)

In this passage the author makes his European reader see the difference in the time concept between Africa and Europe. The African is not obsessed with time. It is only the present that he recognizes and accepts. While the European world functions at the behest of temporality, the African world remains spiritual and therefore eternal.

In a most sarcastic manner the white man is taught the significance of African drumming and music. Clarence has been watching the drummers and the dancers; to him, the drummers are just making a hell of a "noise" while the dancers are only "jumping up and down":

> Leur musique véhémente paraissait être dépourvue de toute
> signification, n'être qu'un tintamarre jeté à la chaleur, jeté au
> ciel. (p. 18)

The beggar then explains this "noise" to him:

> Ces tambours sont des tambours parlants, ils annoncent le roi
> et ils disent que c'est le roi des rois. . . . Ce n'est que chez les
> hommes blancs que la musique est dépourvue de signification.
> (pp. 18-19)

Here the attack on the white man is very direct. It is to
him that music is deprived of meaning, while to the African
it communicates a message. When Clarence suggests later that
he could be a drummer, the beggar bluntly tells him that he is
not qualified for the job, for drumming is a profession for the
noble caste:

> Ce n'est pas là un simple emploi, les timbalaliers sont de caste
> noble, et chez eux, l'emploi est héréditaire, certes vous auriez
> battu du tambour, seulement ce n'est pas ce qui compte: vos
> battements n'auraient eu aucun sens. Là aussi il faut savoir . . .
> vous êtes un homme blanc! (p. 37)

The beggar makes it perfectly clear that the white man is
incapable of producing meaningful music on the African drum.
Camara repeated this idea during the interview with him:

> Starting from the trumpet to the saxophone, to the balafon, if
> you give two groups of Whites and Blacks these instruments to
> make music, the Blacks will give the African rhythm and the
> Whites cannot, even if they tried to copy the Blacks. One will
> always feel the difference. The life within the African rhythm
> can never be interpreted by the white man.[10]

In *Le Regard du Roi*, Camara is really talking about cultural
assimilation, but in his case it is Europe that has to assimilate
from Africa. Speaking of this reversed role, Janheinz Jahn says:

The usual pedagogic relationship of Europe and Africa is here reversed, here the European is the pupil, who must learn justice and pass examination.[11]

Cheik Hamidou Kane: *L'Aventure Ambiguë*

In his answer to my question on audience, Mr. Kane said he had no audience in mind when he wrote *L'Aventure Ambiguë*. He said that he did not even intend to publish the book but he did so at the insistence of friends. When he was later asked to explain the significance of his novel, he put it in the following way:

> Sometimes the white men who have colonized us, particularly the French, think they have to assimilate us. They say to themselves, "These people have no culture, no wisdom, no civilization, therefore we shall give them our culture, our wisdom, our civilization. We shall make them French men with black skin." *L'Aventure Ambiguë* was a warning to the Europeans. It was to tell them that what they are thinking is not possible. It will be wrong for them to try it because it would have catastrophic effects. On the other hand there are some of us who are tempted to say, "What good does it do to be faithful to Africa? African culture does not exist. The only thing we have to do is to become French, British or American. We have to become modernized." To these people, *L'Aventure Ambiguë* is also a warning, it is a kind of mirror for Africans. Samba Diallo's solution is an escapist one, for the problem still remains. But it is possible to retain one's religious beliefs and at the same time become modernized.[12]

In the above quotation, Kane announces his double audience: Europeans and Africans. The novel is therefore structured in form of debate in which the cultural conflict between Europe and Africa is presented and later dramatized by the hero.

In the first half of the novel, the author presents the traditional Islamic society of the Diallobés. Special emphasis is laid on their faith in Islam and in their culture. The Diallobé society is situated in the Middle Ages and the author's purpose is to show the similarity between the Diallobé society and the European society of the same period. The similarity and the equality between the two are dramatized in the personality of the characters. Apart from Demba, who is called a peasant, the rest of the African characters belong to the nobility.

In his description of their physical attributes, the author uses European images that help to make the similarity much clearer to the European reader. Thus, the Chef is likened to "un chevalier du Moyen Age revêtu de sa dalmatique," and he is later referred to simply as Chevalier. Of Samba Diallo, we read of his "origine patricienne, la noblesse de son port, l'élégance racée de son maintien." The heroine is called La Grande Royale and on her visage one discerned "un éclat impérieux."

In Kane's images, one finds a kind of reversed anthropology, that is, using European cultural images to describe African characters. For the average African who knows nothing about European nobility of the Middle Ages, Kane's description of his African characters will not convey any impressions at all. But the author wants his European reader to get the idea that the African nobility is in no way different from its European counterpart and to make it easier for the European, Kane uses images that are familiar to him.

The Frenchmen in the book are also well bred, unprejudiced but rational people. In Africa they meet people of equal social standing as themselves. They display none of the racial arrogance typical of colonialists. They regard the Africans as their equals and when Samba goes to France his friends there never questioned his equality with them. On the part of the Africans there is no feeling of inferiority and they approached and debated with the Frenchmen on their different cultures.

The only distinction between the two parties is that one— Africa—lives in a spiritual world, while the other—Europe—lives in a material world. The tone of the book is thus that of a philosophical conflict between spiritual Islam and material Europe. In the second part of the novel, this conflict is dramatically demonstrated by the hero who is caught between the two worlds as a result of his Koranic and Western educations. His tragedy is his inability to reconcile these two worlds. He tells his Parisian friends:

> Je ne suis pas un pays des Diallobés distinct, face à un Occident distinct, et appréciant d'une tête froide ce que je puis lui prendre, et ce qu'il faut que je lui laisse en contre partie. Je suis devenu les deux. Il n'y a pas une tête lucide entre deux termes d'un choix. Il y a une nature étrange, en détresse de n'être pas deux. (p. 164)

Samba Diallo was sent to Europe to learn the white man's "art de vaincre sans avoir raison." From his childhood he was being trained to be the spiritual leader of his people. In Europe he learns of materialism and communism, both of which he never fully accepted. But his religious faith is greatly challenged. When he goes home he is still undergoing the spiritual metamorphosis which he said had left him in a hybrid state. He is unable to recover his faith and he dies almost a martyr to his faith.

Following Kane's interpretation of his novel, Samba's death is a warning to both the Europeans who want to assimilate Africans, as well as to the Western-educated Africans who want to become Europeanized. It was wrong for Europe to impose her civilization on Africa and it was equally wrong for the African to turn his back on Africa. Throughout the book, a balance between spiritualism and materialism is maintained and the tension between them is so great that the individual caught between them is crushed.

The lesson of *L'Aventure Ambiguë* is "the dangers of assimilation" and Kane meant this lesson for the two parties concerned—Europe and Africa. His two audiences thus controlled the treatment of his subject. A balance is maintained between them; when the European meets the African in Africa, both engage in a debate on the merits of their civilizations, and when the African meets the European in Europe, the same debate continues. In the end neither party wins and the hero who tried to make a compromise between the two is destroyed.

Chinua Achebe: *Things Fall Apart*

Achebe stated in his article "The Role of the Writer in a New Nation,"[13] that the aim of his literary creativity is twofold: artistic and educative. On the educative side, his intentions are to make the Europeans know that "African people did not hear of culture for the first time from Europeans" and to "reeducate" the Africans about their past. Achebe thus announces his two audiences, and he is going to handle his subject in a way to satisfy them. In this article, Achebe is quite definite about his dual audience. But when in the personal interview he is asked to state his audience, he is vague about it. This is a sure sign of development of his awareness regarding the question of audience and the writer's commitment to Africa.

In *Things Fall Apart*, Achebe presents the traditional life and the cultural institutions of Umuofia community. Umuofia is a typical Ibo village and the story is situated in the early 1900s, at the period of the initial contact with the white man.

In his effort to prove to the Europeans that African people have a rich culture, Achebe devotes the greater portion of his novel explaining several Ibo customs, which should in most cases be taken for granted by his African audience. Several critics have commented on the excessive insertion of anthropological material in Achebe's village novels. And in defense of Achebe, Larson says:

> This aversion of literary critics, however, is no doubt due to their equation of anthropological with the local colorists at the end of the last century and at the beginning of this one. However, in a work such as *Things Fall Apart*, where we are not presented a novel of character, the anthropological is indeed important. Without it there would be no story.[14]

As Larson points out, there is no way Achebe could have presented Umuofia society without touching on its customs. But several passages make it very obvious that the author was concerned and more interested in explaining to his European readers those aspects of African customs which he felt would interest them and also those he felt they would not understand without some help from the author.

Among the outstanding examples of unnecessary insertion of anthropology are the stories in chapters nine and ten. For instance, the entire chapter nine is devoted to Ezinma, Okonkwo's daughter. This story provided an excuse for the author to talk of the high infant mortality rate in the area, but particularly to explain the "Ogbanje" phenomenon. There is no equivalent of "Ogbanje" in English, perhaps the closest approximation is the English changling. Achebe describes it as "one of those wicked children who, when they died, entered their mother's wombs to be born again" (p. 74). In the novel, the behavior of the Ogbanje is described in detail. Most of them die and are reborn several times until the necessary rituals are performed to remove the Ogbanje's "*Iyi Uwa*," that is, the bond between an Ogbanje and its world.

This Ogbanje phenomenon is widespread in several African tribes but it is very popular among the Ibos and Yorubas of Nigeria. There was no need for the author to devote a whole chapter explaining such a common thing to his African readers. Apart from that, the story does not add anything to the main plot, for it could easily be detached from the novel and made into a separate story. Its only *raison d'être* then, is that it makes an interesting reading to a foreign audience.

In chapter ten, we find the elders of the village and the "Egwugwu" masqueraders settling a quarrel between a man and his wife. Again, this chapter appears much out of place and even the author seemed aware of it when he makes one of the characters say: "I don't know why such a trifle should come before the Egwugwu," and the author finds the excuse: "Don't you know what kind of man Uzowulu is? He will not listen to any other decision" (p. 89). The intention here is to show the foreigner how village disputes are settled and to point out the important function of the Egwugwu cult. Again in the interview Achebe is asked why he explains commonplace customs such as "Kola breaking" to his presumed Nigerian audience. He carefully avoided the question, and as far as the glossary is concerned, it was done by the publishers who were prompted to do so by the educational value of the book.

As for reeducating the African people on the custom, the need appears rather questionable. For instance, the Nigerian elite audience belongs to Achebe's generation. It is most unlikely that they have already forgotten those customs of which Achebe is reminding them. Besides, most of these customs are very much alive today in the villages. Yet in the interview Achebe insists that there was a need for it and that he has taken it upon himself to reeducate the assimilated Ibos in their customs.

Several passages deal with marriage custom. The settling of bride price is explained in detail. In a passage which has no bearing whatsoever to the entire story, Achebe makes his foreign readers know how very important it is that a bride goes to her husband a virgin. A bride is thus made to swear before the entire members of her husband's family:

> "Remember that if you do not answer truthfully you will suffer or even die at childbirth. How many men have lain with you since my brother first expressed the desire to marry you?"
> "None."
> "Answer truthfully."
> "None."
> "Swear on this staff of my father's."
> "I swear."
> From that day Amikwu took the young bride to his hut and she became his wife. . . . (p. 122)

In a discussion with Professor El Nouty, I pointed out that Achebe's descriptions of marriage custom were overdone and rather unnecessary. Professor El Nouty pointed out that Flaubert also described Emma Bovary's marriage in detail even though his French audience knew about their marriage customs. He further argues that Flaubert's description is termed Naturalism, but when an African writer does the same thing, his own is called Anthropological or at best local color. This tendency of Western critics to equate African customs with local color is part of their practice to downgrade African institutions, El Nouty concludes.

Though there is truth in what El Nouty says, the fact remains that Flaubert's motivation is different from Achebe's. Flaubert needed to show how properly Emma Bovary was married, because the psychological problem of Emma will revolve around this marriage and her betrayal of it. In Flaubert's novel, Emma's marriage is crucial to the development of the plot. In Achebe's case the introduction of marriage and the explanation of bride price do not add anything to the plot. It would have been enough for the author to say that Obierika's daughter got married. He does not need to explain to his African reader the significance of the bride price but he does so, not for the sake of the African reader but for the sake of the non-African audience which does not understand African marriage customs. Furthermore, the African writer finds it necessary to correct the European reader who has learned from Western anthropologists and sociologists that Africans buy wives.

There are many other instances in *Things Fall Apart* where the author describes customs that should be taken for granted by an African reader. An example of this is the presentation of kola, its significance and the rituals surrounding the breaking and eating of it. There is no need to go into details on a practice that is very widely spread in Africa and still very much alive even in the cities. Yet much is made of the kola nut because it makes an interesting reading to foreigners.

In chapter twenty-one we read of a debate between an African and the white missionary. During this debate the white man is made to see the similarities between animism and Christianity.

Akunna: You say that there is one Supreme God who made heaven and earth. We also believe in him and call him Chukwu. He made all the world and the other Gods.

Brown: There are no other Gods. Chukwu is the only God and all others are false. You carve a piece of wood and you call it God. But it is still a piece of wood.

Akunna: Yes it is indeed a piece of wood. The tree from which it came was made by Chukwu as indeed all minor Gods were. But he made them for his messengers so that we could approach him through them. He is like yourself. You are the head of your church.

Brown: No the head of my church is God Himself.

Akunna: I know but there must be a head in this world among men. Somebody like yourself must be head here.

Brown: The head of my church in that sense is in England.

Akunna: That is exactly what I am saying. The head of your church is in your country. He has sent you here as his messengers and servants.

Brown: You should not think of him as a person. It is because you do so that you imagine he must need helpers. And the worst thing about it is that you give all the worship to the false gods you have created.

Akunna: That is not so, we make sacrifices to the little Gods but when they fail and there is no one else to turn to we go to Chukwu. It is right to do so. We approach a great man through his servants. We appear to pay greater attention to the little Gods but that is not so. We worry them more because we are afraid to worry their master. Our fathers knew that Chukwu was the overlord and that is why many of them gave their children the name Chukwu. Chukwu is Supreme.

Brown: You said one interesting thing you are afraid of Chukwu. In my religion Chukwu is a loving father and need not be feared by those who do his will.

Akunna: But we must fear him when we are not doing his will. And who is to tell his will? It is too great to be known. (pp. 164-65).

In the passage above the author's intention to introduce his European reader to the practice of animism is quite obvious. There is also the need to correct the missionary's assertion that African religion is mere fetishism.

From the few instances given, it does appear that Achebe included a lot of anthropological material in his novel not because they added anything to the main plot, but because they made the story more interesting to the European reader—and because such information emphasizes the difference between Africa and Europe just as the bourgeois reader wants it.

On the other hand, the African audience is more interested in following the main story in the book, the fate of Okonkwo, the coming of the white man, and the breaking up of the society due to outside pressure. To the African reader, much insertion of unnecessary anthropological material interferes with the flow of the story and makes it more boring than interesting.

Although Achebe spent the greater part of the time explaining many African customs to his foreign readers, he also tried to satisfy his African readers by telling them how the coming of the white man led to the disruption of native institutions and the final break up of the society into two hostile parties of pagans and Christians. One could therefore say that the author treated his subject matter in a way to satisfy his two audiences even though the European audience had a greater control in regard to the kind of extra materials attached to the major story.

Onuora Nzekwe: *Wand of Noble Wood*

Nzekwu's *Wand of Noble Wood* is one of the most outstanding examples of African novels in which the author makes it obvious that he is writing for a non-African audience. His short novel is nothing short of a precise anthropological document on Ibo customs. The book is arranged in a question/answer form. The author chooses a West Indian to ask questions on various Ibo customs and Peter Obiesie and Reginald, both Ibos, are made to explain the customs to the foreigner.

Here are some examples of answers to Nora's questions:

Nora: Isn't bride price awful? It gives one the impression you buy your wives.

Peter: Bride price is a misnomer. It is applied to the presents a suitor makes to a girl and her parents. . . . It consisted at first of samples of products from his farm. These went to prove that he was strong and hardworking enough for the prospective father-in-law to trust him with the care and welfare of his daughter. (pp. 28-29)

Nora: Can't a man among you ever be free to live according to the dictates of his conscience without always having to be tied down by others?

Peter: But you don't understand. You see, in our social setup we have seniority by age, just as other people do. We also have a system of succession to the headship of the family. . . . Whoever succeeds to the headship is the respository of the fortunes of the family. He is the spiritual head or priest of the family. We call him Okpala and his female counterpart Ada. He takes charge of the Ofo staff which is the symbol of his office. (pp. 31-32)

Nora: Does Ofo staff mean anything more than the symbol of priesthood?

Peter: It is a means whereby the priest comes in contact with ancestral spirits and communes with them. Whoever takes charge of the Ofo is regarded as the abode of ancestral spirits.

Nora: What does it look like?

Peter: It is a short piece of stick cut from the Ofo plant (*Detarium senegalese*) which, when consecreted is a symbol of authority and a guarantee of truth. There are different kinds of Ofo—the family Ofo, the personal Ofo, the Ofo used by medicine men, the cult Ofo and so on. (p. 33)

The book continues in this question and answer form for the first six chapters. From chapter seven to the end of the book, Peter is with his people and Nora is no longer there to ask questions about Ibo customs. But the narrator is still conscious of his foreign audience; therefore, the explanations continue even when they are not asked for. For instance, after presenting kola to his visitors, Peter starts for no apparent reason, to explain the significance of kola in their custom:

Among us, kola nut is a highly valued and indispensable product. Though it is one of the commonest vegetable products seen in Nigeria, it represents in our society a vital social and religious element. Kola nut is a symbol of friendship, the proper offering at meetings and religious occasions.

Many hold that the presentation of kola nut is one proof of the religious disposition of some African peoples. . . . Kola nut is dragged into every aspect of our daily life by our religion which itself permeates every phase of our traditional heritage. (pp. 47-48)

The author is so eager to touch on all aspects of his people's customs that most of the time he has no real justification for introducing his topics. In one of these ridiculous instances Peter suddenly starts to explain "Chi" to his fiancée, a girl from his own village who does not need any lesson on "Chi":

> Chi, according to our traditional religious doctrines, was a genius, a spiritual double connected with every individual's personality. Every individual had a "chi," a guardian angel on whom his success or failure in life depended, for fortune was the result of the application of one's chi to God. But chi had power only over one's material life and matter. (p. 96)

Apart from the brief story of Peter and Nneka's courtship which ended in the latter's mysterious death, there is hardly any plot to Nzekwu's book. To Nigerians and indeed to other African readers, *Wand of Noble Wood* is a boring and naive little book of Ibo customs meant for non-African readers who are interested in learning of African people's customs. The author's desire to explain his native customs to his foreign audience led to a very tactless handling of his subject. Even foreign critics notice that Nzekwu's anthropological explanations are very uninteresting. For example, Gerald Moore comments on Nzekwu's novel in these words:

> Nzekwu has not yet grasped that retelling of anthropological material for its own sake is mere exoticism in a work of creative art.[15]

In his article in *Books Abroad*, no. 40, 1966, Dr. Povey shows how the African writer's awareness of his foreign audience influences the construction of his novel. Povey uses Nzekwu as an example:

> Sometimes this is shown in the unabashed addition of a terminal vocabulary of African words. At other times, pages of anthropological information which could be taken for granted with a local audience are awkwardly inserted in the plot as in the novels of Nzekwu.

In an endeavour to explain to his foreign audience, the religious background of his incidents, his plots become little pegs
on which to hang long explanations of aspects of Nigerian anthropology. The protagonists seem only to act in ways which
allow Nzekwu to inform us about bride price, secret societies,
sacrifices.[16]

Nzekwu's *Wand of Noble Wood* thus gives us a perfect
example of an African novel in which the author's intention to
satisfy his external audience determines his choice of subject
matter as well as the manner of handling it.

Yambo Ouologuem: *Le Devoir de Violence*

Ouologuem's *Le Devoir de Violence* provides a typical example of one other point which Dr. Povey raised in the same
article, that is, the temptation for the African writer "to introduce
the falsely exotic to delight the non-African."[17]

In his novel, Ouologuem paints a most grim and disgraceful
picture of Nakem Ziuko. He traces the history of the Muslim
Saifs from 1202 to 1947. With the possible exception of Isaac
El Heit, who had a short-lived, peaceful reign, the empire of
Nakem knew only tyranny under feudal despots who grew rich
on slave trade. Under these wicked Saifs, all sorts of atrocities
and unheard-of sexual perversities prevailed. For instance, Saif
Moche Gabbai ordered a Herodlike massacre of infants including the unborn. Saif El Haram usurped the throne from his
brother and married his father's widows, including his own
mother! Saif Tsévi seduced his sister and married a bisexual
witch. The same Tsévi and his two brothers were later killed by
the dogs with which they had had sodomic sexual relations. The
author seemed so obsessed with different kinds of sexual acts
that he had to drag homosexuality into his story. And as this
practice is hardly known in Africa, Ouologeum had to make his
African character practice it in France with his Parisian lovers.
The same character, Kassoumi, committed incest with his sister
in Paris because he claimed he did not recognize her, even though
both were adults when they left for France!

Among other improbable incidents in the book are the ones in which the Saif assassinates his enemies by means of vipers that are specially trained to detect the enemy by the smell of his clothes! There is also the fact that the Saif is able to drug and sell slaves under the very eyes of French administrators in the twentieth century!

The only good character in the book is the Frenchman the Reverend Father Henri who tried very often to reason with the Saif and to persuade him to give up his evil ways. To the author's relief, the French forces were able to subdue Nakem and bring "peace" to an area that has known tyranny for over seven hundred years!

Whereas most African writers deem it their responsibility to correct the false images that Europeans have about Africa, Ouologeum made a deliberate effort to corroborate these false impressions in his bid to write a different and intriguing story for a European audience. He capitalized on the European bourgeois craze for the exotic by providing them with a falsely exotic picture of Africa which they nontheless called "Le portrait le plus riche et le plus ambigu d'une Afrique inconnue des Européens."[18]

Though there is enough internal evidence in Ouologuem's novel to show that he wrote mainly to please his European audience, it will be useful to mention some external evidence that would help to reinforce the point. Eric Sellin has written an article entitled: "Ouologuem's Blue Print for Le Devoir de Violence." In this article, Sellin points out the remarkable resemblance between Ouologuem's book and Schwarz-Bart's *Le Dernier des Justes*. From Sellin's comparison, several passages in Ouologuem's book seem to have been copied verbatim from Schwarz-Bart's book. It also appears that Seuil, the publishers, had commissioned Ouologuem to do on Africans, the kind of work that Schwarz-Bart had done on the Jews. The probability of this commission is strongly attested to by the similarity on the cover blurbs of both books.

Here is the description of Schwarz-Bart's book:

Glissant de cette légende à la chronique, puis au romanesque pur, l'auteur nous décrit la vie et la mort souvent dérisoires des justes, leur promenade sanglante au long des siècles Chrétiens.[19]

Ouologuem's book is described thus:

La promenade des Nègres va de la fresque à la chronique puis au romanesque contemporain et au drame souvent dérisoire des Fils de la Nuit.[20]

There is very little or no doubt that Ouologuem wrote at the dictates of his French publishers and editors because they know the kind of books that are popular with their home audience.

Nevertheless, the editors of Seuil deny the allegation that they had commissioned Ouologuem to do a work on Africa similar to that done by Schwarz-Bart on the Jews. In reply to a letter which appeared in the London *Times* "Literary Supplement" of May 19, 1972 (p. 576), Mr. Paul Flamand, one of the chief editors of Seuil, openly denied having any previous knowledge of Ouologuem's novel before it was brought to them for publication.[21] Mr. Sellin who had made the allegation replied to Mr. Flamand's letter, and they corresponded at length on the same issue. In Sellin's letter to the editor of *Research in African Literatures*, vol. 4, no. 1, 1973, he said:

Mr. Flamand has informed me that the editor assigned to the manuscript—Francois-Régis Bastide—did notice in the manuscript prior to publication some structural similarities to *Le Dernier des Justes*, but no one saw harm in that, nor did anyone at Seuil realize the extent of the imitation or that there were other borrowings such as that from Greene. The detail which perturbs me, on the other hand, is the literary devaluation of the authenticity of *Le Devoir de Violence* which so many critics had heralded as the "Great African novel."[22]

After Sellin's apology to Mr. Flamand and Seuil, he nonetheless concludes by saying:

But no number of legal releases will render authentic the alleged Africanness of Ouologuem's book. Although I believe that the publication of this book—presented as it was—put commercialism before literary consequence and was ultimately a disservice to African literature.[23]

In a recent article entitled "Bound to Violence: a Case of Plagiarism,"[24] Robert McDonald exposes the fact that several passages in Ouologuem's novel have in fact been stolen from Graham Greene's novel *It's a Battlefield*. McDonald quoted extensively identical passages in *Le Devoir de Violence* and *It's a Battlefield*. The most striking similarities are found in the scene where Chevalier shows Awa, the African courtesan, around his house (in *Le Devoir de Violence*), and the scene where Mr. Surrogate shows his apartment to Kay Rimmer in *It's a Battlefield*. Here is the passage from *Le Devoir de Violence*:

"I live all alone here" he said sadly and a trifle stiffly. "My wife is dead." (He struck a match, lit an oil lamp, and white walls rose up around them.)

"Take an orange while I light the other lamps." He bent down beside each of the four lamps and the soft flame crackled and purred at the end of his match.

"Not a bad place you've got here," Awa murmured brazenly. "What a lot of books you have."

"Those are the books I have written," the administrator lied.

"It must be wonderful to write."

"One tries to say something. Er . . . would you care to see the rest of the house? It's in excellent taste don't you think? Of course," and here Chevalier lowered his voice, "it lacks the feminine touch." The administrator proceeded from room to room, lighting lamps as he went; and in each room there arose, like sentinels at attention: white panels, paintings on glass, cream-coloured walls, pale, jade-green ceilings. . . . He never looked around him, sensing the silent admiration of this woman who could not have had better taste.[25]

From *It's a Battlefield*:

"I live all alone here," Mr. Surrogate said, a little stiffly and sadly, "my wife is dead." He switched on a light and the white walls rose round him.

"Have a nut while I light the fire?" He knelt and the gentle hissing flames sprang from his match-end.

"It's lovely here," Kay Rimmer said. "What a lot of books you have."

"Those are my own," Mr. Surrogate said.

"It must be wonderful to write."

"One tries to exert an influence. Would you like to see the rest of the flat? It's small, but choice, I think. Of course," Mr. Surrogate added with lowered respectful voice, "it lacks the female touch. A man's den!"

But the word den was a shocking misnomer; Mr. Surrogate went from room to room switching on the lights, and everywhere he went white panelling, cream walls, pale jade walls sprang, like sentries to attention. He never looked around; he was aware behind him of her dumb approval. No woman's taste could have been more adequate.[26]

Mr. McDonald's quotation is long and covers three consecutive pages from Ouologuem's book and four consecutive pages from Greene's book. But the short extract quoted here is enough to prove the point about Ouologuem's plagiarism. That Ouologuem just copied portions of Greene's *It's a Battlefield* cannot be contested. Any slight alteration in phrasing comes from the fact that he translated Greene into French and his own French book is again translated into English.

We find the same glaring evidence of plagiarism in Sellin's comparison of passages from Schwarz-Bart's *Le Dernier des Justes* and Ouologuem's *Le Devoir de Violence*.[27] With all this evidence, and as Mr. McDonald points out: "Mr. Ouologuem has no possible way of proving conclusively that he did write his book."[28]

The reason for citing these examples of plagiarism is not just to question the authenticity of Ouologuem's novel but to show the extent to which an African writer has gone in order to produce a kind of work that sells well in Europe. Ouologuem was quite aware of the popularity of the books he plagiarized; therefore, he hoped that his book would be equally acclaimed by the European audience, and he was right. For he was awarded the coveted Prix Renaudot immediately after the appearance of his novel in 1968. The editors of Seuil who now deny any previous knowledge of Ouologuem's manuscript before it came to them, gave the same publicity and almost word-for-word cover blurb to Ouologuem's novel as they did to Schwarz-Bart's book. They did this because they knew how well their audience received Schwarz-Bart's book.

There are some articles in defense of Ouologuem, such as the one by Seth I. Wolitz entitled "L'Art du plagiat, ou, une brève défense de Ouologuem."[29] This article, even in its defense of Ouologuem admits that he had copied extensively from other European sources. Mr. Wolitz exonerated Ouologeum by saying that every artist has the right to use a model. Wolitz concluded his article by quoting the repartee of Rivarol, "Le génie égorge ceux qu' il pille."

All the defense and exoneration not withstanding, *Le Devoir de Violence* is a sad case of an African novel written for the European market, and because the author was merely interested in capitalizing on the European bourgeois literary taste, he only presented what he felt they would like to read and believe about Africa.

THE COLONIAL EXPERIENCE

Most of the early novels are situated in the colonial period. These novels are often called "protest novels" because they expose and criticize various facets of the colonial regime. Among the popular topics are: the colonial schools and the dilemma of Western-educated Africans; exploitation and unjust imprisonment of Africans by the colonial rulers; and the towns.

The writers' choice of these subjects and the way they treat them seem to show more of a desire to substantiate history than a desire to satisfy the literary taste of this or that particular audience. Very often one notices the writers' effort to present the case of suffering Africa before an international audience. Since most of these novels appeared after Independence, one could not say that they were meant to incite the Africans to rise against the colonial masters. At the same time one could

not say they were meant to prick the Europeans' conscience so
that they would leave Africa alone. The writers' are recording
actual events and the choice of these events does not indicate a
desire to satisfy a "preferred" audience. One could then say
that the topics dealing with colonial Africa are included in
African literature to act as supplement to the history of colonialism in Africa. They are written for the benefit of readers who
would like to verify historical accounts by reading from African
authors who record their own events as participant observers.
In this desire to substantiate history, we find the African writer
looking beyond his local audience for he expects to be read, not
only by his people but by any other reader who is interested in
reading about colonialism in Africa.

The Colonial Schools and the
Dilemma of Western-Educated Africans

The topic of colonial schools occurs very frequently in African
novels. Before the coming of the white man, formal education ex-
isted in the form of Koranic schools in Muslim Africa. In animist
Africa, the initiation rites played the role of school. Here then,
the Western classroom education was introduced by the missionaries who wanted to teach their converts to read the Bible.
The most important subjects were the language of the colonial
masters, writing, arithmetic, and the rudiments of agriculture.
In the French sector, the African languages were not taught and
their use on the school premises was forbidden. In the English
sector, instruction for the first three or four years was in the
mother tongue but after that English became the medium of
instruction for the rest of the academic period.

In both the English and the French schools, the language
of the colonizers posed the most problem for the pupils. The
teachers, particularly the French teachers, were very ruthless in
their method of forcing their language down the throats of
their pupils.

James Ngugi presents a typical English lesson in his *Weep*

Not Child. There one sees the frightened pupils trying to learn the pronouns while the angry teacher is threatening to flog them should they fail to respond correctly (pp. 50-51).

In *Climbié,* Bernard Dadié talks of the *symbole,* a piece of wood, an empty box of matches, anything which is given to the first person who speaks his mother tongue in the classroom or on the playground. The person carries the *symbole* until he hands it over to the next person he surprises speaking his mother tongue. Dadié describes the tense atmosphere created in the school by the presence of the *symbole.*

> Le symbole! vous ne savez pas ce que c'est! Vous en avez de la chance. C'est un cauchemar! Il empêche de rire, de vivre dans l'école, car toujours on pense à lui, on ne cherche, on ne guette que le porteur du symbole. Où est-il? N'est-il pas chez celui-là? Chez cet autre? Le symbole semble être sous le pagne, dans la poche de chaque élève. L'on se regarde avec des yeux soupçonneux. Le symbole a empoisonné le milieu, vicié l'air, gêlé les coeurs![30]

The imposition of the dreaded *symbole* was the effective way which the French teachers devised to check the intrusion of the mother tongue and to minimize the spreading of bad French. In this way the Africans took the learning of French language very serious.

In *L'Enfant Noir,* Camara paints a vivid but shocking picture of a French colonial school. Here the younger pupils live in terror of the older boys. The pupils are subjected to all sorts of harsh punishments at the slightest misbehavior. In the classroom, the pupils are terrified by the blackboard because anyone who made a mistake while writing on it is bound to be heavily punished. Camara describes the pupils' fear in the words:

> We lived in continual dread of being sent to the blackboard. This was our nightmare. The blackboard's blank surface was an exact replica of our minds. When we were called to the blackboard we had to take the chalk and really work, if we were to avoid a beating. (p. 80)

In spite of these harsh treatments, the pupils were eager to learn, because the colonial teachers stressed the point that only those who have been to the white man's school and mastered his language would rule Africa in the future. The fact that the schools promised power and wealth to the educated made many Africans send their children to the colonial schools. Very often the educational career takes the students from their families to the boarding schools or to Europe. By the time he finishes his education the African student finds himself caught between two different cultures neither of which he could fully identify with. In Europe, he is not accepted by those whose culture he has been learning in school, and in Africa he can no longer adapt easily to the local condition. This inability to fit into a particular system is the dilemma of the Western-educated African.

Several African novels deal with the dilemma of the Western-educated African. In Dadié's *Climbié,* the frustrated hero finds it ridiculous and annoying that a very young white man who was just starting his career should sit as a judge in court over him; Climbié and his compatriots had at least fifteen years of service behind them but they remain "fonctionnaires" at the bottom of the scale because the white man is in power both in Europe and in Africa.

Worse than holding subservient position is the cultural alienation from their own people and the rejection by Europeans. The failure to formulate a workable frame of reference which would help them function within the realities of their own countries leads to painful and often tragic ends. The classic examples of the cultural predicament of the Western-educated African are portrayed by Samba Diallo in *L'Aventure Ambiguë,* Obi Okonkwo in *No Longer at Ease,* and to some extent by Jean Marie in *Mission Terminée.*

Samba Diallo dies as a result of his inability to resolve the inner conflict created in him by his newly acquired Western materialism and his previous Muslim spiritualism.

Obi Okonkwo is disgraced because his new Western ideals made it impossible for him to integrate into the system at home:

He was thus "caught in a quicksand of shifting values" and unable "to discern the practical from the ethical parts he defined himself only by negativism."[31]

Jean Marie who had failed his baccalaureat twice was made to realize in the end that his French education left him without a meaningful set of values among his village folks. He had to give it up to adopt the villagers' direct and pragmatic approach to life.

In writing about the colonial schools and their results for the educated Africans, the writers are actually questioning assimilationist principles. To the Europeans, they seem to be saying, "see what you have done to us with your 'superior' education and acculturation." At the same time, they seem to be warning the Africans of the dangers of assimilation, which leave them like the proverbial Ibo bat that belongs to no particular species. On the whole, one could say that the writers have both the European and African audiences in mind when they deal with the problems of the educated African since both parties are involved. However, some authors like Mong Beti in *Mission Terminée*, and Achebe in *No Longer at Ease*, direct more of their attack on or advice to their African elite audience. The elite is made to understand that if he intended to live within the system of his people, he must learn their ways.

Exploitation of Africans by the Colonial Rulers

The theme of exploitation of Africans occurs very frequently in French-African novels. These writers regard it as their duty to attack the system of colonial regime. Though there are English-African novels that criticize some aspects of colonialism, the strong resentment and hostility which mark the Francophone novels are not pronounced. The near absence of protest novels in Anglophone Africa may be accounted for by the British colonial policy of indirect rule.

Unlike the French assimilation, the British indirect rule did not promise automatic citizenship for the colonies and it did

not overtly condemn the entire African culture. A Nigerian
critic, Kolawole Ogungbsan, explains the limited number of protest novels in English Africa thus:

> The British Indirect policy did not alienate the educated African
> from his cultural roots as did Assimilation, there was conflict with
> educated Africans but not intense enough to reach the deepest
> levels of his creativity.[32]

Perhaps Ogungbsan's comment is an over statement because
Achebe has shown in *No Longer at Ease* that the African could
and was culturally alienated. In Achebe's *Arrow of God*, we also
find a very subtle criticism of the colonial policy—the imprisonment of Ezeulu who refused to accept the post of a warrant chief
from the British administrator. In the same novel we read about
forced and unpaid labor imposed on the Africans. In *People of
the City*, Cyprian Ekwensi makes reference to the Enugu coal
miners riot. A whole novel could be written about it.

As of now, James Ngugi's *Weep Not Child* appears to be the
most outstanding novel of "situation" from East Africa. In this
novel, the exploitation of Africans by the white settlers leads
to the Mau Mau insurrection which erupted in Kenya in 1952.[33]

In Francophone Africa, there is a long list of protest novels.
Ousmane Sembène's *Les Bouts de Boise de Dieu*, is a classic
example of African workers rising against their condition. The
story is based on the strike of railroad workers from October,
1947, to March, 1948.[34] The theme of Sembène's novel is universal: the oppression of the working class by their employers.
Les Bouts De Bois de Dieu could be called an African *Germinal*.
Sembène says he is writing solely for his people, but it is doubtful
that the people he has in mind could read his book, because the
majority of them cannot read French. By treating this subject
Sembène demonstrates the similarity among workers all over
the world; therefore, the book will interest the proletariat of
Africa as well as those in Europe. The major differences between
Les Bouts de Bois de Dieu and *Germinal* are (1) the exploited
ones are Africans and the exploiters are Europeans; (2) the

African proletariat win their cause while those in *Germinal* lose theirs. In spite of these differences, Sembène's book is not strictly addressed to African workers but to the entire proletariat of the world. He is therefore writing for two audiences—African and non-African. If it were meant for Senegalese only, he should have written in Wolof, the language of the working class in Senegal.

In *Ville Cruelle*, Mango Beti shows how the African peasantry and workers are exploited by the Europeans. The laborers are underpaid; the farmers have a great deal of difficulty getting their products approved for sale.

Olympe Bhêly Quénum discusses forced labor in *Un Piège Sans Fin*. Here, the French are raising a plantation using forced labor; they summon every male including the respectable elders to come and work in the plantation. Those who protest are severely punished and one of them—Bakari—commits suicide instead of serving the white man.

Achebe also gives a brief description of unpaid labor in *Arrow of God*. Here, the young men go to work without pay on the new road being constructed. In the book we are shown how the white overseer takes liberties with the workers and flogs them when they come late to work. One day, one of the men attacks the overseer for flogging him.

Apart from exploitation of the group, there is also exploitation at the individual level. Oyono gives several instances of this in his novels. In *Le Vieux Nègre et la Médialle*, old Meka lost two sons in the French army. He has also given his land to the mission. For all these, he is cited for a medal from the French governor. His preparations for the occasion and all he suffers after receiving the medal deserve more than all the gold in the Olympic games! Meka loses the medal during the storm that follows the reception. He is arrested for loitering and kept in prison until he is identified as the old man of the medal. It is only after the incident that Meka's confidence in and respect for the white man dies.

In *Une Vie de Boy*, Oyono also shows the exploitation of the "boys" by their white masters. The commandant's wife is astonished to hear the naïve Toundi regret his condition of "boy." He would marry a wife and would like to live like the "Europeans" but the commandant's wife warns him that the present status quo must be maintained:

"Mon pauvre ami, tu as la folie des grandeurs. Soyons Sérieux. Tu Sais que la sagesse recommande à chacun de garder sa place. . . . Tu es boy, mon mari est commandant . . . *personne n'y peut rien*" (p. 89). When Sophie the black mistress of Monsieur Magnol runs away with the money of the administration, the innocent Toundi is arrested and remanded in custody. He is severely tortured so as to make him say where Sophie is. Toundi does not know and he is so severely flogged that he falls sick. He escapes from prison only to die from exhaustion on his way to Spanish Guinea.

Like the "boys," African girls are also exploited. Sophie is an exceptionally high class prostitute-mistress who knows where her lover's key is and with it she steals the money from the safe and runs away. In the majority of the occasions, the girls are just kicked about by their lovers who leave them with half-caste children. We find an example of this in *Un Piège Sans Fin*. In Jean Malonga's *Coeur d'Aryenne* we meet Monsieur Morax whose love affairs with the local women increase the population with mulattoes. In the story of Morax, Malonga depicts the blind racial prejudice and the superiority complex of the white man. Although Mr. Morax could have as many illegitimate children as possible with the native women, when his daughter falls in love with an African he cannot see himself having an African son-in-law, and he vows to destroy the child by his daughter's African lover. In his attempt to carry out his plan, he dies accidentally and his daughter commits suicide.

Unjust Imprisonment of Africans by the Colonial Rulers

Imprisonment is one of the strongest weapons of the colonial masters. An African is sent to prison at the slightest provocation. The prisoners receive the worst kind of treatment imaginable.

In *Things Fall Apart*, six titled men, including the hero Okonkwo, are arrested and remanded in custody by the Commissioner. They had gone peacefully to explain why they had asked the missionary to go away, but there:

> It happened so quickly that the six men did not see it coming. There was only a brief scuffle, too brief even to allow the drawing of a sheathed matchete. The six men were handcuffed and led into the guardroom. . . . The prisoners' barber took down his razor and shaved off all the hair on the men's heads. They were still handcuffed, and they just sat down and moped. At night the messenger came in to taunt them and to knock their shaven heads together. He carried a strong stick, and he hit each man a few blows on the head and back. (pp. 196-97)

The six men were not released until Umuofia village had paid a ransom of two hundred and fifty bags of cowries. It was after this humiliation that Okonkwo vows his revenge on the white man. He carries it out only to hang himself to escape from the white man. In *Arrow of God*, Achebe also shows how the unjust imprisonment of Ezeulu led to his ruin and incidentally to the disintegration of Umuaro society.

Ousmane Sembène describes the state of prisoners in *Les Bouts de Bois de Dieu*. Old Fa Keita, who does not even support the strike, is imprisoned. Fa Keita and the other prisoners are locked in a dark room with buckets of excrement. Any one of them who misbehaves is put in a hole and his skin is slowly burned by scalding water dripping from a heated steel plate. As Fa Keita kneels to pray:

> The commandant's boot caught him in the kidney and hurled him head first into the strands of barbed wire. Little drops of blood flecked the skin of the old man's shoulders and back and sides. (p. 345)

Olympe Bhêly Quénum gives a most incredible story of the prisoner's condition in *Un Piège Sans Fin*. Here, the treatment is such that the prisoners deliberately expose themselves to be crushed by rocks and beams at construction sites. They are closely watched because the rate of suicide is very high. Many prisoners are made to walk around the town bearing a heavy cross and jeered at by a wicked crowd. On one occasion the Reverend Father intervenes and bears the cross for a prisoner, but his action does not save the prisoner who is taken back to prison where he commits suicide. In the prison, the few white prisoners receive a more humane treatment but that does not prevent one of them—Boullin—from letting himself be crushed by a falling rock.

The list could go on and on but the few examples cited represent the general situation. By discussing the grim aspects of colonialism, the African writers are again questioning the colonial intentions and particularly the European sense of justice.

The Towns

The town as opposed to the village is a product of colonialism in Africa. Today the town is the most remarkable feature of modern Africa. White-collar jobs are in the towns and because of that many school dropouts who want to run away from the farms and the poverty of the village troop to the cities to find employment. Once in the city, they quickly lose all the moral discipline of the village because there is no kind of moral ethics to guide the individual and there is no established pattern of norms for social relationships outside the traditional context.

Several African novels are set in the towns. In these novels, the authors present their themes in such a way that the reader is made to notice the sharp contrast between the hectic life of the town and the "pure" and peaceful one of the village. Thus, in every urban novel the town is equated with evil and destruction while the village is good and constructive.

In these novels the authors are largely addressing their local audience and often times these novels are very popular with the town dwellers. An example of a very popular novel is Cyprain Ekwensi's *Jagua Nana*. Ekwensi claims correctly that he is a popular writer for the masses because there is a good deal of evidence to show that the audience of *Jagua Nana* is the Nigerian city dweller. For instance, the moralism of the novel and its entire melodramatic structure indicate the choice of a naïve audience which is being initiated into the novel. The characters speak Pidgin English, the language of the city populace. We do not have any glossary at the end as we find in most African novels, because Ekwensi does not need to explain any local terms or customs to his local audience. He does not need a glossary to eliminate excessive anthropology as we find in Achebe's *Things Fall Apart* or Nwankwo's *Danda*.

However, one very significant fact about Ekwensi's *Jagua Nana* is that in it, we find the African writer's indebtedness to a Western literary tradition even when he sets out to write solely for his local audience. One notices in the novel the influence of American cheap novels and films. For example, Ekwensi's obsession with breasts and bras is very un-African. Unlike America, where we find a kind of breast occultism, in Africa people do not make issues of breasts or of "topless." Girls still go about "topless" and so do elderly women in most African villages. There are traditional dances that are performed "topless" and most of these dances are performed on stage in the big cities. An African woman breast-feeds her baby in public quite unlike her Western counterpart. In short, for the African person, breast is just an integral part of a woman's body and not just a provocative part which is there to tempt the men. In fact, the African male seems to be more attracted by the woman's posterior, which is covered, than by her breast, which is bare. The point here is that the object of curiosity and lust which Ekwensi makes of "breast" in *Jagua Nana* reflects more of American influence than African.

However, Ekwensi knows that people of the city everywhere tend to behave alike and also have similar tastes. He knows how popular the "pop" books are with the Western city populace. He thus predicts correctly that such books would be popular with urban dwellers anywhere else. He first tasted the popularity of the "pop" novel in Nigeria by writing the Onitsha Market type literature. His *When Love Whispers* (1947) was a big success. It was very popular among secondary-school pupils and traders in Onitsha Market. By the time he wrote *Jagua Nana*, he was sure of a large local audience starving for material reflecting their own social condition and environment. In *Jagua Nana*, Ekwensi moves the scene to Lagos, a much larger city with more Western influence. He thus not only enlarges his canvas but embellishes his novel with borrowings from American cheap novels. And as he may have predicted, the novel was an immediate success with the urban populace in Nigeria and indeed with urban dwellers in other parts of West Africa.

Ekwensi's *People of the City* was also very popular with the Nigerian local audience and it is the most representative town novel from Nigeria. In *People of the City* the town is the real antagonist while the hero Sango is a typical unguided young man struggling to make his way in the city. There we see the hero's tribulations as he hunts for lodgings. He combines his reporter assignments with part-time trumpeting at nightclubs, but he is still unable to make ends meet because he has become the victim of a prostitute who drains his pockets under pretext of being pregnant from him. Aina, the prostitute, and Beatrice represent the "hollow" girls of the town, and they are contrasted with Elina the pure innocent girl who was sent from the village to marry Sango. But on seeing Elina:

> Sango felt his heart contract with pain and disillusionment. Pure she must be, innocent, a virgin no doubt, but one whom Sango could never see himself desiring. . . . He cursed himself for his city background which had taught him to appreciate the voluptuous, the sensual, the sophisticated in woman. Elina was none of these. (p. 79)

In the end Sango is very lucky to find a "good" town girl whom he marries and both of them quit Lagos for the Gold Coast to start a new life. But many people in the novel are literally "eaten" by the city. Kofi, the lorry driver, cannot understand why many girls leave the village to waste their lives in the city:

> I have often asked, why do girls leave their happy homes and come here on their own? No brothers, no knowledge of anything, no hope. They just come to the city hoping that some man will

pick them up and make them into something. Not just one man.
You can't find him at the right time. But many men. And some
disease, something incurable picks them up. You see them
dressed, and they are just shells hollow and sick. (p. 145)

The town eats many an innocent people, it is a waste of our
youth. It must stop. (p. 146)

The passage above sums up the fate of the girls who go to
the city hoping for a better life. In the novel, Ekwensi is warning the African youth of the dangers in the city. He is in fact
appealing to them to remain in the "safe" village.

Abdoulaye Sadji

Like Ekwensi's *People of the City,* Sadji's *Maimouna* shows
how the city lures away many innocent people from the peaceful
village. Sadji is criticizing the bourgeois class in Dakar, Senegal,
and the kind of fast life they live. The fate of the heroine is
also a warning to the youths who leave the village to waste
away in the city.

Before Maimouna went to Dakar, she had been living con-
tentedly with her widowed mother in their little village. But
Maimouna's elder sister who lives in the city with her fairly
well-to-do husband, feels that Maimouna has a better chance of
marrying a rich husband in the city. She succeeds in attracting
Maimouna to Dakar. Soon Maimouna is initiated into city life
and she does attract some elderly rich men who sincerely want
to marry her. But Maimouna's heart is set on a well-groomed
young man who is only starting his career. She is secretly taken
to the young man every night by the vicious maid of her sister.
Shortly after, Maimouna becomes pregnant and is sent back to
the village. The young man deserts her and she is left alone with
her mother. Maimouna and her mother catch the small pox
during an epidemic and Maimouna gives birth to a stillborn
baby. Both mother and daughter recover from the small pox,
but Maimouna is very much disfigured. Now, unwanted by any
man, Maimouna settles down to trade like her mother and to
fend for herself.

In Sadji's novel it is the town that destroys Maimouna, and it is the village that restores her to life. The novel is again a plea to the misguided youth who quit the village only to come crawling back after wasting their lives in the city. There are many other novels set in the towns, and the general tendency in these novels is to emphasize the conflict between the traditional society and the modern city. In Ousmane Soce's *Karim* it is to Saint Louis village that Karim returns to find peace and happiness after his escapades with women in the city of Dakar. It is also in the village that Jagua Nana finds a temporary peace before she is drawn back to the city. In Achebe's *No Longer at Ease*, it is the city of Lagos that ruins Obi because he refused to take the advice of his clansmen. In the same novel, Umuofia Union represents Umuofia village. Horton compares the role of Umuofia Union to that of "a maternal octopus always holding out a tempting vision of the absolute security of traditional ties."[35]

By exposing the poor aspects of colonialism, the writers are trying to make the rest of the world know what Africa went through during the period she was colonized. In this case, the novels are there to substantiate history. In the urban novels, the authors are largely addressing their African audience. Yet even in these novels intended for the local audience, the influence of a Western literary taste is evident, as seen in *Jagua Nana*. One could therefore say that both the external and the African audiences influenced the writers' choice of subject matter in the novels based on the African colonial experience.

INDEPENDENT AFRICA

The novels situated in this period are by their contents, a kind of "Face the Nation." The writers are less preoccupied with their foreign audience. They seem to be taking their local audience on a tour of Independent Africa. They want to show them what Africa is really like since the colonial rulers handed her over to the Africans. The popular areas of examination are: bribery and corruption, corrupt politicians, excessive bureaucracy, and neo-colonalism.

A look at the novels of the independent period gives the impression that the writers from West Africa agreed together that each person should present a picture of his country since independence. Thus we have:

Ousmane Sembène	Senegal	*Le Mandat*
Laye Camara	Guinea	*Dramouss*
Ahmadou Kourouma	Ivory Coast	*Les Soleils des Indépendances*
Ayi Kwei Armh	Ghana	*The Beautyful Ones Are Not Yet Born*
Chinua Achebe	Nigeria	*A Man of the People*

Apart from *Le Mandat*, which is not directly concerned with politics, the rest of the novels are patterned in the same way. There is always someone who is not part of it. He could be a passive observer who can only hope for a change, or he can be active enough to take some positive steps to effect a change but in all the cases he never succeeds. When individual or small-group efforts fail, a *deus ex machina* intervenes in form of a military coup.

Bribery and Corruption

Bribery as it now exists in modern Africa was unknown in traditional Africa before the coming of the white man. Its origin goes back to the initial contact of Africans and Europeans. At that time, the interpreters and servants of the white masters demanded "kola" in order to give correct or distorted messages to the master. We find an example of this practice in Achebe's *Arrow of God*, where the messengers from Captain Winterbottom to Ezeulu are offered a "small kola" comprising two cocks and two shillings (p. 191-92).

Corruption of office is also shown in Achebe's *Things Fall Apart* when the messengers of the commissioner increased the ransom money for the release of the prisoners:

The people did not know that fifty bags would go to the messengers who had increased the fine for that purpose. (pp. 180-81)

Bribery and corruption are thus among the by-products of colonialism and they did not end with it. Today they have permeated all levels of society. Bribery is now given in relays from the man at the gate to the big boss secluded in a chamber.

In *No Longer at Ease*, Achebe shows how the process works. Obi, the hero, is convicted and tried in court for receiveing £20 in bribe. His countrymen are not angry that he took the bribe, but they blame him for his lack of experience in the act. They say:

> It is all lack of experience. He should not have accepted the money himself. . . . What others do is tell you to go and hand it to their house boy. Obi tried to do what everyone does without finding out how it was done (p. 13).

In the same novel Achebe explains how the traffic police receive their own bribe. When a policeman came to receive his two shillings from the driver, Obi stared at the policeman, who then did not receive the bribe because

> the policeman was not prepared to take a risk; for all he knew Obi might be a C.I.D. man. So he drove the driver's mate away with great moral indignation. (p. 46)

A few aspects of *No Longer at Ease* show that Achebe is writing for his local audience. For example, he makes frequent use of Pidgin English which the urban people understand. There is no glossary at the end to explain unfamiliar words and he does not explain any customs. He structured his novel in this way because he knows that his local audience will understand his message without the aid of a glossary or explanation of certain terms in parentheses.

In *The Beautyful Ones Are Not Yet Born*, Kwei Armah also describes how policemen receive bribes from drivers:

The policeman looked with long and pensive dignity at the license folder and what was inside it. With his left hand he extracted the money, rolling it up dexteriously into an easy little ball hidden in his palm, while with his right hand he made awkward calculating motions, as if he were involved in checking the honesty of the document he held. (p. 179)

In Soyinka's *The Interpreters*, we also find a sad case of bribery. Here, Sagoe annoys the Board by his bizarre behavior and apparent insolence. Nevertheless, a member of the Board, Winsola, follows him to his hotel to ask for a bribe:

"Well, it is all in your hands, you get my meaning?"
"How much?"
"There are four of us to be . . . seen to, if it was only me
. . ."
"How much? Just tell me how much."
"As you are new, we will make it something for drinks, let us say . . . fifty pounds?" (pp. 88-89)

When Sagoe tells Winsola that he had already been offered the job, the latter becomes furious and tells Sagoe:

On Monday you will receive another phone call telling you that the Board rejected your appointment. You see, the final word is with us. . . . The job is there but you have to secure it. (p. 89)

As these writers point out, there is no honest dealing in Africa. One has to buy his way through everything.

Employment in the new Africa is not always based on qualification but on your ability to oust other contestants by giving more money in bribe to the employers. Achebe tells us in *No Longer at Ease*:

A common saying in the country after independence was that it didn't matter what you know but who you know. (p. 16).

For those who have employment, there is no promotion unless they bribe the people at the top. Kwei Arhma discusses this in detail in *The Beautyful Ones Are Not Yet Born*.

All these writers together decry bribery and corruption. They are addressing their own people and appealing to them to change their ways.

Ousmane Sembène presents the problem of excessive bureaucracy in Dakar. In *Le Mandat*, the hero, Ibrahima, is the prototype of the non-Western educated African who is thwarted by bureaucrats and cheated by corrupt officials. Ibrahima cannot cash a money order sent him from Paris because he has no identification card. He needs a birth certificate, a passport photograph, and a stamp to get his identification card. Ibrahima goes through hell to get these things. After much waiting, he asks to know how long it took to get a birth certificate and he is told:

> Cela dépend. Si tu es connu, ou si tu as des relations, sinon, il n'y a qu à ne pas se décourager, mais si tu as de l'argent alors, là ça va vite. (p. 138)

What Sembène presents in *Le Mandat* is typical of the new nations of Africa. Excessive bureaucracy is one of the effective means the officials use to extort money from people. Here Sembène is directing his criticism to his fellow countrymen as well as to the other countries in Africa where nobody does anything without bribery. To prove further that he is writing exclusively for his countrymen Sembène has decided to write in Wolof in the future and he has already started by publishing his magazine the *KADDU* in Wolof.

Corrupt Politicians

After the exploitation of the people by their colonial masters, the Africans who took over from the white man turned around to exploit their fellow Africans. Getting into politics is the fastest means of getting rich; the election campaign is conducted in a most unethical manner and the masses are lulled with unfulfillable promises. This results in greedy and selfish people becoming rulers of the nations. The only criterion for getting elected is loyalty to the party. But more important than that, the candidate must be "a man of the people"—a man who is ready to play the "people's" game; he must be able to take home to his constituency, their share of the "national cake," for to the masses, the government is an alien body, a "they"; therefore, the government fund is all for grabbing so that each little village must have its own share.

Chief Nanga in Achebe's *A Man of the People* is a typical man of the people. The masses do not mind if their representative is appropriating the fund allocated to them as long as there is a gesture from him that he is going to realize a project in the community. To them, embezzlement is all part of clever politics. While these rotten politics are going on, many powerless intellectuals sit and dream for a change. Some of them try to get into politics in order to change things but the fate of Odili who tried to run a "clean" political campaign in a *Man of the People* clearly shows that the "honest" intellectuals cannot effect any changes because those in authority have all the power and have the ignorant masses behind them.

Armah explores corrupt politics of Nkrumah's Ghana in *The Beautyful Ones Are Not Yet Born*. The hero called "The man" is a passive onlooker. He specifically denounces neo-colonialism and the aping of the white man by the African bourgeoisie:

There is something so terrible in watching a blackman trying at all points to be the dark ghost of a European, and that was what we were seeing in those days. . . . How could they understand that even those who have not been anywhere know that the blackman who has spent his life fleeing from himself into whiteness has no power if the white master gives him none? We knew then, and we know now, that the only real power a blackman can have will come from black people. (p. 80)

In one of the strongest parts of the novel, Armah attacks Ghana's president (Nkrumah) and members of his cabinet directly:

No difference at all between the whiteman and their apes the
lawyers and the merchants, and now the apes of the apes, our
party men. (p. 88)

After a youth spent fighting the whiteman, why should not the
President discover as he grows older that his real desire has been
to be like the white governor himself, to live above all blackness
in the big old slave castle? And the men around him, why not?
What stops them sending their loved children to kindergartens
in Europe? And if the little men around the big men can send
their children to new international schools, why not? . . . All
the shouting against the whiteman was not hate. It was love.
Twisted, but love all the same. (p. 91)

These two passages among many others show very clearly
that Armah was addressing his book to his local audience—Ghana;
therefore, he chose a topic which was uppermost in people's
minds. Armah knew that his strong criticism of Nkrumah's government would land him in jail and to avoid that, he left Ghana.

In *Dramouss*, Camara treats the problem of neo-colonialism.
The hero Fatoma is convinced that the R.D.A. won the election
because it was supported from France. He calls the ex-colonial
masters "hyenas" and the Africans "monkeys." He maintains
that both governors in Dakar and Conakry are controlled from
Paris. The author denounces the highhandedness of the ruling
party in Guinea, and in the novel a group of intellectuals plot
to overthrow the government but they are caught; some of them
are imprisoned for life while some are executed. Fatoma's father
tells him of the fate of most people who plotted against the
government:

Depuis ton départ, beaucoup de tes camarades ont été abattus.
Beaucoup de gens sont en prison. Beaucoup d'autres aussi ont fui.
Notre régime fusile nos enfants pour un oui, pour un non. (pp.
242-43)

Quite unlike his first two novels, *L'Enfant Noir* and *Le Regard
du Roi*, which Camara wrote mainly for the European audience,
in *Dramouss* he is addressing his local Guinea audience. He

wanted the people to know what was happening in their own country. Like Armah, Camara's criticism of his home government has earned him a self-imposed exile so as to avoid imprisonment in his own country.

Ahmadou Kourouma discusses neo-colonialism in the Ivory Coast in his *Les Soleils des Indépendances*. The hero's objection is that independence has brought nothing to the common man. He is particularly angry that his independent country is still largely controlled by French expatriates, including "black Frenchmen" from Senegal and Dahoney:

> Les Toubabs en haut, après les Dahomeens et les Sénégalais, au dessous des pieds, des riens. (p. 89)

In order to change the government, a group of "honest" citizens plan to assassinate the president, but they are caught and imprisoned; however, the "good" president forgives them and buys them off.

As has been shown in the few examples, the novels of the Independent Africa period are mainly criticizing the corrupt governments. The writers' main characters are always "clean" and they act as the champion of the oppressed masses. The novels are an appeal to the nation's politicians to change their ways. On the other hand, the writers are indirectly inciting the people to rise against the corrupt governments. There is hardly any question in these novels of the writers' addressing a foreign audience. They are dealing with local situations that concern their own people. One would therefore conclude that the subject matter and its treatment in the novels on Independent Africa, are determined by the interest of the local audience.

Judging from the novels examined, it has been seen that the African novelists' choice of subject matters and the way they treat them are determined either by the author's intention to satisfy the taste of his external audience or that of his local audience. Since the tastes of both audiences are catered to, it is hard to say which audience controls the writer the more. It

is possible to say in some cases, as in Camara's *Le Regard Du Roi*
or Ouologuem's *Le Devoir de Violence*, that the European bourgeois taste for the exotic controls the writer's choice of subject
and his handling of it. But when one is faced with a book like
Soyinka's *The Interpreters*, it becomes very difficult to say for
whom the writer is writing. One could not, therefore, say that
the subject matter of African novels *en bloc* are dictated by their
European or African audience exclusively, for in most of the
novels, there is an interplay of tastes of both audiences. The most
important thing to note is that, as of the moment, the African
writer is a "committed" artist. He is not writing for writing's
sake. He has a particular intention to satisfy a preferred audience,
European or African; thus it is this audience that influences his
choice of subject and the way he presents it.

NOTES

1. Interview with Cheik Hamidou Kane by author, Abidjan,
   December, 1972.
2. Charles Larson, *The Emergence of African Fiction* (Bloomington: Indiana University Press, 1972), p. 23.
3. Chinua Achebe, "The Role of the Writer in a New Nation,"
   Nigeria Magazine, no. 81 (June, 1964), p. 158.
4. Chinua Achebe, "The Novelist as a Teacher," *New Statesman*, (January 29, 1965), p. 162.
5. Janheinz Jahn, "An Interview with the Editorial Board"
   for *UFAHAMU*, vol. IV, no. 1, (Spring, 1973), p. 36.
6. Claude Wauthier, *The Literature and Thought of Modern
   Africa, A Survey*, (New York: Praeger, 1967), p. 169.
7. Christina A. Aidoo, "Introduction to Armah's *The Beautyful Ones Are Not Yet Born*, (New York: Collier Books,
   1969), p. vii.
8. Interview with Laye Camara by author, Dakar, December,
   1972.
9. *Ibid.*
10. *Ibid.*
11. Janheinz Jahn, *Muntu*, p. 215.

12. Interview with Kane by author.
13. *See* note 3.
14. Larson, *The Emergence of African Fiction*, pp. 43-44.
15. Gerald Moore, "English Words, African Lives," *Présence Africaine*, no. 54, (1965), pp. 94-95.
16. John Povey, "Contemporary West African Writing in English," *Books Abroad*, no. 40 (1966), pp. 253-55.
17. *Ibid.*
18. Review on the cover blurb of Ouologuem's *Le Devoir de Violence.* (Paris: Seuil, 1968).
19. Eric Sellin, "Ouologuem's Blueprint for *Le Devoir de Violence*," *Research in African Literatures*, vol. 2, no. 2 (Fall, 1971), pp. 118-19.
20. Review on the cover blurb of *Le Devoir de Violence*.
21. Paul Flamand, "Letters to the Editor," *Research in African Literatures*, vol. 4, no. 1 (Spring, 1973), p. 129.
22. *Ibid.*, pp. 129-30.
23. *Ibid.*, p. 130.
24. Robert McDonald, "Bound to Violence: A Case of Plagiarism," *Transition*, no. 41, (1972), pp. 64-68.
25. Yambo Ouologuem, *Bound to Violence*, (New York: Harcourt, Brace and Jovanovich, 1971), pp. 54-56.
26. Graham Greene, *It's a Battlefield*, (Heineman; Bodely Head, new ed.), pp. 55-58.
27. Eric Sellin, "Ouologuem's Blueprint for *Le Devoir de Violence*," (*See* note 18).
28. Robert McDonald, "Bound to Violence: A Case of Plagiarism," *Transition*, 41 (1972), p. 68.
29. Seth I. Wolitz, "L'Art du Plagiat," *Research in African Literatures*, vol. 4, no. 1 (Spring, 1973), pp. 130-34.
30. Bernard Dadié, *Climbié*, portion reproduced by Fernand Nathan in *Litterature Africaine*, (Paris: Larousse, 1964), pp. 41-42.
31. Carolyn Nance, "Cosmology in the Novels of Chinua Achebe," *CONCH*, vol. III, no. 2, (September, 1971), p. 133.
32. Kolawole Ogungbsam "Literature and Society in West Afri-

ca," *Africa Quarterly*, vol. XI, no. 3 (October-December, 1971), p. 218.

33. Robert Rotberg, *A Political History of Tropical Africa*, (New York: Harcourt, Brace and World, Inc., 1965), p. 360.

34. Adu Boahen, Introduction to Sembène's *God's Bits of Wood*, (New York: Doubleday and Company, 1970), p. 13.

35. Robin Norton, "Three Nigerian Novelists," *Nigeria Magazine*, no. 70, (September, 1961), p. 221.

5

THE NOVEL GENRE
IN AFRICAN LITERATURE

It is true that Africa had its traditional oral forms of proverbs, poetry and drama, but there is nothing to compare with a sustained work of imaginative creation like the novel.[1]

The novel is the one genre of art that is not Nigerian. . . . The one art that Nigerians have really borrowed.[2]

Nous sommes les héritiers d'une tradition orale . . . on a la tradition du conte, de la légende, mais le roman, livre écrit, que l'on vend, le public Africain ne le connaissait pas.[3]

The above quotations taken from African writers and critics point to the fact that the novel in African literature is a borrowed form. The quotations assume a difference between the novel and other genres—folk tales, epic drama, etc., which exist in traditional African literature. To find the differences between these genres one would have to analyze their various components. But since it is not the purpose of this study to go into such a long analysis, it will be sufficient to look at the findings of established critics who have made the comparisons of literary genres.

Critics like Northrop Frye, George Lukacs, and Rene Wellek do not seem to draw a fast line between the written forms of literature, particularly between the epic and the novel. Rene Wellek says: "The novel as an art form is indeed, in its high form, the modern descendant of the epic."[4]

George Lukacs says:

Entre l'épopée et le roman—les deux objectivations de la grande
littérature épique—la différence ne tient pas aux dispositions
intérieures de l'écrivain, mais aux données historico-philosophiques
qui s'imposent à sa création. . . .

Le roman est l'épopée d'un temps ou la totalité extensive de
la vie n'est plus donnée de la manière immédiate. . . . On s'en
tiendrait à un critère superficiel et purement artistique si l'on
cherchait, dans le vers et dans la prose les seuls caractères décisifs
qui permettent de définir l'épopée et le roman comme des genres
distincts.[5]

Wellek calls the novel "a modern descendant of the epic" and
Lukacs calls it "l'épopée d'un temps." Both critics seem to imply
that the two forms are basically similar, and that the distinction
which is often found between them comes from the historico-
philosophic conditions projected in their creation.

The traditional African literature contains a number of epic
stories. For example, among the Ibos of Nigeria, there is the
epic story of "Eze Iduu na Oba,"[6] which is told for nights without anyone reaching its conclusion. Among the Ijaws, there is
the "Ozidi Saga" which J. P. Clark has compiled.[7] Niane's
Soundjata is the most outstanding example of the epic in traditional African literature to be turned into an epic novel. Other
African oral epics could also be written down.

Since the novel has been called an extension of the epic,
and since the epic exists in African literature, the statement that
the novel is borrowed needs to be further qualified. One would
probably have to go inside the novel to see what aspects of it
are totally absent from the traditional African epic.

Northrop Frye divides the literary genres into two major
groups—Epos and Fiction. The Epos comprises all "works in
which the radical of presentation is oral address" and Fiction is
"the genre of the printed page."[8] Frye sees both as passing
through the same basic stages:

Epos and Fiction first take the form of scripture and myth, then
of traditional tales, then of narrative and didactic poetry, including epic proper, and of oratorical prose, then of novels.[9]

Following the above quotation, one does not know where to draw the line between Epos and Fiction. But Frye does make one other important distinction bsides oral and written forms:

> In Epos, the author confronts his audience directly and the hypothetical characters of his story are concealed. In written literature both the author and his characters are concealed from the reader.[10]

The last distinction which Frye calls "the radical of presentation"[11] is the most important factor that distinguishes the modern African novel from its ancestor the oral epic. Whereas the traditional African literature remained in the Epos stage with the author confronting his audience and telling his story orally, modern literature has reached the Fiction stage with the author hidden from the reader. This is perhaps the distinction that critics of modern African literature have in mind. But this distinction is based on the fact that Epos is oral while Fiction is written. In this case it would not be an overstatement to say that the entire body of modern African literature is borrowed because it is written. It will be more appropriate then to say that the *written* novel is a borrowed form in African literature.

Accepting that the African novelists have borrowed the written novel from the West, several critics including some Africans, infer that the African novelists have altered it to suit their particular vision of life. The Nigerian writer J. P. Clark says:

> The critics have not so much concerned themselves with what our novelists have done to their derived form as with the amount of traditional ritual and modern rottenness and rheum that is to be found in them.[12]

Clark implies that the African novelists have made some important alterations within the novel and that critics have neglected them. But Clark himself did not point out what these changes are. Denis Williams of Guiana seems to be of the opinion that the African novelist cannot adequately express his vision of life without deliberately violating the Western conventions of the novel:

> It is only through a knowledgeable disrespect for the novel, say, a deliberate tampering with the limits which define it as a form, that the African artist can hope to release that mode of his being which he considers particular to himself, and which will be most deeply credible to his people.[13]

Williams does not clearly state whether the African novelist had already tampered with the form of the novel or not. But he maintains that the novelist cannot hope to retain the Western novel form as he found it and at the same time remain intelligible and credible to his people. After his study on the "critical approaches to African fiction" Larson concludes:

> The African writer who has slowly been building up an indigenous reading audience on his own continent has often ignored Western literary demands and relied on his traditional African aesthetics. It is unrewarding, therefore, for the non-African reader and critic to look at any of the three major genres in contemporary African writing—the novel, poetry and drama—solely from the perspective of Western literary criteria and terminology. . . . African novelists are creating new patterns in the traditional literary form.[14]

Larson arrived at his conclusion after studying what he calls the African "situational novels." Incidentally this includes all major novels produced by English- and French-speaking African novelists. Larson maintains that the novelists have created "new unities" which give their fiction "form and pattern." These "new unities" are: insertion of traditional oral tales in the story, use of proverbs, use of anthropological material as a background, and didactic endings. It appears as if Larson has based his judgment mostly on Achebe's novels because most of the things he enumerated are not applicable to many of his "situational novels" such as *Le Regard du Roi, The Voice, Les Bouts de Bois de Dieu, People of the City* and several others. He seems to confuse individual style with a set generic form. What further distinguishes

African novels from European ones are: loose plots, sketchy characterization, and a lack of scenic or atmosphere description. These points will be discussed in more detail later on in this chapter.

To find out if African novels have really deviated from the conventions of the Western novel, a study of Achebe's *Things Fall Apart* and Laye Camara's *Le Regard du Roi* will be made in the light of George Lukacs's *La Théorie du Roman*. For, of all the theories on the novel and the epic, those of Lukacs are the ones that most fittingly describe the majority of the African novels. *Things Fall Apart* has been chosen for study because it is at the moment the African novel which resembles the Lukacsian epic and displays most of its outstanding characteristics. *Le Regard du Roi* is also chosen because it is a perfect example of the *roman* (pure novel) with a little touch of the epic in its denouement.

Lukacs calls the *épopée* and the *roman* "les deux objectivations de la grande littérautre épique." What distinguishes the two is the historico-philosophic ideas which determine their creation. Lukacs gives the conditions necessary for the existence of both:

> Il faut, pour qu'il y ait littérature épique (et le roman est une forme épique), une communauté fondamentale; il faut pour qu'il y ait roman, une opposition radicale entre l'homme et le monde, entre l'individu et la société.[15]

According to Lukacs, the epic is the product of a solid society with a harmonious vision of the world. The novel is the product of a dislocated society with a disintegrated image of the world. The African writers of the twentieth century belong to dislocated societies that have lost the harmonious vision of the world. And the European writers of the nineteenth century, who influenced the African writers the most, also belonged to dislocated societies. Therefore, both the African writers and their models could not produce any epic works because the conditions of their new societies do not favor the creation of real epic. They can only produce novels, a genre properly fitted to develop in a disintegrated society, always in search of a particular truth; a genre that studies the individual in a situation and in perpetual search of harmony. The epic on the other hand concentrates on the destiny of the community as an entity.

Judging from the condition which Lukacs gives for the ex-istence of the epic and the novel, one would then say that the modern African prose writers can only and have so far produced only novels. However, one still finds within the category of the African novels certain works that display very strong resemblances to the epic novel. The most important characteristic of the epic common to many African novels is the emphasis on the fate of the community at large rather than on an individual's destiny.

Following the theory of Lukacs of the *épopée*, *Things Fall Apart* will be considered as a quasi-epic novel. The word "quasi" is used to distinguish Achebe's novel from a true Lukacsian epic novel, for there are certain basic features in *Things Fall Apart* which a true Lukacsian epic novel does not display. Here are some of the basic differences: The object of the epic novel is not to trace the personal destiny of one select individual but that of a community at large. *Things Fall Apart* traces the personal destiny of Okonkwo as well as the collective destiny of Umuofia community. The true epic must thrive in a solid and harmonious society, but *Things Fall Apart* reflects a society in the process of disintegration. Other instances will be cited in the course of the analysis to point out the quasi-epic nature of *Things Fall Apart*. It must be noted that although the author presents a society that is already falling apart, he lays more emphasis on the collective destiny of the people rather than on that of the individual who appointed himself the champion of the dying society. This emphasis on the fate of the community is the most important aspect of the epic novel, and *Things Fall Apart* adheres very closely to it.

Things Fall Apart; A Quasi-Epic Novel

The novel is set at Umuofia, a fictitious place that repre-sents a section of Ibo society of the early 1900s. The author deals with the arrival of white missionaries and colonial administrators in the area. He describes the gradual establishment of Christian Missions and the rupture it created within the traditional social framework.

The most outstanding character of the novel is Okonkwo, who is the embodiment of the social values of Umuofia community. He holds the wrestling championship in Umuofia and the surrounding villages. He has three wives and many children. He has built a flourishing yam barn through crop-sharing. Above all, he has taken the highest title of the land—Ozo—and is aspiring to the last one, which very few people have, when an accident occurs and alters the course of his life. Before that accident, Okonkwo has committed a series of acts the consequences of which are more significant for the community than for him as an individual. Because of the accident, which resulted into an inadvertent murder of a clansman, Okonkwo goes into exile for seven years as stipulated by custom.

While Okonkwo is in exile, white missionaries arrive at Umuofia where they settle and make converts among the rejected and worthless members of the society. Okonkwo is greatly disappointed that his people allowed the missionaries to settle in their village. He hopes to persuade his people to drive the intruders away when he goes home, but even if they refuse, he is determined to do it by himself.

Soon after his return, a native Christian violates a most sacred custom, and this is a good reason to ask the mission to leave. At a meeting of the elders to decide what they are going to do about the situation, a messenger from the District Commissioner arrives to announce that "the white man whose power you know too well has ordered this meeting to stop" (p. 188). Before the messenger can finish his message, Okonkwo draws his matchet and beheads him. From the murmur of disapproval among the people, Okonkwo knows that they will not go to war against the white man. To avoid further humiliation and probably being hanged by the white man, he goes home and hangs himself. As suicide is an abomination in the society, Okonkwo, according to custom, is buried unceremoniously by strangers—the District Commissioner and his messengers.

In the analysis to follow, instances will be taken from the novel to show how very closely it fits into the Lukacsian theory of the epic novel while displaying at the same time certain nonepic features.

The epic individual is relegated to the background; he is important only inasmuch as he is the bearer of a destiny that affects the entire comunity, but he is in no way the hero of the novel. Lukacs states:

> En toute rigueur, le héros d'épopée n'est jamais un individu. De tout temps, on a considéré comme une caractéristique essentielle de l'épopée, le fait que son objet n'est pas un destin personnel mais celui d'une communauté.[16]

In *Things Fall Apart*, Okonkwo is the epic individual but his village, Umuofia, is the hero of the novel. The series of events that occur in his life are important according to the degree to which they affect a larger group, either for their well being or for their misfortune.

The precedence that Umuofia takes over Okonkwo is shown in the opening paragraph of the novel. The first important event in Okonkwo's life—becoming the wrestling champion of the clan, brings fame to him and honor to his village. The fight is described as "one of the fiercest since the founder of their town engaged a spirit of the wild for seven days and seven nights" (p. 7). Here the author announces the birth of the tribe, thus introducing the Umuofia motif which is going to dominate the novel.

In the third paragraph of the first chapter, we have a very brief description of Okonkwo's personality. The next four pages talk of Okonkwo's ne'er-do-well father who died without titles and left his son nothing to inherit. At the end of the chapter we are told how Umuofia has recognized Okonkwo's achievements by appointing him guardian of Ikemefuna, "the doomed lad who was sacrificed to the village of Umuofia by their neighbours to avoid war and bloodshed" (p. 12).

Chapter two emphasizes the Umuofia motif and declares

the worth of the village. The village crier has summoned a meeting of Umuofia elders and "in the morning the marketplace was full. There must have been about ten thousand men there" (p. 14). The powerful orator told them that the people of Mbaino, "those sons of wild animals have dared to murder a daughter of Umuofia" (p. 15). The strength of Umuofia is implied by using the word "dared," but the author later states it clearly:

> Umuofia was feared by all its neighbours. It was powerful in war and in magic. . . . Its most potent war-medicine was as old as the clan itself . . . nobody knew how old. . . . The active principle in that medicine had been an old woman with one leg. . . . It had its shrine in the centre of Umuofia. . . . And if anybody was so foolhardy as to pass by the shrine after dusk he was sure to see the old woman hopping about. And so the neighbouring clans who naturally knew of these things feared Umuofia, and would not go to war against it without first trying a peaceful settlement. (pp. 15-16)

The importance of Umuofia is seen in the fact that a whole chapter is devoted to its description. For instance, in two consecutive pages, Umuofia is mentioned nine times. Only a brief reference is made to Okonkwo's prosperity and how "his whole life was dominated by fear, the fear of failure and of weakness" (p. 16). Chapter three tells of how Okonkwo rose from nothing to become a wealthy farmer. But much of the chapter is again devoted to his worthless father.

In chapter four, Okonkwo commits an act whose consequences would be more significant for the Umuofia community than for him. It was said that "Okonkwo was provoked to justifiable anger by his youngest wife" (p. 30), so he beat her during that week of peace and thereby violated an ancient custom. The priest of the earth goddess warns him:

> The evil you have done can ruin the whole clan. The earth goddess whom you have insulted may refuse to give us her increase and we shall all perish. (p. 32)

Here the importance of the act is weighed by its repercussion on the whole clan. The fact that Okonkwo was "provoked to justifiable anger" does not exonerate him, so he is told to make the necessary sacrifices to propitiate the offended earth goddess for the safety of the clan.

Chapters five and six are devoted to communal activities in Umuofia. There is the celebration of the New Yam Festival during which the entire village watches a wrestling match. The beating of the drum symbolizes the strenth of Umuofia:

> The drums were still beating, persistent and unchanging. Their sound was no longer a separate thing from the living village. It was like the pulsation of its heart. It throbbed in the air, in the sunshine, and even in the trees, and filled the village with excitement. (p. 44)

Okonkwo appears briefly again in chapters seven and eight because he commits another act which is only important for the village's welfare and not for his own personal gratification. The oracle has ordained that the lad in Okonkwo's keeping should be killed. Okonkwo is warned by the priest not to have a hand in it since the lad calls Okonkwo "father." But Okonkwo's fear of being thought weak forces him to go with the group and he is the one whose matchet deals the fatal blow to the lad. When his friend Obierika blames him for taking part in the killing, he claims that he did it in obedience to the oracle. He says to his friend: "If we were all afraid of blood, it would not be done. And what do you think the oracle would do then?" (p. 64). The agony that Okonkwo suffers after the incident shows the amount of precedence that the interest of the community takes over the private feelings of the individual:

> Okonkwo did not taste any food for two days after the death of Ikemefuna. He drank palm wine from morning till night. . . . He did not sleep at night. He tried not to think about Ikemefuna, but the more he tried the more he thought about him. . . . Now and then a cold shiver descended on his head and spread down his body. (p. 61)

Okonkwo suffers privately but his personal suffering is not the concern of Umuofia. His own friend is less concerned about him than he is about the repercussion that his act might have on his family. He tells Okonkwo: "What you have done will not please the Earth. It is the kind of action for which the goddess wipes out whole families" (p. 64). Again the importance of Okonkwo's act is measured by the effect it would have on a larger group, this time, his entire family or lineage, as Lukacs says:

> La signification que peut revêtir un événement dans un monde clos de cette sorte reste tour jours d'ordre quantitatif: la série d'aventures à travers laquelle se manifeste cet événement ne tire son poids que de l'importance qu'elle prend pour le bonheur ou le malheur d'un grand complex organique peuple ou lignée.[17]

From the second half of chapter eight to chapter twelve, Okonkwo is pushed to the background, and emphasis is on life in the village. The author describes traditional marriage and divorce. Two chapters are devoted to Okonkwo's daughter, Ezinma and her struggle for life. The author digresses into the story of Ezinma and her mother in order to show the high infant mortality rate that exists in the community. At the beginning of chapter thirteen there is the description of the traditional burial ceremony. In these chapters much anthropological material is woven into the narrative because it is the only way to show the rich life and culture of Umuofia before its invasion by a foreign culture. Through the description of the life cycle, from birth to marriage and death, with all the rituals that surround them, Umuofia is concretized as an organic entity which is comparable to Lukacs's community:

> Et la communauté est une totalité concrète, organique et, par là, riche en elle-même de sens.[18]

The totality of Umuofia is achieved through the epic technique that chronicles the events in the community's life from birth to death: "l'épopée façonne une totalité de vie achevée par elle-même."[19] The birth of Umuofia was announced at the beginning of the novel, its death begins with the sacrilegious unmasking of the Egwugwu and is consummated through Okonkwo, who epitomizes its values.

Chapter thirteen is very crucial to the development of the novel. It is here that the accident occurs to change the course of Okonkwo's life. The chapter also ends the first part of the story as well as the first part of Okonkwo's life. It opens with "the esoteric language of the ekwe—GO-DI-DI-GO-GO-DI-GO. DI-GO-GO-DI-GO—summoning Umuofia Obodo Dike—the land of the brave, it said this over and over again" (p. 113), as if to emphasize the point that Umuofia is indeed the main character of the story.

During the burial ceremony which follows, Okonkwo reappears but only to commit an inadvertent murder, which has great consequences for him, his family and the community. His rusty gun explodes and kills the son of the dead man:

> The confusion that followed was without parallel in the tradition of Umuofia. . . . The only course open to Okonkwo was to flee from the clan. It was a crime against the earth goddess to kill a clansman, and a man who committed it must flee from the land. . . . He could return to the clan after seven years. That night he collected his most valuable belongings into head-loads. . . . And before the cock crowed Okonkwo and his family were fleeing to his motherland. (p. 117)

This time the event is accidental but its consequences are great for Okonkwo and the rest of the community. He has committed a "female crime" and if the earth goddess is not placated, the life of the entire community is endangered. Okonkwo must go into exile in order to be considered fit to rejoin the Umuofia community. His property must be ritualistically destroyed so that the land may be properly cleansed. Thus, after the accident the necessary steps are taken to safeguard the community; but Okonkwo loses all the wealth that he has accumulated through hard work.

Several critics see the accident which led to Okonkwo's exile as a pure tragic incident in the life of the man, because it led to the isolation of a man from a world into which he has been trying desperately to integrate. In Lukacsian terms, the incident does not belong to the category of the tragic. Lukacs describes the tragic crime in these words:

> Dans la tragedié, le crime est soit un détail sans importance, soit un symbole, soit un simple élément de l'intrigue, requis et dé- terminé par des exigencies techniques, soit l'éclatement des normes terrestres, la porte par laquelle l'âme trouve accès à elle- même.[20]

Okonkwo's "female crime" does not fit in Lukacs's definition of a tragic crime because the accidental murder of a man is not a detail without importance. It is not a symbol. However, it could be an element of intrigue just as any other incident in any story form part of the intrigue. But definitely the accident is not "a door through which Okonkwo's soul finds access to itself." If anything, it is a door through which Okonkwo's soul is torn out. Because, from then on we find a conflict within the man. His aspirations are foiled and Okonkwo's exile is spent in bitterness and regrets. The tensions that build up in him will lead him to commit other acts which will only add to the series of events which make up the epic universe.

On the other hand, Okonkwo's crime will fit into Lukacs's epic world

> où la violation des normes indiscutées entraine nécessairement une vengeance, laquelle exige d'être vengée à son tour, et ainsi de suite à l'infini, ou bien elle devient la parfaite théodicee où le crime et le chatiment pèsent d'un poids égal, de même nature dans la balance du jugement divin.[21]

The "female crime" is called a violation against the earth goddess and she necessarily requires to be avenged; therefore,

> as soon as the day broke, a large crowd of men from Ezeudu's quarter stormed Okonkwo's compound dressed in garbs of war. They set fire to his houses, demolished his red walls, killed his

animals and destroyed his barn. It was the justice of the earth goddess. . . . (p. 117)

By destroying Okonkwo's compound and property, the men from Ezeudu's quarter have symbolically avenged their son whom Okonkwo killed. The action is also a vengeance and "justice of the earth goddess." It is significant to note that the avengers are "dressed in garbs of war," a sign that they are fighting a war of revenge. The vengeance will continue because the seven years of exile did not change Okonkwo's character. His obsession with manly power increased. He spent the seven years preparing for his vengeance against the times. His desire to prove himself again will force him into more reckless acts until finally the vengeance reaches the stage of theodicy.

The exile may have isolated Okonkwo physically from his people but it did not totally cut him off from them. His friend Obierika paid him visits and brought him the money he realized from the sale of his yams. During these visits his friend told him all that had been happening during his absence. The stories about his people increase his desire to rejoin them. In this we see that Okonkwo's crime did not result in complete and total isolation of the hero from his society. On the other hand it brought him closer to his people in that he was ever with them in spirit through his longings to go back to them. His situation is that of an epic individual described by Lukacs:

Le fait d'être porteur de ce destin, pour le héros, loin de l'isoler l'attache bien plutot par un reseau de liens indissolubles à la communauté.[22]

Okonkwo's destiny is strongly linked with his community. He can only realize himself within it. Lukacs insists that the world in which the individual stands apart from his fellows in order to realize himself is strongly opposed to the epic world. The determination of a personality depends on the interaction between the individual and the group:

La personne et la physionomie individuelle naissent d'un equilibre dans le conditionnement réciproque de la partie et du tout, non d'une reflexion polémique sur soi de la personnalité solitaire et fourvoyée.[23]

The seven-years' exile is a technical device which the author uses to introduce the important aspect of the epic novel. This is the arrival and the establishment of the missionaries in Umuofia. This corresponds to what Lukacs calls "l'intervention d'éléments étrangers" in the epic world. From chapters sixteen to twenty-five, the author discusses the "intervention" and the activities of the foreign elements.

According to Lukacs, the foreign elements can safely attach themselves to the central hold without disrupting the equilibrium already established. And their presence does not threaten the unity of the whole because both live as separate organic entities:

C'est sans péril que des éléments étrangers peuvent se joindre au noyau central: il suffit que des réalites concrètes entrent en contact pour que se nouent entre elles des relations concrètes, en sorte que ses éléments étrangers, par l'eloignement que leur confère la perspective et leur plenitude continue, ne menace en rien l'unité de l'ensemble tout en gardant le caractère evident d'une présence organique.[24]

Most of the quotation above applies to the establishment of missionaries in Umuofia. It is without peril that the new religion attaches itself to the core of the community, because religion is what holds the people of Umuofia together. Within a short time the missionaries establish contact with the people by making converts among them. Umuofia elders looked at the missionaries from a distance and this prevented them from knowing the magnitude of the strangers' strength. They did not take the mission seriously; therefore, the "unity of the whole" did not seem to be in danger, but this was only at the initial stage, for the author later deviates from Lukacs's theory of the epic novel. In Achebe's novel, the foreign elements are very destructive indeed. They safely attach themselves to the central hold of Umuofia—religion—and then destroy it:

> The white man is very clever. He came quietly and peaceably with his religion. We were amused at his foolishness and allowed him to stay. Now he has won our brothers, and our clan can no longer act like one. He has put a knife in the things that held us together and we have fallen apart. (p. 162)

By making the foreign elements destructive, Achebe alters Lukacs's theory to suit his own artistic purpose. As a quasi epic, we have the intervention of foreign elements but rather than attach themselves harmlessly to the established order and become part of it, Achebe's foreign elements turn around and destroy the established order. In this deviation we see the capacity of the African writer to modify what he has borrowed and to create features that are quite authentic.

What happened after Okonkwo's return from exile helps to emphasize the point that the Umuofia community is the hero of the novel, proving therefore, in Lukacsian terms, that *Things Fall Apart* is more of an epic novel than anything else.

Throughout his exile, Okonkwo was planning for a great return to his fatherland. But to his great mortification, his return did not cause the stir that he had anticipated:

> Umuofia did not appear to have taken any special notice of the warrior's return. The new religion and government and the trading stores were very much in the people's eyes and minds . . . they talked and thought about little else, and certainly not about Okonkwo's return. (p. 167)

In addition to this disappointment, Okonkwo's plans to initiate his two sons into the Ozo title are also thwarted because he returned two years too early so he had to wait. If he had been able to do it immediately after his return, that would have drawn attention to him and would have shown that he could catch up with the times. To add to these disappointments, Okonkwo returns to find a much changed Umuofia. Most of the values he is striving to regain are now becoming obsolete and even some respectable members of the society have joined the strange religion which he was hoping to wipe out from Umuofia. Because of all these:

> Okonkwo was deeply grieved. And it was not just a personal grief. He mourned for the clan, which he saw breaking up and falling apart. (p. 168)

Okonkwo's reaction is very significant because it clearly shows that the fate of his community is more important to him than his own personal losses. By his reaction Okonkwo himself proves that Umuofia and not he is the hero of the novel.

An event which will lead to a chain of vengeances occurs again in chapter twenty-two. An over zealous native Christian dared unmask an "Egwugwu" in public. Symbolically the culprit "has killed an ancestral spirit and Umuofia was thrown into confusion" (p. 171). This crime is committed against the community and not against the man carrying the mask. Umuofia is greatly agitated and

> that night the mother of spirits walked the length and breadth of the clan weeping for her murdered son. It was a terrible night. . . . It seemed as if the very soul of the tribe wept for a great evil that was coming—its own death. (p. 172)

Here the author spells it out that Umuofia is the hero of the novel. The tribe is personified and it weeps for its imminent death. The weight of this crime is much heavier than that committed by Okonkwo. It led to the death of an ancestral spirit and this is more significant to the people than the death of a human being. The reaction of the people has a marked tragic ring to it. The weeping of the mother of spirits was "a strange and fearful sound, and it was never to be heard again" (p. 171). The note of finality announces the tragic consequences to follow:

> On the next day all the masked Egwugwu of Umuofia assembled in the market place. . . . It was a terrible gathering. For the first

time in living memory the sacred bull-roarer was heard in broad
daylight. . . . From the market place the furious band made for
Enoch's compound. (p. 172)

Umuofia goes to avenge itself. The missionary refuses to
hand over the culprit who is hiding in the mission. The church
is burnt down and the mission is asked to leave. In turn, the
church seeks redress, so the commissioner intervenes on her behalf. Umuofia delegates, among whom was Okonkwo, are imprisoned by the commissioner. In prison they are manhandled
and humiliated. Umuofia pays a ransom and the men are freed.
But Okonkwo vows his revenge. He must rid Umuofia of the
white men even if he has to do it all alone.

Umuofia elders meet to decide what they would do about
the white men. The commissioner's messenger arrives to stop
the meeting. Okonkwo draws his matchet: "It descended twice
and the man's head lay beside his uniformed body" (p. 188).
Okonkwo's crime, again, is important for the whole group because
it could call down the wrath of the white man on the entire
community.

They have heard stories about the great power of the white
man, and the story of Abame which has been wiped out by the
white man is still very fresh on their minds. They disapprove
of Okonkwo's action and they ask, "why did he do it?" They
know that the white man will come for revenge; therefore, they
do not stand behind Okonkwo. However Okonkwo does not
wait for the white man's revenge. He goes home and hangs
himself. He thus completes Lukacs's cycle of revenge. For in
the end, vengeance becomes a perfect theodicy in which the
crime and the punishment are of equal weight—it is a life for a
life.

Okonkwo's death is not exactly the end of the novel. It is
just one of those moments of great intensity found in the epic
novel. Undoubtedly it is the summit of the whole moment but
it never signifies more than the denouement of the great tensions.[24]

The novel continues but only to lay more emphasis on the
importance of the community. Here it is through the point of

view of the commissioner that the insignificance of Okonkwo is made clearer. The district commissioner reflects on how much he is going to write about Okonkwo in his book. The author comments on the commissioner's decision:

> The story of this man who had killed a messenger and hanged himself would make an interesting reading. One could almost write a whole chapter on him. Perhaps not a whole chapter but a reasonable paragraph, at any rate. There was so much else to include, and one must be firm in cutting out details. He had already chosen the title of the book, after much thought: THE PACIFICATION OF THE PRIMITIVE TRIBES OF THE LOWER NIGER. (p. 191)

The story of Okonkwo can only be given a paragraph but the title of the book is the tribe. The story is on "the primitive tribes of the lower Niger," a much larger group. Okonkwo is only one man among many; therefore, his story should not be made to occupy more space than is necessary; the emphasis should be on the group and not on the individual.

Judging from the analysis so far made, one could say that *Things Fall Apart* fits fairly well into the theory of the epic novel in which the community and not the epic individual is the hero. In spite of some indications that tend to lean the novel a little toward the tragic, Achebe himself seems to interpret his novel in Lukacsian terms. In an interview he said:

> I mean my sympathies were not entirely with Okonkwo. . . . Life just has to go on and if you refuse to accept changes, then tragic though it may be, you are swept aside.[25]

Achebe implies that change is inevitable and as such an individual must be prepared to accept it. It was also indicated in the novel that the community was beginning to adapt to the new situation and that they welcomed the gain which the building of the trading store by the white man brought to them. Okonkwo himself was afraid that Umuofia was not going to fight the white man. We know that Okonkwo died, but we really do not know what happened to Umuofia. Okonkwo's death is symbolically identified with that of Umuofia because he is the one individual who strongly identifies with it to the extent that he is ready to give up his life for it. He elected himself the defender of the traditional values of Umuofia, but in this he was not supported by the community which he tried desperately to protect.

Several other African novels could be interpreted as epic novels in Lukacs's terms. In most of these novels, the fate of the community is more important than that of the individual. For instance, Achebe's other novels are concerned with the welfare of a larger group than that of the hero. In *Arrow of God*, it is the unity and safety of Umuaro that is at stake and not the personal ambitions of Ezeulu. When Ezeulu goes insane at the end, the people mock him and most of them nonchalantly join the new religion in order to save their harvest and avoid starvation. In *A Man of the People*, Odili's attempt to gain a seat in the election is not for his own personal aggrandizement, but in order to save the nation from the corrupt politicians. In *No Longer at Ease*, it is Umuofia union that feels the greater impact of Obi's disgrace. They send him to study in England so that he will come home and uplift the name of Umuofia, but instead he drags it to the dust because of his lack of experience.

Other political novels like Armah's *The Beautyful Ones Are Not Yet Born*, Kourouma's *Les Soleils des Indépendances*, and Camara's *Dramousse*, are concerned for the well-being of the entire nation.

Kane's *L'Aventure Ambiguë* is another important novel which could be very closely interpreted as an epic novel. The Diallobé society is a very strong one with its rich, Muslim culture. Samba Diallo is the epic individual whose destiny is closely linked with that of the community. He is the one to lead the people spiritually in the future. His entire life is in preparation for the sacred function of the Maitre—the conscience of the nation.

A foreign element intervenes in the form of the white man and his school. Samba is sent to France to learn the methods with which he would protect the nation from the intruders. Samba loses his faith and a new Maitre is chosen to be the spiritual leader of the nation. When Samba dies, his death is no longer significant for the community, because a new Maitre has been appointed before that. But his death is a warning to those Africans who feel they could make a synthesis of African and European cultures. In this way his death is indirectly significant for the people, because it tells them to be more careful.

In James Ngugi's *Weep Not Child*, it is the entire Kikuyu tribe which is threatened and in fact destroyed by the foreign elements. The supposed hero, Njoroge, is an insignificant personage who is so helpless that he attempts to commit suicide. He stands as a passive onlooker while his community struggles for existence. He had dreamed of greater things but the fate of his people at the hands of the foreign elements has thwarted his ambitions. In defense of the tribe, his brothers and his father have been killed.

The important deviation which these novels make from Lukacs's theory is that the foreign elements which are supposed to integrate harmlessly into the society, turn around and destroy it.

African writers are charged for lack of detailed character development of the heroes. Okonkwo is the same irresolute man from the beginning to the end. Ezeulu is the same ambitious man, only that he goes insane at the end. Odili is the same ineffective picaro to the end, and Obi remains confused and undefined. Samba Diallo undergoes some changes in Europe and loses his faith but he remains the same *raisonneur*.

That African writers do not present "rounded" characters or that their characters are not developed psychologically is nothing new in literature. One can get European novels where characters are either underdeveloped or are mere caricatures. In Dickens's novels, for example, we find caricatures and allegoric types. His *A Tale of Two Cities* is a novel without a specific human hero and none of the numerous characters in the novel is developed in detail. We find famous French writers like Zola presenting static, recurrent characters. If one goes back to the sixteenth century, one finds that the characters in Rabelais's works are not developed in detail.

It would be incorrect to attribute the lack of detailed characterization in African novels to inferior skill on the part of the writers. The African writers at the moment are "committed" artists. They are still concerned with the problems facing Africa since her contact with the Western world. Their novels deal mostly with the fate of the community as an entity rather than the destiny of one individual in a society. This shifts the emphasis from the individual to the group; therefore, a character is given as much description as would enable the reader to identify him within the larger group. One would then say that it is the nature of the novels that determines the presentation of the characters.

The mistake that European critics of African novels make is that they compare characterization in African novels with that in the twentieth-century European psychological novels in which the investigation of character is very crucial to the entire novel. In these novels one finds that action has moved from exterior to interior, that is, into psychoanalysis of the individual's mind.

One has to remember that the majority of the African novelists are influenced by European authors of the nineteenth century or earlier and not by the twentieth-century novelists. If African novelists must be compared with their European counterparts, it would be more justifiable to compare them with their models. The point here is not to show that the African novelists have not developed their characters because their European models have not done so. The fact is that evidence, from close analysis of their works, shows that they select from their models only those features that are necessary in their own artistic creation. They have chosen the novel form because it provides a large canvass for the presentation of the enormous experience of Africa and her peoples. The novelists' preoccupation at the moment is not character study of individuals but the exposition of the experiences of the entire group.

There is the question of loose plots. This again is due to the nature of the novels. Lukacs explains the loose nature of the epic novel by saying that the epic by its very nature remains indifferent to all architectonic constructions,[26] and that the series of events that constitute the epic are articulated but never tightly closed.[27] If the majority of the African novels fall within the category of the epic, one would then not hold it as a deviation from the conventions of the Western novel which they have borrowed.

There are some African novels that are very loose in their plot and some that have no plots at all. This does not mean that they are epic. For instance Nzekwu's *Wand of Noble Wood*, is almost plotless because the author was more concerned with the explanation of his culture to the reader than with the construction of one definite story. In this case it is the particular author's inability or immaturity in his art, or perhaps a "deliberate tampering" with the conventions of the Western novel in order to remain "intelligible and credible to his people," as Denis Williams says.

Soyinka's *The Interpreters* has no plot in the conventional style. The movement of the narrative is very difficult to follow because it is not progressively arranged. The entire story is a series of flashbacks. There is no central personage whose destiny could be followed closely to the end. However, it fits into the stream of the Western *nouveau roman à la* Robbe-Griellet, it is more of *une tranche de vie* which actually does not follow any definite pattern. Here one would not blame Soyinka's book for its lack of plot, because the author followed closely the kind of Western novel which he set out to write.

Again, if several African novels have loose plots or no plots at all, one could not attribute it to artistic incompetence but rather to the artist's privilege to deal with only those features that are relevant or necessary to his own creation. Since most of the novels deal with the life of the group and not the biography of an individual alone, it would be superfluous to compile a daily chronicle of the life of a people in a way to produce a tightly knit plot around which revolves one main issue to be resolved in the end.

Where we have a particular issue as in Sembène's *Le Mandat*, then we have a more tightly knit plot. And even in his *Les Bouts de Bois de Dieu*, in which the whole community in involved, we have a fairly close plot woven around the issue of the strike, which is resolved in the end. One has to admit once more that the kind of subject matter plays a vital role in the nature of the plot. The effort of many African writers to pile up the life experiences of a whole group of people results in a frescolike plot instead of one solid plot around which the entire story is woven.

Scenic descriptions *à la* Balzac are lacking in most African novels. One has to remember that Balzac and his associates believe in *le milieu definit l'homme.* Therefore the Western novelist who believes that the milieu affects the character of the personage spends a great deal of time describing the paysage and the atmosphere. The African writer who is not strictly concerned with portrayal of character does as much description as is necessary for his work. Thus we have more anthropological material, which takes the place of scenic description as well as local color. The anthropological material appears most often in the novels set in the village, and they are necessary to show the life of the people, but inevitably this life is a set of customs and traditions.

Without seeking to justify the scarcity of scenic and atmosphere descriptions in African novels, there is actually no reason why African novelists should be measured with the yardstick of milieu describers like Balzac or verbal painters of paysage like Bernardin de Saint Pierre, Chateaubriand, or Thomas Hardy. The Africans could have been influenced by some other writers like Stendhal, who gives very little space to description, or Paul Bourget, whose *roman à idée* is much closer to the African novelists' committed writings and calls for little or no descriptions.

Scenic description appears in some African novels when it is necessary to illustrate a point. For example, in Armah's *The Beautyful Ones Are Not Yet Born,* one finds several passages of very impressive descriptions of milieu. Such is the description of the banister in the office where the hero works:

> The banister had originally been a wooden one, and to this time it was still possible to see, in the deepest of the cracks between the swellings of other matter, a dubious piece of deeply aged brown wood. And there were many cracks, though most of them

did not reach all the way down to the wood beneath. They were no longer sharp, the cracks, but all rounded out and smooth, consumed by some soft, gentle process of decay. (pp. 11-12)

This passage, and others like the dustbin overflowing with refuse or the politician escaping through the latrine hole, emphasizes the filthy surroundings which form the motif of the novel.

In Kane's *L'Aventure Ambiguë* we find several passages of scenic description of the little village during the twilight hour. But these descriptions are not just there for their own sakes. Kane uses these descriptions to emphasize the Diallobé people's profound faith in their God and also their feeling of oneness with their cosmic world. This feeling of union with the universe is shown in the reaction of people like Samba Diallo, the *chef*, and even Jean Lacroix when they watch the setting sun.

On this occasion, Samba Diallo's face is called "un visage de basalte" because he is petrified by the setting sun:

Le soleil se couchait dans un ciel immense. Ses rayons obliques, qui sont d'or à cette heure du jour, ses rayons s'étaient empourprés d'avoir traversé les nuages qui incendiaient l'Occident. Le sable rouge, éclairé de biais, semblait de l'or en ébullition.

Le visage de basalte de Samba Diallo avait des reflets pourpres. De basalte? C'était un visage de basalte, parce que aussi il était comme petrifié. (p. 70)

Paul Lacroix also comes to realize the mysteries of the universe as he watches the sun set in the African village.

A l'horizon, il semblait que la terre aboutisait à un gouffre. Le soleil était suspendu, dangereusment, au dessus de ce gouffre. L'argent liquide de sa chaleur s'était résorbé, sans que sa lumière eut rien perdu de son éclat. L'air était seulement teinte de rouge et, sous cet éclairage, la petite ville soudain paraissait appartenir à une plante étrange. (p. 86)

In these descriptions, Kane juxtaposes light and color to create the effect of mystery. At the same time he uses the descriptions to heighten the significance of his fundamental theme which is the infinite majesty of God and the insignificance of man.

One could cite more instances of scenic or atmosphere descriptions in African literature, but the few cited go to show that the African writer is quite capable of describing a setting when he feels that it is crucial to convey a particular idea or message. That quite a number of African writers do not spend time on unnecessary description is because they are yet "committed" artists engaged in treating the most pressing problems of the continent. A writer like Achebe for example is more interested in describing for the reader the kind of humiliation and ill-treatment which Okonkwo and five elders received in prison rather than describing the guardroom in which they were held prisoners. Likewise, he describes the killing of Ikemefuna in the forest instead of describing the scene and the atmosphere in the forest. For this author, interest is centered on the fate of the individuals rather than on the milieu in which they suffered their fate.

Le Regard du Roi: A "Roman"

On the title page of this novel one finds a quotation taken from Kafka:

> Le seigneur passera dans le couloir, regardera le prisonnier et dira:—celui-ci, il ne faut pas l'enfermer à nouveau; il vient à moi.[28]

With this quotation in mind, the reader goes into the novel searching for parallels between Camara's novel and Kafka's works. Incidentally one finds a number of them. The most outstanding of these is the sleep-walk and dream motif which persists from the beginning to the end of the novel. The numerous confusing corridors of the Hall of Justice and the roundabout march in the forest, all recall the labyrinth in Kafka. The word labyrinth is actually used in the novel and Clarence describes the paths in words that emphasize their confusing nature: "Ce sentier est un tunnel, il a la lueur incertaine d'un tunnel, . . . Ces éternelles allées et venues! . . . Je devrais faire des marques, semer des cailloux blancs, ou briser des branches, ou cocher les arbres" (pp. 88-89). Finally there is the basic theme of quest which is found in Kafka's *The Castle*.

Camara does not deny Kafka's influence or that of any other European writer, but he is annoyed that critics have made too much of the resemblances between his novel and those of Kafka, very often neglecting the difference between their works. In an article: "Kafka et Moi," Camara wrote:

> Kafka m'a-t-il influencé? Je ne pretends pas n'être fils de personne: des orphelins de cette sorte n'ont jamais existé qu'en imagination . . . Dira-t-on que j'ai plagié Kafka en empruntant sa technique plutot que celle de Balzac ou de Stendhal? C'est probable. On ne le dirait ni pour Balzac ni pour Stendhal. On ne le dirait, ni pour Passos ni pour Jules Romains, si j'avais emprunte leur technique unanimiste, ni pour Dujardin ou James Joyce, si j'avais choisi le dialogue intérieur. Mais on le dirait pour Kafka, pourquoi?[29]

Whether Camara plagiarized Kafka or not, is unimportant; the important thing is that the latter's influence on him has been shown in *Le Regard du Roi*. Both men have produced works which fall within the category of Lukacs's *roman*. The object of this study is to find out how close to or far away from the *roman* Camara's novel is, as defined in Lukacs's *La Théorie du Roman*.

Le Regard du Roi tells a long but straight forward story of a white man's adventures in a particular corner of Africa. The hero, Clarence, has gambled away all his money among his fellow Europeans. He owes money to all of them and he is thrown out of the hotel because he has no money to pay. He wanders off to the African quarters. Here people are celebrating and waiting for the arrival of the king. Clarence believes that if he meets him, the king would give him some employment because he is a white man. The African to whom he told this is amused at his presumptions because he knows that the king does not receive just anybody; he then asks Clarence:

> "Croyez-vous donc que le roi recoive n'importe qui, jeune homme?"
> "Je ne suis pas n'importe qui. Je suis un blanc!"
> "Un blanc?"
> "Je ne suis pas un blanc?"
> "Les hommes blancs ne viennent pas sur l'esplanade!" (p. 12)

Nevertheless Clarence is hopeful that a personal interview with the king will assure him of employment. The king comes but Clarence cannot reach him because of the dense crowd. A beggar tells him that the king will eventually go south, and he advises Clarence to go there and wait for him. The beggar offers to take him there. That night both of them and two dancing boys—Noaga and Nagoa—proceed south. After what appears to be a circling around in one spot in the forest, the four travelers reach their destination at the village of Aziana. Here Clarence is sold to the Naba by the beggar, but Clarence does not know that he has been sold. The beggar tells him that the Naba will keep him till the king arrives. Clarence wonders how they could keep him free of charge.

The beggar tells him that he could render some light services, and Clarence is not sure that there is anything he can really do. He does not know that the service he will render will be to breed half-caste children for the Naba. Arrangements are made whereby a different woman visits him every night. Clarence is unaware of this because each night his hut is filled with highly scented flowers and herbs which have a narcotic and aphrodisiac effect. He thinks he sleeps with his woman, Akissi, but he does not understand how she changes so much every night: "Drôle de femme! Pas un jour elle n'est la même. N'etait ce pas étrange? C'était incomprehensble" (p. 135). Finally the king comes and Clarence is received by him.

Le Regard du Roi belongs to the third category of *roman*

discussed in Lukacs's *La Théorie du Roman*. This is called: "Le roman éducatif du renoncement conscient qui n'est ni résignation ni désespoir."[30]

Camara's novel is the story of the education of Clarence in African ways of life. The education is accomplished through a gradual and conscious renouncement of his indigenous culture. Clarence had to have this education so as to be able to integrate into the new world around him. There is resignation on his part but the interplay of hope and despair guide his march toward his ideal—the meeting with the king.

The basic form of the novel corresponds to that described by Lukacs:

> La forme extérieure du roman est essentiellement biographique. La figure centrale de la biographie n'a de sens que dans sa relation à un monde d'idéaux qui la dépasse . . . mais ce monde n'a lui-même de réalité qu'autant qu'il vit en cet individu et par la vertu de cette expérience vécue.[31]

The novel is biographic in form even though we are not told much about Clarence's life in Europe before he comes to Africa. But we follow his life adventures from the time he arrives on the coast of Africa to the time he meets the king. As an individual, Clarence is almost undefinable. He is not totally a fool, yet one could not call him an intelligent man. Clarence finds himself in an African world which the author presents as ideal and superior to that which the hero had known before. This ideal world very much surpasses Clarence and does not make any sense to him. Everything that happens here appears incomprehensible and contrary to his own common sense. For example, at the esplanade where the crowd is waiting for the king, Clarence notices that the tall people are standing in front while the shorter ones are behind. He feels that if the short people got in front, they would have the opportunity to watch the spectacle without blocking the vision of the tall people behind. But since the position here is different he concludes: "Mais peut-être cette ville appartient-elle à un pays où aucune chance jamais n'était donnée" (p. 10). In the evening he sees a fresco in the reception hall and the two dancing boys give him two different interpretations of it. One says the king is killing his unfaithful vassals, the other says the king is killing faithful vassals because they are the ones worthy of being killed, for guilty blood will desecrate the altar. Clarence is exasperated by this explanation and he scolds the boy: "Quel conte me faites-vous la?" It does not make any sense that the king should kill his faithful vassals. After thinking it over, he feels that there may be some sense to it but he quickly changes his mind and finally he is completely confused:

> Eh bien, oui le raisonnement de ce Noaga, pour peu qu'on y réfléchit, était. . . . Ton raisonnement est juste, non ce raisonnement ne pouvait être juste: il heurtait le bon sens! Ou plutot il était juste sans l'être. . . . Quelle sottise! Ce qui est injust peut-il être juste? . . . C'est juste une sottise. (p. 31)

In a hotel, Clarence buys some food for himself and his three companions. He watches them eat rice with their fingers and he wonders how they are able to do it. He tries unsuccessfully to eat with his fingers and finally gives up and drinks only palm wine. He pays for the food with his coat. Later he is arrested and accused of having taken back his coat, which he did not. The judge tells him to give the hotel keeper his shirt and trousers. Clarence is so surprised at the judge's decision that he asks him if he could stand by and watch him go out naked. The judge tells him that there is no law against nudity in the country. Clarence manages to escape with his clothes on.

In all this, one sees that Clarence's relation with the African world resembles that described by Lukacs. There is a radical opposition between Clarence and the African world. In the first place, he is a white man in the midst of black people. More important than that is the cultural difference between the two groups. The ideal world of Camara's novel is such that admits no compromises. Consequently Clarence has to give up his Western culture in order to become part of the new world in which he now finds himself.

It is at Aziana that his education in African ways of life

takes place. He lives in a little hut with his woman. He learns to eat the local food and drink a lot of palm wine. He finds that people here always close their eyes when thinking, so he does so whenever he wants to think deeply about anything. Now he takes his bath in public because he has become less conscious of nudity. He wears the African *boubou* and eventually he prefers to go nude to the extent that on the day the king comes he bluntly refuses to put on his *boubou* and indeed approaches the king stark naked! Thus, he is slowly stripped of his Western civilization and values. His racial superiority complex disappears and his *prise de conscience* occurs at the moment when he realizes that he is unworthy to meet the king.

In the Lukacsian sense, this ideal world takes on reality for Clarence by virtue of the experiences he has acquired in it. His march toward his goal, the experiences that follow from it, and his final self-awareness, all fit into that of the hero of a *roman*:

> La somme des expériences vécues par le héros est organisée par l'orientation que prend la marche du héros vers le sens de sa vie qui est la conscience de soi.[32]

The personage of Clarence and the object of his search are just what one finds in the theory of the *roman*:

> Le héros du roman est un être problématique, un fou ou un criminel, parce qu'il cherche toujours des valeurs absolues sans les connaître et les vivre intégralement et sans pouvoir, par cela même, les approcher. Une recherche qui progresse toujours sans jamais avancer.[33]

Clarence's behavior borders on the insane. He is in quest of an absolute value which he does not understand, because the king whom he wants to meet is an absolute value, the embodiment of Africa's mystical world. For instance, when Clarence perceives the king's face at the esplanade he is totally overwhelmed by it and the mysterious nature of the king's smile baffles him so much that he does not know what to call it:

> Mais était-ce bien un sourire qui se jouait sur les lèvres? C'était cette sorte de sourire qu'on voit aux idoles, lointains, enigmatique et où il entre peut-être autant de dédain que de bienveillence, le reflect d'une vie intérieure sans doute, mais de quelle vie? Peut-être de cette vie-la justement qui est audelà de la mort . . . Est-ce cette vie que je suis venu chercher? Peut-être cette vie-là, oui. (p. 22)

Perhaps the king's smile betrays an inner life. "But what life?" Clarence wonders, evidently it is a life which is not of this world. He is not sure that this is the life he has come to look for, perhaps it is. After this first experience with the king's person, Clarence's illusion and despair increase. But hope leads him south where he continues to search for his ideal. Here his search is in the form of waiting an indefinite time. Thus the search progresses without moving forward.

The hero of a *roman* is also called a criminal. At Adrame, Clarence is arrested for taking back his coat which he gave the hotel keeper in lieu of money. He is dragged before the judge and on the way he sees his fellow white people and tries to hide his face; they see him and declare him guilty before he is ever judged:

> Voyez comme il baisse la tête. La baisserait-il si bas s'il n'était pas coupable? Personne ne me fera admettre que cet individu n'est pas coupable. (p. 66)

Clarence protests before the judge that he is innocent and in the end he escapes without giving his shirt and trousers to the man, as the judge decided. He is surprised to find his coat with the two boys. The coat is mended and given back to him and he is happy to have it back. He feels no regrets that he did not pay what he owed.

The most dominant features of *Le Regard du Roi* are summed up in Lukacs's definition of the *roman*: "Le roman est la forme de la solitude dans la communauté, de l'espoir sans avenir, de la présence dans l'absence."[34] Clarence has been thrown out into a strange world. He is isolated from the black community by his race and culture. While he waits for the beggar to bring him word from the king, he thinks of his loneliness:

> Je suis seul, aussi seul que dans l'instant ou l'hôtelier blanc me mettait à la porte . . . Seul! Je me trouve chaque fois un peu plus seu! (pp. 35-36)

In spite of this feeling Clarence feels and hopes that his deliverance lies in this strange world incarnated by the king:

> C'était malgré tout, sur le roi qu'il comptait pour être delivré. Oui, le roi viendrait et le délivrerait. . . . C'était insensé, et c'était vrai néanmoins ce frêle et fol espoir demeurait au plus profond de Clarence: Le roi viendrait s'asseoir sous la galerie, et le délivrait! (p. 210)

His is a slim and foolish hope because no one is sure when or whether the king would ever come. Even if the king does come there is no guarantee that Clarence will be able to meet him:

> Pourrait-il, dans le sud, aborder le roi plus facilement que dans le nord? Et quelle apparence y avait-il que les circonstances fussent plus favorables dans le nord? (p. 26)

Clarence's hope is one without future though he has been assured that when next the king comes he would sit in the gallery just opposite Clarence's hut. Clarence is amused by the word "next" because he is sure there will never be a "next" time: "Quand y aurait-il une prochaine fois? Jamais, peutêtre! il ne viendra pas" (p. 210). The state of hope/despair persists and is further reinforced by the absence/presence of the king. Physically absent, the king is ever-present in the people's minds and so is he in the mind of Clarence.

The time element in *Le Regard du Roi* is exactly that which Lukacs attributes to every authentic novel. Time is seen as a process of continuous degradation and an obstacle between the hero and his ideal.[35] The entire life of Clarence in Africa is a continuous degradation, because Clarence is a "superior" white man in the midst of "inferior" African people. At first he is proud of his European superiority complex. He is sure that the king will give him employment because he is a white man. The Africans themselves seem to acknowledge the white man's superiority, because they are surprised to see Clarence in their midst. When Clarence tells the beggar that the king will give him a job because he is a white man, the beggar looks at him spitefully and says: "Les hommes blancs ne viennent pas sur l'esplanade!" Clarence thinks about this and agrees that white men would not be found rubbing shoulders with Africans in the sun:

> Non, cette esplanade n'était pas un endroit ou des hommes blancs se fussent risqués. . . . Les blancs n'eussent pas toleré ce coudoiement de la populace noire. (p. 12)

From the moment when Clarence is thrown out of the hotel for white people, his degradation starts. It is the first time that a white man has been thrown out. He has no face to go back to the European quarter because he owes practically everybody there some money. He is thus rejected by his own group so he joins the "inferior" group. As if that were not enough, a mere beggar offers to speak on his behalf before the king. Clarence is angry at the beggar's impudence but in the end he finds that he has no other choice. The beggar takes him to a very dirty hotel and after looking at the dirt, Clarence concludes that, perhaps, that is the only place he has the right to be. He regrets that he did not drown himself instead of landing on the coast of Africa: "Je ne regrette qu'une chose, c'est de ne m'être pas jeter à la mer avant de débarquer sur ce rivage" (p. 43).

The final degradation is when Clarence is sold to the Naba by the beggar in exchange for a woman and a donkey. His work will be that of a "cock" for the Naba's harem. He thus becomes a breeder-animal without knowing it. He does not understand why Samba Baloum calls him a cock and feels him all over as a man does to an animal or an object he wants to buy:

Il poussait Clarence devant lui avec sa badine et le palpait en geignant.

"Un vrai poulet! On sent les os partout."

"Je n'aime pas qu'on m'appelle un poulet."

"Je ne peux pourtant pas vous appler un coq? Après tout qu'en sais-je? M'est avis pourtant que ce coq le naba l'a acheté comme un chat dans un sac."

"Je ne me suis pas vendu." (p. 127)

Clarence makes the most ironic statement in the novel; he says that he has not sold himself! He is told to take a good rest because he will start work that night. From that night on, a different woman is sent to his hut. Sometimes he feels the difference and he keeps wondering why Akissi assumes different shapes and moods every night. After a while the harem is filled with half-caste babies.

In the end it is the wicked master of ceremony who tells Clarence to his face that he was sold and that he has been sleeping with a different woman from the harem every night. Clarence falls back into deep introspection. He thinks over his nightly debaucheries with the supposed Akissi and he is thoroughly ashamed of himself!

Je me laisse vivre, si je me limais les dents comme les gens d'Aziana on ne verrait plus de différence entre eux et moi. Il y avait la couleur de la peau, oui. Mais quelle différence était-ce là? C'est l'intérieur qui compte. . . . Je suis exactement comme eux. (p. 152)

This is the ultimate degradation for Clarence. He is now exactly like these "inferior" people, his color not withstanding. "It is the inside that counts," he says. From that day he decides to go completely nude but Akissi tells him that it will be preferable to wear the *boubou*; she says to him: "Si tu n'es pas un blanc" and Clarence cuts her short: "Tu veux dire que je suis plus noir qu'un noir? Tu peux le dire. Je m'en moque bien" (p. 153). The same day Clarence is taken by the dancing boys to witness a trial against the master of ceremony for revealing

the secret of Clarence's position to him. Clarence hears everything said about him, but he dismisses the whole thing as stupid
bagatelle!

However after witnessing the scene Clarence decides to pass
by the harem to verify what the master of ceremony has said.
There he sees women carrying half-caste babies; still he wonders
where they came from. Samba Baloum explains to him that
Negro children look like that at birth and only change with
exposure to the sun. But Clarence is not satisfied with the
explanation so he says: "J'aurais juré que c'étaient des sang-
mêlé" (p. 165).

In his dream he sees the women showing him the babies
and telling him that they are his children. When he wakes up,
he realizes the truth. Self-awareness takes place and he is completely annihilated. He decides to change: he will not take his
bath in public any more, he will go and live in the desert. He
goes into the forest and there he thinks of his degradation. He
considers himself a beast and does not expect the king to look
at him:

> Mais pouvait-on, même par seule pitié, jeter le regard sur une
> bête? Le roi se détournerait de cette bête immonde, il s'en
> détournerait avec horreur. (p. 195)

After considering the possibility of not being seen by the
king, Clarence wishes that death would come and deliver him:
"Si la mort pouvait me délivrer" (p. 195). He shakes himself
and feels that he is going insane: "Je deviens fou."

In addition to being a process of degradation for Clarence,
time has been the major obstacle between him and his ideal.
If only he knew when the king would come he would be better
prepared to meet him. Clarence is thus condemned to waiting
indefinitely.

This degradation is just the negative aspect of temporality,
for according to Lukacs, this same degradation has a positive
effect. It is a passage from an inferior form to a superior one
which is also more authentic. In *Le Regard du Roi*, the aim of

the author is to strip Clarence of his European culture which he considers unsuitable for his life in Africa. He wanted to clothe Clarence in a new and more authentic African form. After his degradation Clarence himself declares that he is now blacker than black people. But by becoming "black" in spirit, Clarence is now ready to accept the "ideal" African world. Moreover, it is through this degradation that Clarence attains self-awareness, which is the ultimate aim of the *roman*.

Clarence's self-awareness makes him see that he is unworthy to approach the king. This feeling of Clarence is again the author's objective—to make him realize that the grace he is going to receive from the king is not given for his own merit, but by the king's voluntary choice and benevolence. On the day the king arrives, Clarence bluntly refuses to go out and see him because he feels that he is so impure that he smells. He stays in his hut but the "radiance" of the king penetrates the hut and Clarence sees it and wonders where it comes from: "Mais d'où vient cette lumière?" At that moment he lifts up his face and sees the king's gaze fixed on him, beckoning him. All naked, Clarence is drawn toward the king by a power beyond him. The king envelops him in his big coat and Clarence is seen no more. Thus Clarence is symbolically absorbed by Africa— the king.

The ending of the novel is the only important deviation that Camara makes from Lukacs's theory of the *roman*. Because in Lukacs's terms the ideal is never attained. If it is, it would cause a rupture between the hero and the world around him. His search is described as

une recherche problématique et démonique qui ne saurait aboutir puisque l'aboutissement serait précisément de la rupture entre le héros et le monde et par cela même, le dépassement de l'univers romanesque.[36]

Clarence attains his ideal but this does not result in a rupture between him and the African world, instead he is positively absorbed into it. Since this rupture does not take place,

Camara's hero has not gone beyond the universe of the *roman*, he has only become part of it. Camara has pointed out this major difference between his novel and Kafka's works in the same article "Kafka et Moi":

> Mes personnages savent mieux que moi ce que sont cette angoisse, ces tourments, ce désespoir, mais il vient toujours un instant ou ils atteignent le bonheur, et alors ils l'atteignent pleinement, tandis que les personnages de Kafka, eux, ne l'atteignent qu'à demi ou pas du tout, et quand bien même ils s'imaginent l'atteindre, ils ne l'atteignent que provisoirement.[37]

The deviation which appears in Camara's denouement is very important, because by it, *Le Regard du Roi* incorporates an important aspect of the Lukacsian *èpopée*—a world of harmony and peace, a world that has a meaning and an answer to people's problems. At the beginning of the novel this harmony is hidden from Clarence because of his racial prejudice and distorted image of Africa. But when he integrates into the African society, he finds its harmony as it is epitomized by the king. Camara deliberately chose to give his novel a different denouement from that of a typical *roman* because he wanted to point out particularly to his European readers that Africa holds the answer to their problem—the search for peace and harmony; that Africa is ready to stretch out her redeeming hand to Europe if only Europe would be humble enough to accept it just as Clarence did. However this unusual denouement, which gives Camara's novel some semblance of the epic, does not alter the fact that *Le Regard du Roi* is a typical *roman* produced by a writer from a dislocated society.

Apart from this difference in denouement, Camara's novel follows the Lukacsian theory of the *roman* almost to the letter. Lukacs says that the hero dies symbolically when he attains his self-awareness. There is a point in the *roman* at which the hero becomes passive, but this passiveness comes from "la relation du héros avec son âme et sa relation avec le monde environnant."[38] Clarence becomes passive when he realizes the kind of life he had been leading at Aziana. He gives up completely all hopes of ever becoming a better man.

Lukacs calls the *roman*: "l'épopée d'un monde sans dieu."[39] In this world without God, life is deeply fixed in its own immanence. People only aspire to live. God is completely absent in the world of *Le Regard du Roi*. In fact, God's place is taken symbolically by the king who is quasi divine. He is an eternal and redeemer king; on him alone Clarence trusts his deliverance. The only thing we know about Aziana people is that everybody is waiting for the king. Their life is fixed. For instance we see Diallo ever making his axes; Akissi's daily routine is to fetch water for Clarence's bath and pound the millet for the meal. There is Clarence whose occupation is to sleep with a different woman every night. The world of *Le Regard du Roi* is not like that of *Things Fall Apart* or *Arrow of God* where people are actively engaged in different activities.

All the important aspects of Lukacs's *roman* are found in *Le Regard du Roi*. One would just be laboring the point by discussing other minor aspects of the novel found in Camara's book. A careful study of *Le Regard du Roi* in the light of *La Théorie du Roman*, shows that it is a pure novel by all Western standards despite the slight alteration in its ending.

Contrary to the epic novel the plot of the "pure novel" is more compact. Camara's novel differs in its plot from most African novels which fall within the category of the epic novel. The plot of *Le Regard du Roi* is compact. The *fil conducteur* is the quest, and the reader never loses sight of Clarence. He is constantly interacting with the rest of the characters in the novel.

The African novels studied earlier do not go into detailed characterization because they are more concerned with the entire group than with the individual. It is not easy to consider these novels as one-character novels. For example it would be more appropriate to entitle *Things Fall Apart*, *Umuofia* than to call it *Okonkwo*; but one can easily call *Le Regard du Roi*, *Clarence*; and it would not hurt the novel because the whole intrigue is centered around him.

The characters in the epic do not often change at the end
of the novel and they do not very often introspect. Clarence is
ever introspecting and through it he knows his true self, which
he hates and decides to change. He stops bathing in public and
he goes to live the rest of his life in the desert except that the
strong desire to meet the king brings him back to his hut. There
is every indication that Clarence would be a new man after he
enters the king's service.

Speaking of characterization in Le Regard du Roi, Larson
says:

> It is surprising how little we actually know of Clarence, and yet
> it is possible to think of the book as a one-character novel.[40]

Clarence is a problematic individual, a criminal, and nothing
short of a mad man. In this case it is fairly difficult to know a
great deal about the character of a maladjusted person except
that he is mentally unstable. We do not know what Clarence
was in Europe. He says he never gambled, but we find him a
gambler in Africa. We also find him an accomplice in theft.
It is true that Clarence is intoxicated when he sleeps with the
women but when he later realizes what he has been doing, he
admits that he has always been weak:

> J'étais faible, personne n'a été plus faible que moi, et la nuit
> J'étais comme une bête. . . . Pourtant je n'aimais pas ma
> faiblesse J'aurais voulu rejeter cette faiblesse, et j'aurais voulu
> n'être pas cette bête. (p. 252)

If one says that Clarence is not deeply studied psychologically
one could not say that he is a type like most characters in
African epiclike novels; he is not a stereotyped white man but
a unique character. Other characters in the novel are not studied
in detail but they are vividly portrayed. For instance, the sound
of Baloum's name alone is enough to describe his round and
very soft body. Clarence says that Baloum's hands are so soft
that they could not scrub off the dirt from his back. The Naba
is the man who speaks with his beard. Diallo is the conscientious

philosopher-artist through whom the author describes the African concept of time and art. Akissi is the chameleon woman who behaves like an automat and says just the necessary things. She knows what goes on in the hut every night but she never reveals anything to Clarence. The king is described by contrasts: "Il est jeune et il est fragile, mais il est en même temps très vieux et il est robuste. (p. 21)" Gold is the symbol of the king's love for the people and it is the gold that chains him to them. He gives his favors to any one, irrespective of race or worthiness.

Camara's novel differs from other African novels because the anthropological material in his novel is subtly woven into the fabric of the novel. In *Le Regard du Roi*, the anthropological material could hardly be separated from the main plot. The characters themselves, by their functions, are part of the anthropology. But these individuals are not just inserted for local color; each of them plays a definite role in Clarence's life. Unlike other African novels, anthropological material does not replace scenic or atmosphere description. There are several passages of scenic description in *Le Regard du Roi*, an example of which is the depiction of the esplanade at the very beginning. There are numerous passages describing the atmosphere of the novel. The most powerful of these is the persistent odor motif. Here is the description of the odor of the South:

> L'odeur mêlait intimement aux parfums des fleurs les exhalaisons du terreau. C'était là assurement une odeur bizarre et même suspecte, pas désagreable, ou pas nécessairement désagreable, mais bizarre, mais suspecte; un peu comme l'odeur opaque d'une serre chaude et de fleurs décomposées; une odeur douceâtre, entêtante et inqietante, mais plus enveloppante que robutante, étrangement froleuse, oui, et—on s'effraie de l'avouer —attirante, insidieusement attirante; une odeur en vérité ou le corps et l'esprit, mais l'esprit surtout, insensiblement se dissolvaient. On l'eût très exactement qualifiée d'emolliente. (p. 86)

Among the most impressive scenes in the novel are the final paragraphs where Clarence approaches the king. This scene has been called "one of the most beautiful passages in all African literature."[41]

From the preceding analysis, one could say that *Le Regard du Roi* is structurally a perfect example of the *roman* in African literature in spite of the little touch of the epic in its denouement. At the same time it is a perfect example of the influence of the European audience whose taste and literary tradition greatly influence the African writer.

As has been shown, the African novel adheres very closely to its Western model be it epic novel or pure novel (*roman*). However, when Chinua Achebe and Ezekiel Mphahlele were questioned about this close identity, neither writer would agree without qualification: Achebe claims to have added some new dimensions to the Western novel while Mphahlele feels that his *Down Second Avenue* is something different from the Western autobiographical novel. Achebe first:

QUESTION: So you think you have added any new dimensions to the novel?

ACHEBE: Yes, obviously.

QUESTION: Which ones?

ACHEBE: Well, it's easier to say than to define. I don't think anybody reading my novel can be in any doubt that he is dealing with things from a different environment, culture, history and tradition, say different from Virginia Woolf, from Europe and American tradition. And this new dimension is what I call a non-Western humanity—seeing the human predicament from a non-Western standpoint. For instance, emphasis on community as opposed to individual. The whole community is engaged in the drama. And there is also the individual. This element of community is very important but it is constantly underrated.

QUESTION: This new dimension of yours seems to deal with the content rather than the form of the novel?

ACHEBE: Well, I don't know. I have a problem with drawing a

line between form and content. I don't think you can alter the content without altering the form.[42A]

(Invariably but quite unconsciously, Achebe is only affirming Lukacs's definition of the epic novel whose essential characteristic is the emphasis on communal rather than on individual destiny. In this case it is difficult to regard Achebe's emphasis on the community as a new dimension brought into the fixed form of the Western novel.)

QUESTION: How do you think you have deviated or added anything to the conventional Western novel?

MPHAHLELE: The autobiography I wrote was cast in a novelistic frame even though it is a true story. I deviated slightly and I did that to make it more readable instead of a straightforward autobiography. At the same time I deviated from the traditional novel which is why so many English critics didn't like it, because it was not a traditional novel. It is quite something else and I deliberately did that in order to say things the best way I wanted.

QUESTION: How does your book actually differ from the traditional novel?

MPHAHLELE: It is not traditional because I speak in the first person and a number of other things that I talk of confirm the personal view of the narrator.

QUESTION: In other words, *Down Second Avenue* is neither a novel nor a pure autobiography?

MPHAHLELE: You could say that. Indeed I don't know if we can drastically do anything to the novel as it exists. We are still writing narratives of one kind or another. I don't think we can do much to it because we are telling stories. On the other hand we can do a lot to it only when we have an immediate audience of Africans, and through an African publisher can we experiment more with the form of the novel.

QUESTION: Why not experiment at the moment?

MPHAHLELE: At the moment I can't because when I do no

one will want to publish it. I know what I would want to do but I can't do it unless I get an African publisher.[42B]

Here again the new dimension added by Mphahlele is not easily detectable though it is termed "something else." As for his speaking in the first person in an autobiographical novel, that can hardly be called an innovation. But the role of the external audience is very crucial here. Because in order to be published the African writer is forced to ape the Western form at the expense of expanding his own creative abilities.

WHY THE NOVEL?

Most African writers are of the opinion that the novel is not the best means to reach the African masses whom they claim to be their reading audience. Apart from the fact that the *written* novel is foreign to this audience, the majority of the people cannot read either English or French. In this case, it seems that the best way to reach them would be visually, using the cinema, television, and dramatizations on the stage.

The following are responses from some of the authors on the question, "Why the novel?"

QUESTION: Do you think the novel is the best vehicle you could have used to reach your African audience?

NGUGI: Definitely, no. In fact I don't think the novel is necessarily the most effective means for reaching the people. I can think of other art forms that are more direct, like the film—the most direct art form which can reach people at grass-root levels. But the film is not what an individual writer decides on. One must have money, equipment, and other gadgets which come into it. All this again makes it a minority occupation by the way it is produced. Writing is more of a public art form than the film.

QUESTION: For you, then, the novel is a convenient means rather than the best means?

NGUGI: It's more of a ready-made art form that is there to be used. But if the government is interested in investing in the film industry, then we can reach more people.

QUESTION: Since the African audience does not have the tradition of the novel, why do many African writers choose the novel?[43A]

MPHAHLELE: I think the novel has got that thing which is so close to the reader—which is to present human life in its reality, and social realism is something that we want very badly. And it seems to me the nearest would be the novel. The poem for instance is something else. The way I see it, the novel naturally deals with conflict, and the poem does not so much deal with conflict as unity. In a novel you are always aware of a conflict and dissimilarity. And our African lives have got so many conflicts so that we would naturally select the novel to present those conflicts; particularly, when we first began writing we did it in order to present the situation of conflict.

QUESTION: In choosing the novel you are automatically excluding the African masses.

MPHAHLELE: Yes, what it means is that the immediate audience is made up of the enlightened people who can understand the novel. But I don't think we are dealing with a highly educated people. And the language in which it is written is simple, not an intellectual horseplay and it does capture a number of readers if it is well written. The novel we produce today is too long and complex; it presents a slice of life, too many characters to be accounted for. It is not suitable for a larger reading public.

QUESTION: You do not then think the novel is the best way of getting your message across to the people?

MPHAHLELE: I was thinking the best way to reach a larger audience is through the pictures, such as what Sembène is doing in Senegal. But I am not sure that writers are ready to explore this avenue open to them.

QUESTION: Why have you chosen the novel?

ACHEBE: I don't know. Most recent things I have done are short stories and poems, no novel since 1967. The next thing I

will do is to publish a book of critical writings. So I don't
know. The novel was the first thing that came to me, perhaps.
I can't say why I am better at the novel.

QUESTION: Wouldn't you say it's because you can get more
things into the novel than you can, say, into a poem, and
you can alter the novel to suit your own creative purpose?

ACHEBE: But you can do it with other genres. Doing this kind
of work, it's not really how much you can get into it.

QUESTION: I am thinking in terms of the novel being flexible.
Is it not a flexible medium?

ACHEBE: But so is a poem.

QUESTION: I don't think so. Do you really think a poem has
the flexibility of the novel?

ACHEBE: I suppose you are right. The novel is a kind of catch-
all genre; it's new too, so it's possible to do things with it.
But I think it is overrated. I think one can do things with
poetry, too, so long as you are not trying to write like somebody else, to continue some other tradition that's not really
yours. I think one can do all sorts of things with any genre
if one isn't obsessed with copying, with unities. It just happened that when I wrote the four novels at a row, that was
how I was feeling at the time. When the situation changed
I just switched to poetry. That's what I found appropriate
at that time.[43B]

After discussing the inappropriateness of the novel Mr. Kane
and Mr. Camara particularly praised the dramatists and especially
Ousmane Sembène for his recent move over to the cinema. The
drama and the cinema attract the populace and even if the
piece, like *Le Mandat*, is in French, they understand the actions
because they are based on their own experience with the new
bureaucracy. Mr. Kane narrated to me his experience at Abidjan
where he watched a huge crowd of semiliterate and illiterate
people rushing to see Sembène's *Le Mandat:*

> I was there and I saw how the audience reacted even though it
> was a film about Senegal. They felt that it was their own prob-
> lem.

Mr. Kane's words echo those of Wole Soyinka when he commented on the reaction of the masses to his play *A Dance of the Forests*:

> But what I found personally gratifying and what I considered the validity of my work, was that the so-called illiterate group of the community, the stewards, the drivers—the really un-educated non-academic world—they were coming to see the play every night. . . . If you allowed them, they always felt the thing through all the way, and they came night after night and enjoyed it tremendously.[44]

This shows that the African writer has a large local audience which understands what he is talking about, but the writer loses this audience when he transmits his message through a strange medium. Mr. Kane concluded by saying:

> Perhaps the novel is just being used for the moment because it is necessarily obliged to address a preferred audience. The African audience belongs to an oral tradition and it is an audi-ence that has not been to school. Perhaps it would be necessary to return to oral tradition. . . . The novel is a very narrow avenue.[45]

The phrase "at the moment" and "preferred audience" are very significant. At the moment, the writers are writing for a preferred audience. Because, from the answers given by most of them, they are very much aware that the novel is not the best medium for reaching their supposed African audience. They also know that the film has great potential to capture a large African audience, but most of them are not prepared to venture into the movie industry for lack of funds. Thus there seems to be no alternative to the novel, because it is the most convenient ready-made art form available to them.

As Mphahlele remarked, the major problem facing the writers is the lack of a literate audience. If they are assured of an audi-ence that is trained to appreciate the novel, there would be no objections to their writing mainly novels. While not blaming the writers for the inappropriateness of the genre they are using, one has to point out that their assumption of writing for an African audience is very questionable. Because judging from language, subject matter and its presentation, and now the novel genre, one cannot but admit that the African writers are essentially addressing a bourgeois audience of Europeans and the African elite which is also the bourgeoisie in Africa. By using the novel to reach this "preferred audience" one could, in fact, say that the writers are actually using the best vehicle. For it is an accepted fact that the bourgeoisie prefers the novel to other genres because they could sit at home and read it. Besides their preference for the novel, it is a well-known fact that the development of the novel is attributed to the influence and demand of the bourgeoisie. Lukacs says,

> On savait en effet, depuis toujours, que le roman était la principale des formes littéraires correspondant à la société bourgeoise et que son évolution était étroitement liée à l'histoire de cette société.[46]

For the African writer who claims to be responsible to his community, the novel is not the best means of communication because most members cannot read. However it must be pointed out that the modern African writer has a preferred audience that is more interested in reading the novel than going to sit in a cinema to watch a popular film. Moreover, at the initial stage of African literature, the aim of the writers was to explain Africa to the Western world and secondly, as Achebe said, "to reeducate the people." From the attention that African literature is receiving outside Africa, one could say that the writers have succeeded in their first objective. It is doubtful whether they have succeeded in reeducating the culturally alienated African elite who are supposed to look back on the African past and identify with it. However, as far as the African populace is concerned, the writers are yet to start reaching them through other means, because they cannot reach them through the novel.

Apart from the fact that this bourgeois audience prefers the novel, there are perhaps some other reasons why the African writers prefer it to other genres that are found in traditional

African literature. One of the reasons is the nature of the novel itself. The novel offers a wider scope for personal literary creation than most other genres with strictly defined rules. Gide called the novel "a game that has no rules."[47] As "a personal direct impression of life,"[48] there is no limit to what the novelists can put down as personal impression of life, provided the reader is interested in the story. D. H. Lawrence said: "You can put anything you like in a novel so why do people always put the same thing? Why is the *vol au vent* always chicken?"[49]

Since the novel is so capable of taking in so much, the African writers found it their best means to present the vast experience of Africa and its people before and since the contact with the Western world. It also appears that the only rule a novel has to observe is that suggested by Henry James—to be interesting: "The only obligation to which in advance we may hold a novel without incurring the accusation of being arbitrary, is that it be interesting."[50]

In conclusion, one could say that in genre as in language and subject matter, the African writer is again controlled by the literary taste of his audience. However, in genre, it is the European audience which controls him the more. For although we find certain modifications, as in the ending of *Le Regard du Roi*, consistency of sketchy characters and few detailed scenic descriptions, these modifications are not enough to conclude that the African novel is not an offshoot of the European novel, or that the writers are not catering to the taste of a largely preferred external audience.

NOTES

1. Koawole Ogungsban, "Literature and Society in West Africa," *African Quarterly*, vol. XI, no. 3, (October-December, 1971), p. 216.
2. J. P. Clark, "Our Literary Critics," *Nigeria Magazine*, no. 74 (September, 1962), p. 80.
3. Interview with Cheik Hamidou Kane by author, December, 1972.

4. Rene Wellek and Austin Waren, *Theory of Literature*, (New York: Harcourt, Brace and World, Inc., 1949), p. 212.
5. George Lukacs, *La Théorie du Roman*, Edition Gonthier, (Berlin, 1963), p. 49.
6. Information by Dr. A. U. Ogike. The Story of "Eze Iddu na Oba" is well known in Iboland but I did not know that it was based on actual historical events: the wars between the King of Iddu and the Oba of Benin. Dr. Ogike is an Ibo from Orhu Nigeria.
7. Ruth Finnegan, *Oral Literature in Africa*, (London: Oxford University Press, 1970), p. 108.
8. Northrop Frye, *Anatomy of Criticism*, (Princeton: Princeton University Press, 1957), p. 248.
9. *Ibid.*, p. 250.
10. *Ibid.*, p. 249.
11. *Ibid.*, p. 246.
12. J. P. Clark, "Our Literary Critics," *Nigeria Magazine*, no. 74, (1962), p. 80.
13. Denis Williams, "The Mbari Publications," *Nigeria Magazine*, no. 75, (December, 1962), p. 69.
14. Charles Larson, *The Emergence of African Fiction*, pp. 25-26.
15. George Lukacs, *La Théorie du Roman*, p. 171.
16. George Lukacs, p. 60.
17. *Ibid.*, p. 61.
18. *Ibid.*
19. *Ibid.*, p. 54.
20. *Ibid.*, p. 55.
21. *Ibid.*
22. *Ibid.*, p. 61.
23. *Ibid.*
24. *Ibid.*, p. 78.
25. Robert Serumaga, "Chinua Achebe Interviewed," *Cultural Events in Africa*, no. 28, (March 1967), p. i-iv.
26. Lukacs, *La Théorie du Roman*, p. 62.
27. *Ibid.*, p. 61.
28. Laye Camara, "Kafka et Moi," *Littérature Africaine*, 2nd ed., Ferrand Nathan, p. 37. Quoted from Dimanche-Matin,

Nouvelles des Lettres, 2 Janvier 1955.

29. *Ibid.*
30. Lukacs, p. 175.
31. *Ibid.*, pp. 72-73.
32. *Ibid.*, p. 76.
33. *Ibid.*, p. 176.
34. *Ibid.*, p. 171.
35. *Ibid.*, p. 176.
36. *Ibid.*, p. 175.
37. Laye Camara, "Kafka et Moi." See note 28.
38. Lukacs, p. 86.
39. *Ibid.*, p. 84.
40. Charles Larson, *The Emergence of African Fiction*, p. 225.
41. *Ibid.*, p. 223.
42[A]. Interview with Chinua Achebe by author, September, 1974.
42[B]. Interview with Ezekiel Mphahlele, Philadelphia, September, 1974.
43[A]. Interview with James Ngugi, Nairobi, December, 1974.
43[B]. On the same interviews with the respective authors.
44. Donatus Nwoga, "The Limitations of Universal Criteria." This paper was presented at a conference on African writing at Dalhousie University, Halifax, Nova Scotia, May, 1973. The same paper was read in a Seminar on African Literature at UCLA and published in *UFAHAMU*, vol. IV, no. 1 (Spring, 1973), pp. 10-31.
45. Interview with Kane.
46. George Lukacs, p. 173.
47. H. E. Hugo, *Aspects of Fiction*, "André Gide: Imaginary Interviews No. 8," (Little, Brown and Company, Boston, 1962), p. 167.
48. Paul West, *The Modern Novel*, vol. 1, (London: Hutchinson & Co.) Second edition, 1965, p. 27.
49. David Daiches, *The Novel and the Modern World*, (Chicago: University of Chicago Press, 1960), p. 140.
50. H. E. Hugo, *Aspects of Fiction*, p. 86. Extract taken from Henry James *The Art of Fiction*.

CONCLUSION

In relation to writers in other parts of the world, the position of the African writer is unique on account of language and history. We have for the first time a group of writers committed to dualism of audience. The African elite and the European bourgeois who make up this audience exert varying degrees of influence on his writing even though to some extent they tend to have similar tastes.

The use of European languages in African literature seems to pose the most serious problem at the moment. As has been explained in the study, the adoption of European languages is explainable by the colonial factor. As colonized peoples, Africans attended European-type schools where they learned the languages of the colonizers and acquired some of their culture and inherited their literary tradition. The result is that when the Western-educated African started to express his African experience through literature, he had to do so in the European language and literary tradition which predefine what is acceptable and appropriate.

In the study we find that the majority of Francophone African writers tend to write classical French because the French language by its nature is very rigid. A few writers have tried to modify or "Africanize" their French, but these writers have either been refused publication in France or severely criticized by French critics. Most of the writers including Senghor and Camara confessed that the exigences of French limit their creative scope.

The Anglophone writers appear to be in a better position because the English language is less rigid in its demands on quality. The English publishers and audience do not seem to frown on modification or innovation within the framework of

241

the English language and quite often they find such variety a reason for praise. The result is that we have a number of African novelists who have published works not written in orthodox English. For example, Achebe has created a new prose style in English now identified with him. The favorable criticism he received from the English critics and reading audience has led several Nigerian writers to emulate his style. Amos Tutuola with his "eccentric" English also received encouragement from his British audience and in fact his peculiar English is regarded as his most valuable quality as his stories are often very ordinary. In his *The Voice* Okara's simulation of Ijaw into English resulted in a kind of English which appears absurd to most Nigerian readers. But like other innovators, Okara has received favorable criticism from English critics.

Given the freedom to experiment with English, the African writers have ample opportunity and a wider scope to exercise their literary talents. It is ironic, however, that in spite of the apparent "permissiveness" of English, the Anglophone writers are in the same position as their Francophone counterparts. They depend on the approval or disapproval of their European readers because to a great extent their experiments are deemed good or bad, depending upon how they please a London sophisticated audience.

To eliminate the great influence which the European audience exercises over the writer through language, several African critics and writers feel that the only way is to write in African language. But as the discussion on language usage has shown, this is probably not a possible option at present, for the setup of the new nations of Africa shows that a sudden switch from European to African languages is not likely to happen in the near future.

Equally in choice and presentation of subject, the writer is influenced by his double audience. The choice of subject has been limited to Africa because the audience seems to be interested only in Africa though for different reasons. The African audience wants to read a balanced if not an all too good account of Africa. The European prefers novels which present Africa as an exotic land. The writer is thus under pressure to produce something acceptable to both audiences. Sometimes a novel is written exclusively for one audience. A typical example of this is Ouologuem's *Le Devoir de Violence* whose subject matter and its presentation are determined by the taste of the European audience. In most novels set in precolonial and colonial Africa we find some writers trying to satisfy the taste of both audiences in the same book. Examples of this are Achebe's *Things Fall Apart* and Kane's *L'Aventure Ambiguë*. In novels set in Independent Africa, one notices a near absence of influence by the European audience in subject matter and attitude. The writers are concerned with their corrupt home governments. The trend in these novels suggests that the writers can do without the European audience as far as subject matter and attitude are concerned.

A genre form has always been defined after European styles; therefore, in genre as in language, the writers still have to contend with the European influence. It has been shown that the written novel is a Western literary form. As long as the Africans write novels, there will always be the tendency for critics to measure African literature by Western literary standards. And the result is that African novels are categorized according to how close they come to or how far they deviate from the Western novels.

Already several Western critics have outlined some common characteristics of African novels; viz; lack of detailed characterization, very little or no scenic descriptions, and loose plots. The critics seem to attribute these idiosyncrasies to lack of skill. The study shows that this is not true because some writers like Camara can have "good" plots and good scenic descriptions when the work calls for such. The main reason for the present apparent idiosyncrasy is due to the fact that contemporary African literature is still in transition. The authors are yet writing as committed artists. Their immediate preoccupation is to present to their international audience the experiences of Africa from her initial contact with the Western world to the present day. To carry out this objective, the majority of African novelists write what Larson describes as "Situational Novels." In these novels the writers concentrate more on the experiences and destiny of the entire community. The effort to include everything in one novel often results in loose plots. Since the concern is to show how rich African culture is and how much it has suffered from foreign encroachment, little time is given to detailed or psychological development of individual characters and the description of the milieu. On the whole, it is found that the nature of the African novels determines their treatment and this in turn is affected by audience.

Analysis of Achebe's *Things Fall Apart* and Camara's *Le Regard du Roi* following the Lukacs's *La Théorie du Roman*, shows that African novels remain very close to their European models in spite of few modifications. In genre, therefore, we have an imprint of Western literary tradition which will, perhaps, always remain with African literature.

In the overall estimation of influence of readership on writing, the study reveals that the African novelist is not a free artist, because he is controlled in almost every aspect of his writing by his audience. And of his African and European audiences, the latter exerts more influence over him in language, genre, subject, and partly through the control of publication.

BIBLIOGRAPHY

WEST AFRICAN NOVELS IN FRENCH

Beti, Mongo. (Under the pseudonym, Eza Boto). *Ville Cruelle*, Paris: Editions Africaines, 1954.

_____. *Mission Terminée*. Paris: Correa, 1957.

_____. *Le Pauvre Christ de Bomba*. Paris: Laffon, 1956.

Bhêly-Quénum, Olympe. *Un Piège Sans Fin*. Paris: Librairie Stock, 1960.

Boni, Nazi. *Crépuscule Des Temps Anciens*. Paris: Présence Africaine, 1962.

Camara, Laye. *L'Enfant Noir*. Paris: Plon, 1953. Translated: *The Dark Child*, by J. Kirkup and E. Jones. New York: Doubleday, 1969.

_____. *Le Regard du Roi*. Paris: Plon, 1954.

_____. *Dramousse*. Paris: Plon, 1966.

Dadié, Bernard. *Climbié*. Paris: Seghers, 1956.

_____. *Un Nègre a Paris*. Paris: Présence Africaine, 1959.

_____. *Patron de New York*. Paris: Présence Africaine, 1964.

Diop, Birago. *Les Contes D'Amadou Koumba*. Paris: Présence Africaine, 1961.

_____. *Les Nouveaux Contes d'Amadou Koumba*. Paris: Présence Africaine, 1964.

Fall, Malik. *La Plaie*. Paris: Editions Albin Michel, 1967.

Hazoumé, Paul. *Doguicimi*. Paris: Larose, 1938.

Kane, Cheik Hamidou. *L'Aventure Ambiguë*. Paris: Julliard, 1961.

Kourouma, Ahmadou. *Les Soleils des Indépendances*. Paris: Suil, 1970.

Loba, Ake. *Kocoumbo, L'Etudiant Noir*. Paris: Flammarion, 1960.

Niane, Djibril T. *Soundjata*. Paris: Présence Africaine, 1960.

Nokan, Charles. *Violent Etait Le Vent*. Paris: Présence Africaine, 1966.

Ouologeum, Yambo. *Le Devoir de Violence*. Paris: Seuil, 1968.

Owono, Joseph. *Tante Bella, roman d'aujourd'hui et de demain*. Yaounde (Cameroun): Librairie au Messager, 1959.

Oyono, Ferdinand. *Une Vie de Boy*. Paris: Julliard, 1956.

————. *Le Vieux Nègre et la Médaille*. Paris: Julliard, 1956.

————. *Chemin d'Europe*. Paris; Juilliard, 1960.

Sadji, Abdoulaye. *Maimouna*. Paris: Présence Africaine, 1958.

————. *Nini, Mulatresse du Sénégal*. Paris: Présence Africaine, 1947.

Sembène, Ousmane. *Le Docker Noir*. Paris: Nouvelles Editions Debresse, 1956.

————. *Oh Pays, Mon Beau Peuple!* Paris: Le Livre Contemporain Amiot Dumont, 1957.

————. *Les Bouts de Bois de Dieu*. Paris: Le Livre Contemporain, 1960. Translated: God's Bits of Wood by Francis Price. New York: Doubleday, 1970.

————. *Le Voltaique*. Paris: Présence Africaine, 1962. Presence Africaine, 1966.

Socé, Ousmane. *Karim, roman Senegalais*. Paris: Nouvelles Editions Latines, 1937.

WEST AFRICAN NOVELS IN ENGLISH

Achebe, Chinua. *Things Fall Apart*. Greenwich, Connecticut: Fawcett Publications, 1959.

————. *No Longer at Ease*. Greenwich: Fawcett, 1969.

————. *Arrow of God*. London: Heinemann, 1964.

————. *A Man of the People*. New York: Doubleday and Company, Inc., 1969.

Aluko, T. M. *One Man One Wife*. Lagos: Nigerian Printing and Publishing Company, 1959.

————. *One Man One Matchet*. London: Heinemann, 1964.

Amadi, Elechi. *The Concubine*. London: Heinemann, 1964.

————. *Great Ponds*. New York: John Day and Company, 1969.

Arhma, Kwei A. *The Beautyful Ones Are Not Yet Born.* Toronto: The Macmillan Company, 1969.

―――. *Fragments.* New York: Collier Books, 1971.

Dipoko, Mbella. *A Few Nights and Days.* London:Longmans, 1966.

―――. *Because of Women.* London: Heinemann, 1969.

Duodo, Cameron. *The Gab Boys.* London: Fontana, 1970.

Ekwensi, Cyprian. *Jagua Nana.* New York: Fawcett World Library, 1969.

―――. *People of the City.* London: Heinemann, 1963.

―――. *Beautiful Feathers.* London: Hutchinson, 1963.

Konadu, Asare. *A Woman in Her Prime.* London: Heinemann, 1967.

―――. *Come Back Dora!* Accra: Anowuo Educational Publications, 1966.

Nwankwo, Nkem. *Danda.* London: Heinemann, 1964.

Nzekwu, Onuora. *Wand of Noble Wood.* New York: The New America Library, 1963.

―――. *High Life for Lizards.* London: Hutchinson, 1965.

Okara, Gabriel. *The Voice.* New York: Africana Publishing Corporation, 1970.

Soyinka, Wole. *The Interpreters.* New York: The Macmillan Company, 1970.

Tutuola, Amos. *The Palm Wine Drinkard.* New York: Grove Press, 1953.

―――. *My Life in the Bush of Ghosts.* London: Faber, 1954.

―――. *Simbi and the Satyr of the Dark Jungle.* London: Faber, 1955.

BOOKS

Abrams, M. H. *A Glossary of Literary Terms.* New York: Holt, Rinehart and Winston, 1971.

―――. et al. *The Norton Anthology of English Literature.* New York: W. W. Norton and Co., 1962.

Angoff, C. and Povey, J. *African Writing Today.* New York: Manylands Books, 1969.

Auerbach, Erich. *Mimesis: The Representation of Reality in Western Literature.* Princeton: Princeton University Press, 1968.

Basden, G. T. *The Niger Ibos.* London: Frank Cass and Co., Ltd., 1966.

Beardsley, M. C. *Aesthetics: Problems in the Philosophy of Criticism.* New York: Harcourt, Brace and World, 1958.

Booth, Wayne C. *The Rhetoric of Fiction.* Chicago: Chicago University Press, 1961.

Brench, A. C. *The Novelists' Inheritance in French Africa.* London: Oxford University Press, 1967.

Conrad, Joseph. *The Heart of Darkness.* New York: W. W. Norton and Co., 1963.

Daiches, David. *The Novel and the Modern World.* Chicago: University of Chicago Press, 1960.

Danzieger, M. and Johnson, W. S. *An Introduction to the Study of Literature.* Boston: D. C. Heath and Company, 1966.

Finnegan, Ruth. *Oral Literature in Africa.* London: Oxford University Press, 1970.

Fishman, J. A. *et al. Language Problems of Developing Nations.* New York: John Eiley and Sons, 1968.

Frye, Northrop. *Anatomy of Criticism: Four Essays.* Princeton: Princeton University Press, 1971.

Gide, André. *Voyage au Congo.* Paris: Gallimard 87 ed., 1927.

Gleason, Judith I. *This Africa.* Evanston: Northwestern University Press, 1965.

Goldman, Lucien. *Pour une Sociologie du Roman.* Paris: Gallimard, 1964.

Hardy, Barbara. *The Appropriate Form: An Essay on the Novel.* London: The Athone Press, 1964.

Hugo, H. E. *Aspects of Fiction.* Boston: Little, Brown and Company, 1962.

Jahn, Janheinz. *Neo-African Literature: A History of Black Writing.* New York: Grove Press, 1969.

_____. *Muntu: The New African Culture.* Translated by Majorie Greene. New York: Grove Press, 1962.

James, Henry. *The Art of Fiction*. New York: Oxford University Press, 1948.

————. *The Art of the Novel*. New York: Scribners Sons, 1948.

Kesteloot, Lilyan. *Les Ecrivains Noirs de la Langue Française: Naissance d'une Littérature*. Université Libre de Bruxelles, 1965.

————. *Anthologie Négro-Africaine*. Verviers (Belique): Marabout Université, 1965.

Larson, Charles. *The Emergence of African Fiction*. Bloomington: Indiana University Press, 1971.

Laurence, Margaret. *Long Drums and Cannons*. New York: Praeger, 1969.

Lukacs, George. *La Théorie du Roman*. Berlin: Edition Gonthier, 1963.

Malonga, Jean. *Coeur d'Aryenne*. Paris: Présence Africaine (Trois Ecrivains Noirs), série speciale no. 16, 1965.

Macneice, Lows. *The Poetry of W. B. Yeats*. London: Oxford University Press, 1941.

Moore, Gerald. *Seven African Writers*. London: Oxford University Press, 1962.

Ngugi, James. *Weep Not Child*. London: Heinemann, 1964.

Obiechina, E. N. *Onitsha Market Literature*. New York: Africana Publishing Company, 1972.

Obioha, R. I. *Money Hard To Get*. Onitsha (Nigeria): All Star Printers.

Ogali, O. A. *Okeke The Magician*. Aba (Nigeria): Okeudo Printing Works.

————. *Veronica, My Daughter*. Onitsha: Appolos Brothers Press.

Pageard, Robert. *Littérature Négro-Africaine*. Paris: Le Livre Africain, 1966.

Palmer, Eustace. *An Introduction to the African Novel*. New York: Africana Publishing Corporation, 1971.

Pieterse, Cosmo, and Duerde, Dennis. *African Writers Talking*. New York: Africana Publishing Corporation, 1972.

Poulet, Georges. *Les Chemins Actuels de la Critique*. Paris: Union Générale d'Editions, 1968.

Ratner, Moses. *Theory and Criticism of the Novel in France, from L'Astrée to 1750.* New York: De Palma Printing Company, 1937.

Rothberg, Robert. *A Political History of Tropical Africa.* New York: Harcourt, Brace and World, 1965.

Saintsbury, George. *A History of the French Novel.* Vol. II. London: Macmillan, 1919.

Sainville, Leonard. *Anthologie de la Littérature Négro-Africaine, romanciers et conteurs,* Vols. I & II. Paris: Présence Africaine, 1963.

Senghor, L. S. *Liberté 1: Négritude et Humanisme.* Paris: Editions du Seuil, 1964.

_____. *Poèmes.* Paris: Seuil, 1964.

Soyinka, Wole. *Five Plays.* London: Oxford University Press, 1964.

Stallknecht, N. P. and Frenz, Horst. *Comparative Literature: Method and Perspective.* Chicago: Southern Illinois University Press, 1971.

Stanzel, Franz. *Narrative Situations in the Novel.* Translated by J. P. Pusack. Bloomington: Indiana University Press, 1971.

Tibble, Anne. *African English Literature.* New York: October House, Inc., 1965.

Uba, E. *The Broken Heart.* Onitsha: Providence Printing Press.

Wauthier, Claude. *The Literature and Thought of Modern Africa: A Survey.* Translated by Shirley Kay. New York: Praeger, 1967.

Wellek, Rene, and Warren, Austin. *The Theory of Literature.* New York: Harcourt Brace and World, 1949.

West, Paul. *The Modern Novel,* Vols. I & II. London: Hutchinson University Library, 1967.

Zola, Emile. *Germinal.* New York: Charles Scribner's Sons, 1951.

Zwerdling, Ales. *Yeats and the Heroic Ideal.* New York: New York University Press, 1965.

_____. *Camara Laye. Littérature Africaine,* No. 2, Paris: Fernand Nathan, 1964.

_____. *Olympe Bhêly-Quénum. Littérature Africaine,* No. 4. Paris: Gernand Nathan, 1967.

————. *Mongo Beti. Littérature Africaine,* No. 5. Paris: Fernand Nathan, 1964.

————. *Birago Diop. Littérature Africaine,* No. 6. Paris: Fernand Nathan, 1964.

————. Bernard Dadié. *Littérature Africaine,* No. 7. Paris: Fernand Nathan, 1964.

————. *Ferdinand Oyono. Littérature Africaine,* No. 8. Paris: Fernand Nathan, 1964.

————. *Aime Césaire. Littérature Africaine,* No. 9. Paris: Fernand Nathan, 1967.

————. Seydou Badian. *Littérature Africaine,* No. 10. Paris: Fernand Nathan, 1968.

ARTICLES

Achebe, Chinua. "English and the Writer," *Transition,* No. 18 (1965), pp. 27-30.

————. "The Novelist as a Teacher." *New Statesman,* (January 29, 1965), pp. 161-62.

————. "The Black Writer's Burden," *Présence Africaine,* English ed., XXXI, 59 (1966), pp. 135-40.

————. "The Role of the Writer in a New Nation," *Nigeria Magazine,* No. 81 (1964), pp. 157-160.

Alexander, P. "The Politics of Language," *Africa Report,* (July-August 1973), Vol. 18, pp. 16-20.

Banttam, Martin. "African Literature II: Nigerian Dramatists in English and the Traditional Nigerian Theatre," *Journal of Commonwealth Literature,* No. 3 (1967), pp. 99 ff.

Case, Frederick. "The Cultural Predicament of L. S. Senghor," *Literary Studies,* (Fall 1970), Vol. I, No. 4, pp. 15-24.

Dathorne, O. R. "African Literature: Writers, Publishers and Their Public," *Books,* No. 361, (1965), pp. 180-88.

————. "African Literature IV: Ceremony in Okigbo's Poetry," *Journal of Commonwealth Literature,* No. 5, (1968), pp. 82-88.

Dobert M. and Nwanganga Shields. "Africa's Women: Security in

Tradition, Challenge in Change," Africa Report, (July-August, 1972), pp. 14-19.

Echeruo, J. C. "Traditional and Borrowed Elements in Nigerian Poetry," Nigeria Magazine, No. 89, (June, 1966), p. 142ff.

Egudu, R. N. "The Nigerian Literary Artist and His Society," UFAHAMU, Vol. IV., No. 1 (Spring 1973), pp. 59-72.

Ekwensi, Cyprian. "African Literature," Nigeria Magazine, No. 83 (1964), pp. 294-99.

_____. "The Dilemma of the African Writer," West African Review, July, 1956, pp. 701-04.

Emenyonu, Ernest. "Achebe: Accountable to our Society," Africa Report, (May, 1972), pp. 14-19.

Ferguson, John. "Nigerian Drama in English," Modern Drama, (May 1968), pp. 10-26.

_____. "Nigerian Prose Literature in English," English Studies in Africa, 9:1:66, pp. 43-60.

_____. "Nigerian Poetry in English," Insight, No. 18, October-December 1967), pp. 231-235.

Gerald, Albert. "Elegies Nigeriennes," Revue Generale Belge, XCI, (1963), pp. 37-49.

_____. "Cyprian Ekwensi, Romancier de la Ville Africaine," Revue Generale Belge, IC, (1963), pp. 91-105.

_____. "The Neo-African Novel," Africa Report, Vol. IX., (July, 1964), pp. 13-15.

Giles, Raymond H. "African Studies Depend on a New Black History," Africa Report, (November-December, 1972), pp. 35-37.

Grant, Stephan H. "Publisher for the Many," Africa Report, (January, 1972), pp. 26-27.

Horton, Robin. "Three Nigerian Novelists," Nigeria Magazine, No. 70, (September 1961), pp. 218-225.

Irele, Abiola. "The Tragic Conflict in Achebe's Novels," Black Orpheus, No. 17 (1965), pp. 24-32.

Ita, J. M. "Negritude: Some Popular Misconceptions," Nigeria Magazine, No. 97 (June-August, 1968), p. 117 ff.

Jahn, Janheinz. "African Literature," Presence Africaine, Eng. ed., XX No. 48, (1963), pp. 47-57.

Jeffares, N. A. "The Author in the Commonwealth," *Nigeria Magazine*, No. 95 (1967), pp. 35-55.

Johnson, Babasola. "The Books of Amos Tutuola," *West Africa* (April 10, 1954), p. 322.

Jones, Eldred. "Nationalism and the Writer," *New Statesman*, (January 29, 1965), pp. 151-56.

Kennedy, Jean. "The City as a Metaphor," *Africa Report* (April, 1972), pp. 27-29.

Knipp, Thomas R. "Two Novels from Kenya," *Books Abroad*, Vol. 39, (1965), pp. 411-13.

Lerner, L. D. "The Influence of Europe," *West African Review*, (June, 1952), p. 599 ff.

Lindfors, Bernth. "Five Nigerian Novels," *Books Abroad*, XXX-XXIX (Autumn, 1965), pp. 411-13.

—————. "Achebe's African Parables," *Presence Africaine*, No. 66, (1968), pp. 130-36.

Mazuri, Molly. "Suicide and Society in some African Fiction," *Literary Studies*, Vol. 1, No. 4 (Fall, 1970) pp. 61-71.

McDonald, Robert. "Bound to Violence: A Case of Plagiarism," *Transition*, No. 41, (1972), pp. 64-68.

Mohome, Paulus. "The African Writer and International Recognition," *Literary Studies*, Vol. 1, No. 4, (Fall 1970) pp. 97-99.

Moore, Gerald. "English Words, African Lives," *Presence Africaine* English ed., XXVI, No. 54 (1965), pp. 90-101.

—————. "African Literature, French and English," *Makerere Journal*, No. 19 (1963), pp. 29-34.

Mphahlele, Ezekiel. "Writers in Search of Themes," *West African Review*, (August, 1962), pp. 40-41.

Mutiso, G. C. "Women in African Literature," *East African Journal*, Vol. 8, No. 3 (March 1971).

Nance, Carolyn. "Cosmology in the Novels of Achebe," *CONCH*, Vol. III, No. 2 (September, 1971), pp. 121-35.

Nwoga, Donatus. "Onitsha Market Literature," *Transition*, No. 19 (1965), pp. 26-33.

—————. "The Limitations of Universal Literary Criteria," *UFAHAMU*, Vol. IV., No. 1 (Spring, 1973), pp. 10-31.

Obiechina, Emma. "Through The Jungle Dimly; European Novelists on West Africa," *Literary Studies*, Vol. L., No. 4 (Fall, 1970), pp. 113-23.

_____. "Transition from Oral to Literary Tradition," *Presence Africaine*, No. 63 (1967), pp. 140-61.

_____. "Cultural Nationalism in Modern African Creative Literature," *African Literature Today*, No. 1 (1968), pp. 24-35.

Ogungbsan, Kolawole. "Literature and Society in West Africa," *Africa Quarterly*, Vol. XI, No. 3 (October-December, 1971), pp. 220-23.

Okwu, E. C. "A Language of Expression for Nigerian Literature," *Nigeria Magazine*, No. 91 (1966), pp. 289-92.

Olumide, Olawole. "Amos Tutuola's Reviewers and the Educated Africans," *New Nigeria Forum*, 1, 3, (October, 1958), pp. 5-16.

Omolara, Leslie. "Chinua Achebe: His Vision and Craft," *Literary Studies*, Vol. 1, No. 4 (Fall, 1970), pp. 33-47.

_____. "African Aesthetics and Literature," *UFAHAMU*, Vol. IV., No. 1 (Spring, 1973), pp. 4-7.

Povey, John. "The Quality of African Writing Today," *Literary Review*, No. XI (Summer, 1968), pp. 403-21.

_____. "Contemporary West African Writing in English," *Books Abroad*, 40 (Summer 1966), pp. 253-60.

_____. "African Literature in English," *Books Abroad*, 41 (Autumn, 1967), pp. 417-19.

Ravenscroft, Arthur. "African Literature V: Novels of Disillusion," *Journal of Commonwealth Literature*, No. 6 (January, 1969), pp. 120-37.

Renato, Berger. "Review: Négritude et Humanisime," *Nigeria Magazine*, No. 95, (December, 1967), p. 318 ff.

Rubadiri, David. "Why African Literature," *Transition*, No. 15 (1964), pp. 39-42.

Rubin, J. Steve. "Laye: Commitment to Timeless Values," *Africa Report* (May, 1972), pp. 20-26.

Salami, Adebisi. "Defining a Standard Nigerian English," *Journal* of Nigerian English Studies Association (November, 1967), pp. 99-105.

Sellin, Eric. "Ouologuem's Blueprint for *Le Devoir de Violence*," *Research in African Literatures*, II, No. 2 (1971), pp. 117-20.

Sermuaga, Robert. "Chinua Achebe Interviewed," *Cultural Events in Africa*, No. 28, (March, 1967), p. i-iv.

Shelton, Austin J. "Some Problems of Intercommunication," *Journal of Modern African Studies*, II (1964), pp. 394-403.

Soyinka, Wole. "The Writer in an African State," *Transition*, No. 31 (1967), pp. 11-13.

Stock, A. G. "Yeats and Achebe," *Journal of Commonwealth Literature*, No. 5 (1968), pp. 106-11.

Stuart, Donald. "African Literature III: The Modern Writer in His Context," *Journal of Commonwealth Literature*, No. 4 (1967), pp. 114-29.

Treadgold, Mary. "Writers in Search of Themes," *West African Review* (May, 1962), p. 57 ff.

Warner, Alan. "A New English in Africa," *Review of English Literature*, IV (April, 1963), pp. 45-54.

Wright, Edgar. "African Literature I: Problems of Criticism," *Journal of Commonwealth Literature*, No. 2 (December, 1966), pp. 103-12.

UNPUBLISHED MATERIALS

Lindfors, Bernth Olof. *Nigerian Fiction in English, 1952-1967*. A dissertation submitted in partial satisfaction of the requirements for the degree Doctor of Philosophy in English. University of California, Los Angeles, 1969.

Ogike, Aloysius Uche. *Traditional Africa in Franco-West African Novels*. A dissertation submitted in partial satisfaction of the requirements for the degree Doctor of Philosophy in French. University of California, Los Angeles, 1973.